Indian Reminiscences

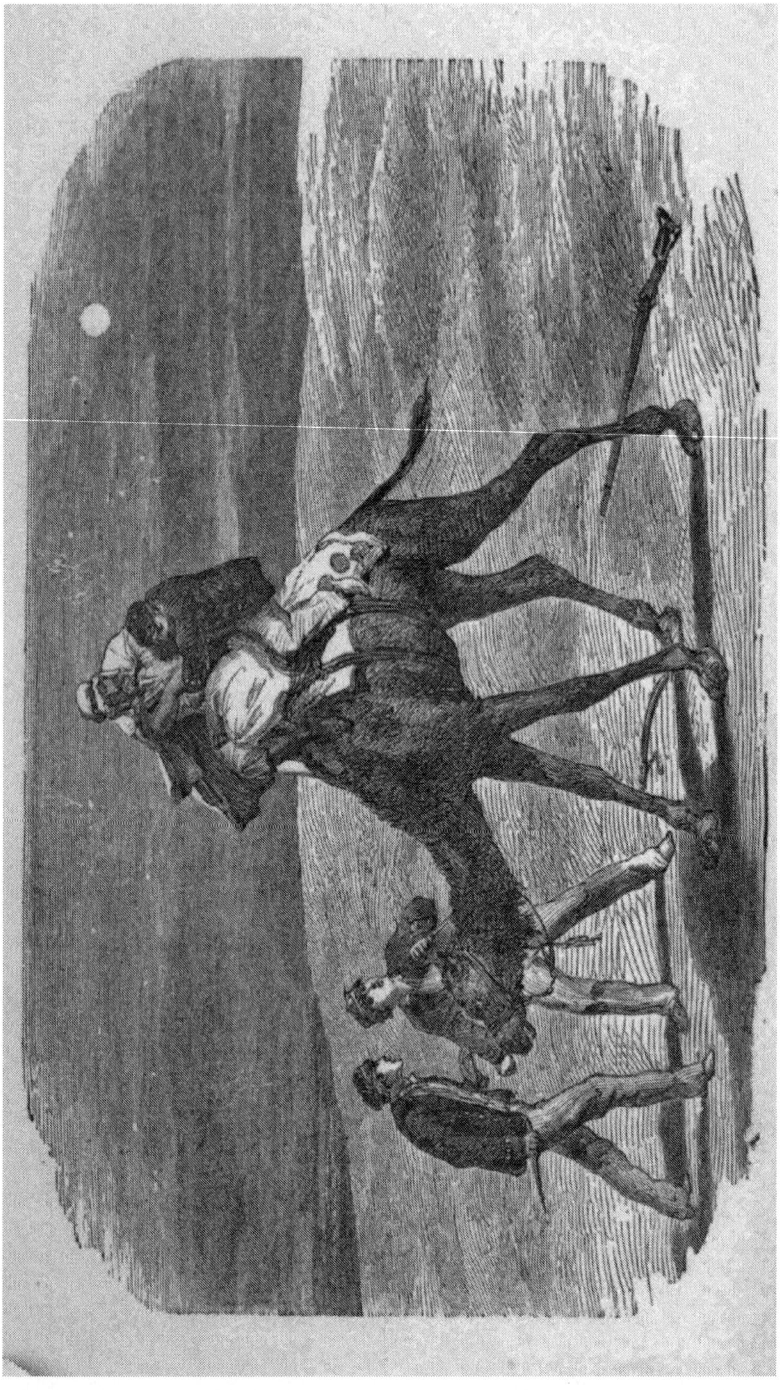

INDIAN REMINISCENCES.

BY

Colonel S. DEWÉ WHITE,

LATE BENGAL STAFF CORPS.

LONDON:
WM. H. ALLEN & CO., 13, WATERLOO PLACE, S.W.
PUBLISHERS TO THE INDIA OFFICE.
1880.

[*All rights reserved.*]

Gift of
Prof. A. C. Coolidge

LONDON:
PRINTED BY WOODFALL AND KINDER,
MILFORD LANE, STRAND, W.C.

PREFACE.

I MAY inform any wishing to know why my "Indian Reminiscences" has been so long in making its appearance, that, considering my position, it would have been unadvisable for me to have had such a book published during the time of my service in India. Moreover, I could not have composed my narrative of the great Sepoy Revolt immediately after that event so dispassionately and advantageously as I have now done. And in the next place, after my final departure from India, I was engaged in writing two works, the first volume of the most important of which—my History of the Reign of Charles I., the Commonwealth, and Protectorate of Oliver Cromwell—will, I trust, ere long be sent to the Press. I now hopefully await the verdict of public opinion on this my first literary production, and I shall be exceedingly glad if, in addition to affording interest to the reader, it turns out a useful and profitable book in a religious point of view.

S. DEWÉ WHITE.

SOUTHSEA,
23rd March, 1880.

CONTENTS.

CHAPTER I.

PAGE

Departure from England—Life on Board Ship—Practical Jokes—A Challenge to fight a Duel—Pleasant Stay at the Cape of Good Hope—Dangerous Return to Ship—Outrageous Conduct of the Captain — His Extraordinary Humiliation—Escape from a Shark—Touch at Madras—Arrival at Calcutta—Funny Adventure at Barrackpore—Taken by Steamer to Allahabad—Taken ashore at Dinapore—Dangerous Illness there—A good Samaritan—Exchange my Regiment—Serve through the Sikh Campaign of 1845-46—Descriptions of Battles of Moodkee and Ferozshah—Sir Hugh Gough—Rank Worship—Petty Warfare at Watch-tower—Battles of Buddiwal, Aliwal, and Subraon—Remarks on War—Personal Feelings—March on Lahore—Submission of the Sikhs—Annexation of Jullundur Doab—British Protectorate of the Punjaub—Stationed at Hoshiapore—Expedition to Cashmere—House broken into by Robbers—Ordered to Bareilly—Visit Nynee Tall, Simla—Its Charm—Description of Mussoorie—2nd Sikh War—Chillianwallah—Goojerat—Sir Charles Napier sent out—Victory of Goojerat—Annexation of the Punjaub—Koh-i-Noor—Dhuleep Singh—Suppression of Duelling—March to Berhampore—Exchange my Regiment—Reason of 1

CHAPTER II.

Suggestiveness of the Truth of the Bible in Things that may be Seen in India—General Remarks on the Folly of Infidelity as Contrasted with Christianity—Objection regarding the Apparent Discrepancies of the Bible answered—Reply to the Cavils of Scientific Men—The Objections of Infidels cannot stand the Test of a thorough Examination—Actual Experience the most convincing Evidence of the Truth of the Bible—Meeting with the Subject of this Sketch, E. S., at Bareilly—Want of Christian Society at Bareilly—Next door neighbour with E. S. at Barrackpore—Description of Barrackpore, and the wretched state of Locomotion in India at this Period—Sketch of Calcutta, and its accessible Health Resort,

Darjeeling—Ensign S—— engaged to be Married—The Engagement broken off—His Downward Career—Fires into my Room—Tried by a Court Martial—His narrow Escape—Does not Profit by the Warning—Leaves Barrackpore—Scene presented in his vacant Room—Again tried by a Court Martial, and dismissed the Service—Enlists as a Private Soldier . . 22

CHAPTER III.

A Season of Trial—Gross Favouritism contrasted with Injustice and Oppression—Dangerous Illness—Slander—Narrow Escape of being Shot at Target Practice—Report the Matter—No Enquiry—Regimental Order thereon—Placed under Arrest on a false Charge—Released by Commander-in-Chief—Misrepresentation—My Vindication approved of by His Excellency—I appeal to the Commander-in-Chief against the Regimental Order and the Offence against my Life at Target Practice—Placed under Arrest by Commanding Officer—Brigadier's arbitrary Proceeding—I appeal to the Commander-in-Chief against it—Lord Dalhousie's singular Conduct towards me—Tried by General Court Martial—Regarded as a ruined Man—Anecdote—Favourable Results of my Court Martial—Regimental Order directed to be Cancelled, &c.—Remarks—The Need of a Lawyer to conduct General Court Martials—Active and Unjust Part taken against me by Lord Dalhousie—Divine Protection—My triumphant Escape—Systematic Persecution—Arrival at Benares—Description of the Place—Practical Use of Prayer—Dead Set made against me at Benares by my Commanding Officer and the Officers commanding the Station and Division—I appeal against them to the Commander-in-Chief—My signal Triumph over them all—My Case noticed very favourably by the Press—Frustration of a Spiteful Design against me—Promoted to Lieutenant—Receive Prize of a Thousand Rupees—Join 3rd European Regiment at Chinsurah—Fresh Troubles—Lose my Temper—Severe Punishment—Its Grievous Results—Take my Furlough to England—Nearly wrecked off the Cape—A Week's Stay at St. Helena—Description thereof—Meet with nice Christian Society there—Arrival in England—Hear of my Brother's Death in the Crimea—Return to India with Recruits—Dangerous Illness—Providential Disappointment at Cawnpore—Arrival at Agra just before the Outbreak of the Mutiny 43

CHAPTER IV.

Origin and Cause of the Great Sepoy Revolt—Personal Knowledge of this Matter—The Greased Cartridges—Ridiculous Fears of the Sepoys—Their Obstinate Belief in a Lie—Disgraceful

CONTENTS. ix

Policy of the Indian Government righteously Punished—Remarkable Character of this Divine Retribution—Retrospect of former Mutinies—Lord Dalhousie's Undignified and Unenergetic Treatment of the Mutinous 38th Regiment in 1852—Circumstances favourable to a General Revolt—Paucity of Europeans for the Defence of an Extended Frontier—Dalhousie's Mischievous and Impolitic Annexation of Oudh—"Right of Lapse"—Its unfairness—Sattarah, Nagpore, and Jhansi—First Appearance of a Mutinous Spirit at Berhampore and Barrackpore—Premature Outbreak and Massacre at Meerut—Remarkable Inactivity of the European Troops—Mutiny and Massacre at Delhi—Proclamation of King of Delhi—Description of Agra—Taj Mahal—Council of War at Agra—Grand Parade of Troops—Lieutenant-Governor harangues them—Mutiny at Ferozepore—Useless Proclamations of the Governor-General and Commander-in-Chief—Scindiah's Devoted Loyalty—Sepoys rise at Alygurh, Etawah, and Mynpoorie—Lieutenant-Governor's Injudicious Manifesto—Cancelled by Earl Canning—Mutiny at Muttra—Intended Rise and Massacre at Agra—Blessing of United Prayers of Earnest Christians—Remarkable Intervention of Divine Providence in our Favour—The Native Regiments at Agra are Disarmed—Organization of a Volunteer Force—The Untrustworthiness of the Agra Police—Mutiny at Gwalior—Our Isolation at Agra—Retirement of the Ladies and Children into the Fort—The North-West Provinces in a Blaze of Revolt—Mutineers at Jhansi, Hissar, Nusseerabad, Neemuch, Bareilly, Moradabad, Shahjehanpore—Touching Scene at the Massacre near Aurungabad—Revolt at Futtehgurh—Flight of the English—Mutiny at Cawnpore—Unparalleled Misery of the English besieged in Wheeler's Entrenchment—Dhoondhoo Punt, Nana Sahib—His old Grudge against the English—The Amazing Treachery of the 6th Regiment N.I. at Allahabad—Sepoys rise at Azimgurh—Outbreak at Benares and Jaunpore—Mutiny at Jhansi—The ill-used Ranee of Jhansi's Revenge—Atrocious Massacre—Mutinies at Nowgong, Jullundur, Phillour, and Rohnee—Retributive Effects of Wrong-doing in Oude—Sepoys rise at Lucknow, Seetapore, Mohumdee, and Fyzabad—Terrible Sufferings of Mrs. Mills and other Fugitives—Revolts at Sultanpore, Bareitch, and other Stations—All Classes in Oude rise in Insurrection against the Usurped Power of the British Government in their Country—Commander-in-Chief dies of Cholera—Mutinies at Indore—Holkar's Noble Reply to the Mutineers—Revolt at Mhow—Sepoys rise in the Vicinity of Agra 82

CHAPTER V.

Imperilled Condition of Agra—Mutiny of the Kotah Contingent—Fight with the Neemuch Brigade at Shahgung—Description of the Battle—Our Defeat with Terrific Loss and Retirement

CONTENTS.

into the Fort—Great Dismay there—Remarkable Saying of the Lieutenant-Governor—Awful Conflagration and Massacre at Agra—Terrible Disorder outside the Fort—Hardships—Devoted Attention paid to the Wounded—Life inside the Fort—Adoption of Precautionary Measures—Causes for Expecting an Attack—Our Native Christians rise in Public Estimation—A Melancholy Day—Arrival of the News of the Cawnpore Tragedy—Successive Arrivals of Messengers with Gloomy Tidings—State of Affairs before Delhi—Desperate Condition of the Besiegers—Particulars of the Cawnpore Massacre—Wonderful Escape of Lieutenants Thomson and Delafosse—Subsequent Atrocious Massacre of the Women and Children—The Mythical Story of Miss Wheeler—Gloomy Forebodings—Sir Henry Lawrence's Defeat and Death—Sir Henry's dying Words—Sir John Lawrence's View of the Situation—Natives Expect our Ruin—God the Source of all Comfort to the Christian in such Seasons of Gloom—Execution of Martial Law at Agra—Energetic Course adopted in the Punjaub—Disarming of Regiments at Meean Meer (Lahore) and Peshawur—Mutineers blown from Guns—Mutiny at Jhelum—Mutineers Fight with a Wing of H.M. 24th Foot—Severe Loss of the Latter—Subsequent Destruction of these Mutineers—Mutiny at Sealcote—Destruction of these Mutineers—Eminent Service rendered by the Punjaub Officials—Despatch of Sikh Troops from the Punjaub to Delhi—Arrival of Nicholson—Victory of Nujufgurh—Havelock's Victories—Futtehpore and Aong—Defeat of the Nana Sahib—Reoccupation of Cawnpore—Havelock's Advance into Oude—His Victories—The grievous Necessity to fall back—Brigadier Niel's stern Justice—Havelock defeats the Nana at Bithoor—A Native Regiment crosses Bayonets with British Soldiers—Havelock's precarious Position at Cawnpore—Koonwur Sing's Insurrection—Wake's Defence of Arrah—Defeat of Captain Dunbar by Dinapore Mutineers—Major Eyre defeats Dinapore Mutineers—Relief of Arrah—Mutiny of the 27th Bombay N.I.—Mutinous Conduct of 8th Madras Native Cavalry—Mutiny at Segowlie—Sepoys of Ramgurh Battalion and Jodhpore Legion rise—Despatch of a Force from Agra—Sudden Attack of Ophthalmia—A miserable Night in Command of the Advance Guard—Battle near Alygurh—Sent into Agra with Sick and Wounded—Personal Violence offered me by a Junior Officer—Unjust Adjudication of the Case by my Commanding Officer—I appeal against this to Commander-in-Chief—Placed under Arrest—Extreme Injustice of this Proceeding—Deprived of the Means of Grace for nearly five Months—Religious Consolations—Impartial Testimony of an Officer of my Regiment—Sympathy of the Editor of the *Mofussulite*—Death of Mr. Colvin—News from the Punjaub—Annihilation of the Mutinous 51st Regiment N.I.—Arrival of Siege Train at Delhi—Preparations for the Assault—The Hazardous Nature of the Undertaking—Hear at Agra of the Capture of Delhi. 115

CHAPTER VI.

Description of the Assault and Capture of Delhi—Death of Nicholson—Capture of the King—Captain Hodson shoots three Princes—Colonel Greathed's Pursuit of the Mutineers—Brigadier Showers' Successes—Mutiny of Regiments after the Escalade of Delhi—Nagode, Jubbulpore, Deoghur, Chittagong, Dacca, and Julpigoree—Havelock's Victorious Advance to Lucknow—Sir James Outram—His Grand Chivalry—Commander-in-Chief's Remarkable Order thereon — Outram's Bravery—Sore Peril of the Besieged—Relief of Lucknow— Great Mortality of the Garrison—Surprising Loyalty of the Faithful Sepoys—Battle of Agra—Strange Refusal of Permission to go out to the Battle with my Regiment—Complete Defeat of Mutineers—Lady Nurses—Their Devotedness— Troubled State of Rajpootana—Repulse of Colonel Lawrence —Murder of Major Burton—Defeat of Captain Tucker— English still Besieged at Lucknow—Arrival of Sir Colin Campbell at Cawnpore—Advance of Commander-in-Chief— Captain Peel and the Naval Brigade—Warlike Operations— Desperate Fighting at the Secunder Bagh—Second Relief of Lucknow accomplished—Withdrawal of Non-combatants from Lucknow—Death of Havelock—Defeat of General Windham at Cawnpore—Arrival of the Commander-in-Chief—He defeats the Enemy—Their Defeat again by Grant—Pious Despatch of the Victor—Defeat of Jodhpore Legion—Seaton's Victories of Gungaree and Puttialee—Tried by Court Martial—Injustice of the whole Proceedings—Cruel Sentence—Remarkable Circumstances following it—Condition of Affairs at Agra—Departure of Siege Train—Leave Agra with my Regiment—Letter from Head-Quarters—Commander-in-Chief declines to confirm Sentence of Court—Hard Usage and extreme Unfairness—Appeal to Commander-in-Chief—Authorities refuse to forward it—I trust in the Lord—Lord Clyde comes to Gwalior in 1859—My Interview with him—Its happy Results—Continuation of the Narrative of the Events of 1858—Re-occupation of Futtygurh— Advance of Commander-in-Chief to Lucknow—Outram repels Repeated Attacks—Jung Bahadur's Diversion in our Favour —Brigadier Frank's Victories at Chandah, Humeerpore, and Sooltanpore—Sir Hope Grant takes Meeangunge by Storm— Great Strength of the Enemy at Lucknow—Huzrut Muhul the Begum—·Operations against Lucknow—Storming of Queen's Palace and Imambara—Unexpected Capture of Kaiser Bagh—Immense Loot—Outram's March through the City— Conquest of Lucknow—Escape of the Rebels—Excessive caution of Commander-in-Chief—Remarks on the Character of Outram 147

CHAPTER VII.

Commander-in-Chief's Operations in Rohilcund—Defeats Rebels and Captures Bareilly—Brilliant Campaign of Sir H. Rose— Defeats Tantia Topee near Jhansi—Captures the City—Takes the Fort by Storm—Victories of Koouch and Gulowlie—Capture of Calpie—Doings of our Column in co-operation with Sir H. Rose—Engagement at Sheregurh Ghaut—Narrow Escape of being Shot in Bed—Defeat of the Maharajah of Gwalior by Tantia Topee—Flight of Scindiah to Agra—We March to Dholpore—Remain there, though Ordered to Gwalior—Sir H. Rose captures Gwalior—Napier's Victory over Tantia Topee—Successful Operations of the Columns of Showers, Stuart, and Rowcroft—Disaster of Colonel Milman—Victories of Lord Mark Kerr, Sir E. Lugard, and Brigadier Douglas—Second Disaster of Arrah—Victories of Lugard, Havelock, Roberts, and Whitlock—Blunder of Walpole—Victories of Walpole, Hope Grant, Seaton, and Jones—We return to Agra—Illness—Placed under Arrest—Released by the Brigadier—Transferred to the Service of the Crown—Queen's Proclamation—Cold Weather Campaign of 1858-59—Defeats of Tantia Topee—Serve under Brigadier Showers—Battle of Dowsa—Complete Suppression of the Revolt—Operations of Lord Clyde—Victory of Sir Hope Grant—The Nana and other Leaders driven into Nepaul—Remarks—Ordered to Gwalior—Curse of Drinking and Debt Exemplified—Ordered to Futtygurh—Description of an Indian March—Leave my Regiment to take up an Appointment at Benares—Ordered to Barrackpore—Stationed there—Bitten by a Widow—Awfully sudden Death of an Acquaintance from Drinking—Capricious Conduct of Commanding Officer—Ordered back to my Regiment at Futtygurh—Serious Embarrassment—Interview with Sir Hugh Rose—His kind Consideration of my Hard Case—Appointed Garrison Interpreter, Fort William—Pleasant Life at Calcutta 189

CHAPTER VIII.

Amalgamation Scheme arrives in Calcutta—Its Unsuitability to me—My Regiment (3rd Europeans) becomes 107th Foot—Visit Chota Nagpore—Spread of Christianity among the Coles—Their Extraordinary Belief in the Power of Witches—Arrival of Cannibals in Calcutta—The dreadful Cyclone—Become Lieutenant and Brevet Major under Government Scheme of 1864—Illness—Resign my Appointment—Appointed to Convalescent Depôt, Darjeeling—Fierceness of Rats there—Severe Affliction—Promoted to Captain—Suicide of a Gentleman in the Ranks—Obtain Leave to England—Leave my Baby at a Ladies' School—Strange Affair there—Nearly Wrecked in a Hurricane—Stay at St. Helena—Arrival in England—Promoted to Major—Two Months' Continental Tour—Return to India—Last Voyage round the Cape—Remarks—Arrival at Calcutta—Suicide there of a Fellow-Passenger—Apply for the vacant Appointment of the Persian Translatorship to Government—Disappointment for want of Interest—Ordered to Gwalior—Appointed Interpreter to 92nd Highlanders at Jullundar—Strange Case of Suicide—Promoted to Lieutenant-Colonel—Resign the Interpretership—Visits to Simla and Mussoorie—Apply for an Appointment—Fair Reply—Take Furlough to England—Stay at Delhi—Description of the Palace—A Week at Bombay—Remarks on Missionary Work in India—Thoughts about Indian Servants—Overland Journey to Genoa and through Europe—Retirement from Service . 217

CHAPTER IX.

Narrative continued of E. S. the Atheist—Our Final Meeting in Calcutta—E. S. takes his Discharge—His Bright Prospects Ruined by his own Folly—He Re-Enlists—His Wretched Death—Remarks—Concluding Argumentative Remarks . . . 249

GLOSSARY

OF

WORDS IN COMMON USE IN BENGAL PRESIDENCY WHICH OCCUR IN THIS WORK.

AB (*pronounced* aub, *as Punjaub*), five waters or rivers. DOAB, a district between two rivers.
ABAD, inhabited as a town, like ALLAHABAD, the City of God.
ANNA, four copper coins called pice, making a sixteenth part of a rupee.
AYAH, nurse.
BABA, child.
BABOO, Hindoo title equivalent to Esquire.
BAGH, garden; as BADSHAH BAGH, king's garden.
BANG, an intoxicating potion.
BAWURCHEE, cook.
BAZAR, market.
BEARER, valet-de-chambre.
BEGUM, queen or princess.
BHEESTIE, water-carrier.
BRAHMIN, a man of the priestly caste worshipped by the Hindoos.
BUDGEROW, a sailing vessel on the Ganges.
BUDMASH, a vagabond of the worst description.
BUGGEE, a covered gig.
BUHADUR, a high-sounding title of oriental eulogy.
BUKHSHEESH, a present.
BUNGALOW, a house.
CHOWKYDAR, a native servant who watches against thieves, on the principal of "set thief to watch thief," the chowkydar belonging to their caste.
CHUPATTY, a thin cake of unleavened bread, the ordinary food of the natives.
COOLIE, a punkhah-puller. *See under* PUNKHAH.
DAWK, Indian post. GAREE DAWK, a journey by coach.
DHOBY, the manservant that washes the clothes.
FERINGHEE, a European. But it is disrespectful to speak of an English gentleman as a Feringhee.
FUKEER, a native mendicant held in considerable esteem.
GARREE, a carriage drawn by horses.
GHAZEE, a devoted Mussulman who fights for the Mohamedan faith.

GURH, a fort, as Azimgurh.
HAVILDAR, a native sergeant.
JEMADAR, a native lieutenant.
KHIDMUTGAR, a servant who waits at table.
KUCHERY, a court of justice.
LOÓT, plunder.
LOTA, a brass drinking-vessel used by the natives.
MATER, a sweeper, who belongs to the lowest caste.
MEM SAHIB, the mistress of the house.
MUSJID, mosque, as the Jumma Musjid of Delhi, being to Delhi what St. Paul's is to London.
NAICK, corporal
NANA, grandfather. A term of respect amongst the Mahratas, as Nana Sahib, given to Dhoondoo Punt of infamous memory.
NAWAB, a viceroy or ruler of a principality, as the Nawab of Rampore.
NUDDEE, a river.
POOJA, idolatry.
PORE, a town, as Serampore, or literally Serie-ram-pore, the city of the illustrious Ram.
PUNKHAH, a huge fan hooked in the ceiling, which in the hot weather is pulled day and night to promote a cool current of air, and to drive off the mosquitoes.
RAJA, a Hindoo king, as the Raja of Bhurtpore.
RYOT, a peasant.
SAHIB, master.
SEPOY, a native soldier.
SHAHZADA, prince.
SOWAR, trooper.
SUBADAR, a native captain.
SULAM, a common salutation of " Peace be to you ! "
SYCE, a groom.
TALL, a lake, as Nynee Tall.
TALOOKDAR or ZUMEENDAR, a landholder. These landholders may be regarded as the nobility of the country.

INDIAN REMINISCENCES.

CHAPTER I.

Departure from England—Life on board Ship—Practical Jokes—A Challenge to Fight a Duel—Pleasant Stay at the Cape of Good Hope—Dangerous Return to Ship—Outrageous Conduct of the Captain—His extraordinary Humiliation—Escape from a Shark—Touch at Madras—Arrival at Calcutta—Funny Adventure at Barrackpore—Taken by Steamer to Allahabad—Taken ashore at Dinapore—Dangerous Illness there—A good Samaritan—Exchange my Regiment—Serve through the Sikh Campaign, 1845-46—Descriptions of Battles: Moodkee, Ferozshah—Sir Hugh Gough—Rank Worship—Petty Warfare at Watchtower—Battles of Budiwal, Aliwal, and Sobraon—Remarks on War—Personal Feelings—March on Lahore—Submission of the Sikhs—Annexation of Jullundar Doab—British Protectorate of the Punjaub—Stationed at Hoshiarpore—Expedition to Cashmere—House broken into by Robbers—Ordered to Bareilly—Visit Nynee Tall—Simla—Its Charm—Description of Mussoorie—Second Sikh War—Chillianwallah—Goojerat—Sir Charles Napier sent out—Victory of Goojerat—Annexation of the Punjaub—Koh-i-Noor—Dhuleep Singh—Suppression of Duelling—March to Berhampore—Exchange my Regiment—Reason of.

On the 2nd or 3rd December, 1844, I left England on board the ship C—y, as a cadet in the E.I.C.S. My fellow-passengers were two young officers, and two other young fellows, besides the ship doctor, who was always ready for any kind of fun. I had only recently left school, and being totally inexperienced in the ways of the world, I became their butt, so that they appeared to enjoy themselves amazingly at my expense. Now, had they contented themselves with merely chaffing me, provoking as even that is, I might possibly have borne it; but to be incessantly the object of their practical jokes; to have salt put in my wine, and on one

B

occasion even gunpowder inside a cigar I ventured to smoke till it exploded; to have hard peas propelled through a peashooter with stinging force against the different features of my face; to be tied fast to the ladder till they chose to release me, whenever I attempted to mount aloft; to have my chair suddenly withdrawn the moment I was about to sit upon it, amidst laughter at my fall to the ground—all this was enough to provoke to desperation one by nature hot-tempered! It will therefore be easily understood that I led a dog's life on board ship, for not only were these games carried on during the day, but even at night they would not let me alone; since sometimes they would come into my room when I was fast asleep and rub my face over with burnt cork, so that when I awoke and looked in the glass, I found myself turned into a regular Christy minstrel!

At other times I would find myself in the middle of the night dragged out of my bed by a cord attached to my big toe; and once, by a wicked device concocted by the passengers and the Captain of the ship, they made me furiously drunk. Moreover, I was barbarously treated crossing the Line. At last I could not stand it any longer, so in a fury, I sent them a challenge to fight a duel at the first place we landed.

This instead of awing them only excited their merriment. I had a pretty dull time of it on board ship, for there was not much to take off my thoughts, and the interest in marine sights, such as watching the enormous albatrosses and other birds as they flew fearlessly by, wears away after a time. It was therefore a great relief when we arrived in February at the Cape of Good Hope, where we remained ten days. Landing at Cape Town, I put up at a boarding-house, or a hotel, for I don't know which it would be called. This town, which is the capital of Cape Colony, is situated in a valley between Table and Lion Mountains. It is celebrated for its sherry, which is absurdly cheap—only sixpence a quart bottle, if I remember right. Table Mountain is an interesting object to see. It is a stupendous mass of naked rock, rising almost perpendicularly about 3,580 feet, and when the clouds are low, they occasionally present the appearance of a white cloth spread over and hanging down its side.

The Cape, however, is that sort of a place, so it has struck me, that one would get tired of before long; though my sojourn there was very pleasant. It was not too hot to go about during the day, for I frequently hired a horse and rode to the lovely vineyards of Constantia, distant I should think from Cape Town about ten or twelve miles. I was quite charmed with the place. It was indeed a very pretty sight, and thoroughly enjoyable. I stayed to the very last at Cape Town. Finally, late in the evening, I went to the beach and hired a boat to take me on board my ship, lying about three miles from the shore, and was to leave very early the next morning. Having taken my seat, the boatmen pulled away; they rowed first in one direction and then in another, but they could not find the ship. At length the head boatman worked himself into a perfect frenzy at not being able to find the vessel; besides which I expect he was half drunk if not worse, because at last, strange as it may seem, he threatened in a rage to throw me overboard. And now I must relate a very remarkable circumstance: though I did not know at all where the ship was lying, yet the thought struck me that it might be in one particular direction. Acting on the idea, I said to the boatman, "Pull in that direction," adding (if I rightly remember), "and then if you don't succeed in finding the C—— you may do what you like with me." The man obeyed, and to my inexpressible joy I arrived safely on board. Who can say but that my life may not have been saved by that happy suggestion? I can't help thinking that the merciful God put this thought into my head. We took three passengers on board, a Major and his wife, and Captain

MacV——, who preached extempore sermons to us on Sundays, causing thereby a sort of religious revival, in which I so far partook that I felt impressed by his earnest addresses. But it is time now to narrate that which wrought a great change in the feelings of the passengers towards me, transforming two of them from persecutors into sympathizing friends. A Mr. H—— (who I believe was going out as a clerk in a merchant's office) one day snatched the hat off my head and hung it up near the stern for the Captain, who had a gun in his hand, to aim at; the latter immediately shot it into the sea. I felt excessively annoyed, as this was the only hat or cap I had left, and being in a regular passion I gave way to a torrent of abuse directed against the Captain, and at the same time snatching up his shot-bag, I sent it after my hat. The skipper now in his turn became furious. The first thing he did was to rush at me and knock me down with a single blow, for he was a very powerful man. Then in a mad fury he tried to throw me down the companion ladder; but with all my strength for very life I clung to the steps and prevented him accomplishing his fierce purpose. He then came and stamped upon me. At last, when I did come down, he confined me to my cabin for a day or two. Such an outrage, committed on a passenger, a mere youth, aroused much compassion and sympathy. Those that had teazed me without mercy before, now became my comforters. I made up my mind what to do when I landed, and that was to prosecute the Captain for the assault and unlawful imprisonment.

My intention coming somehow or other to the ears of the Captain of the ship, filled that hard-hearted man with the greatest alarm, and he had good cause to feel so, for had I carried out my intention, it would, I should think, have ruined him. His well-grounded fears led him to humiliate himself in an extraordinary manner, in the hope of softening my resentment. For he actually threw himself at my feet, and implored my forgiveness, which I was induced to extend, by the mediation of Captain MacV——, who urged the duty of forgiveness in a Christian point of view. I have nothing further to say of the skipper, except that he once certainly saved my life. It was when there was not a breath of wind, and the ship being becalmed, I was undressing for a plunge into the sea, that the Captain, coming up in the very nick of time, stopped the rash act I was just about to commit; and well for me was it that he did so, for if he had not, a horrid shark that appeared about a minute afterwards would undoubtedly have satisfied the craving of its appetite at my expense. We touched at Madras, as we had to land there the two passengers from the Cape. I went on shore to see what was to be seen; but though I have been there twice, I can't help thinking Madras a dull and uninteresting place. There are, of course, Fort St. George and Government House, and some other handsome public buildings. But Madras is entirely wanting in that animated appearance which is to be seen in Calcutta and Bombay. The most exciting thing there, as far as my experience goes, is the going through the tremendously heavy surf in a Maṣoolah boat. We in the Bengal Presidency are accustomed to speak of Madras as the benighted presidency. Nothing worth mentioning occurred during the rest of the voyage. A few days afterwards we reached the pilot station at the Sandheads, then passing Saugor Island we sailed up the Hoogly, to make or mar our fortunes in a land where, beyond a handful of Europeans, there is so little to remind one of home; still there was something very exhilarating in the idea of having done for ever with school and being one's own master, and of acquiring military renown at some future time.

We arrived at Calcutta on the 24th of April, but I lost a day's pay by not reporting myself at Fort William till the 25th of April. As I was only a few days in Calcutta, and don't remember much about my short visit there at that time, I shall reserve a description of the metropolis of British India to that future period of my narrative when I come to speak of my return to the presidency five years afterwards. The three principal events of my short stay there were—first, the purchase of uniform, and then, as soon as it was ready, which was quickly the case, the strutting about in it to be saluted for the first time by the soldiers. The swallow-tailed full dress coat, and that article which we used to call the "coal scuttle" full dress cap, were then in vogue. The intrinsic value of these things is small; it is the workmanship that one has to pay so enormously for.*

The second incident was the kindness shown to me by the banker to whom I presented my letter of credit, which, such was Indian hospitality in those days, proved to me a letter of recommendation.

The third occurrence was a flying visit I paid to the neighbouring military station of Barrackpore, where late in the evening I surprised the officers of one of the regiments there by marching right into their mess house whilst they were sitting down to dinner, under the impression that it was an hotel. However, they no doubt saw at once that I was a griff, since they hospitably overlooked my ignorant impertinence, gave me a good dinner, and a bed for the night. After which I returned to Calcutta, and took my passage by steamer for Allahabad. But before reaching that place I was taken dangerously ill of typhoid fever. The doctors on board took me ashore on reaching Dinapore, and placed me there in an unfurnished bungalow, then, having hastily hired for me some servants, and having placed me under the medical care of the surgeon in charge of the station, they proceeded on their journey. Shall I ever forget that time? No, never, as long as life lasts. The

* My experience has been that a uniform in good condition only fetches a shilling in the sovereign when disposed of.

doctors on board the steamer had given it as their opinion—so I subsequently learnt—that I should not outlive the twenty-four hours. It is hardly possible to imagine any condition more deplorable than mine then was. I, a mere stripling, who at home had been accustomed to every comfort, was now, to all appearance, dying of typhoid fever in an empty bungalow (the only article of furniture being a borrowed bed); with no loving mother or kind friend at hand to soothe my sufferings, which must have been great, when it is considered that it was about the middle of May, when the hot winds are at their height. And I was all alone, except that I was surrounded by the stolid apathetic faces of a lot of heathen servants picked up in a hurry, who, I believe, only waited for the breath to leave my body to make off with whatever they could lay their hands on. But, worse than all, I felt I was not ready to die—there was the weight of unpardoned sin. This was most awful! The night that followed is stamped upon my memory as though branded with a red-hot iron. I think, mentally and physically, I bore all that the human frame is capable of bearing without actual dissolution. I really felt I was dying, and seemed to see earthly things passing away. And, oh! the awful thought that oppressed me that I was not ready to meet my God! I wept all night, praying incessantly that God would have mercy on me and restore me to health, vowing that then I would live to Him. God in his infinite mercy heard my cry, or I should have been eternally lost. He inclined the heart of an officer in the 66th Regiment N.I. to take compassion on me. This officer acted the part of a good Samaritan, took me to his own comfortable house, and procured a European soldier to wait on me. This and the judicious treatment of the doctor was blessed to my recovery in due course of time. I have had many hair-breadth escapes since, but have never been nearer inside the portals of death than on this occasion. In due time I left Dinapore* to join the regiment I had been posted to. But I shortly afterwards exchanged into the 59th Regiment N.I., stationed at Meerut, and with this regiment I served through the first Sikh campaign of 1845-46, which, with its origin, must now be briefly related.

The cause of this war was the unmanageable turbulence of the Sikh soldiers, whose military ardour was directed to the invasion of British India. We were now, for the first time in India, about to encounter an enemy possessing the personal courage of Europeans. My regiment formed part of the Meerut Force, under Sir John Grey, which was sent on to the frontier in hot haste to meet the threatened danger.

For the first time in my life I slept one whole night on the ground on this march to join the main army. Our brave chief, Sir Hugh Gough, whose fingers itched to fly at the invaders at once, engaged the enemy under Lall Singh at Moodkee on the 18th December, 1845. The English were victorious, and the Sikhs were driven from their positions with great slaughter, and with the loss of seventeen pieces of artillery. Our loss in killed and wounded amounted to eight hundred and seventy-two, but we lost two Generals, Sir John McCaskill and Sir Robert Sale, who were both slain. Flushed with the victory won, Sir Hugh, probably thinking with the immortal Shakespeare that "the fewer men the greater share of honour," attacked the enemy without waiting for the reinforcements which were close at hand (21st December, 1845). I was not present at this battle because my regiment did not arrive on the spot till a day or two after it was all over. We then heard the particulars of that fearful day of carnage. How Sir Henry Hardinge had waived his superior official rank and served under his subordinate as second in command. How they both on

* Nineteen years afterwards I met an officer in Calcutta who spoke to me about this illness, and he told me that the deplorable way I was brought into Dinapore made a great impression on his mind. This struck me as being such a singular incident that I immediately recorded it in my diary, which I had kept up ever since my first arrival in India.

that day (the 21st), at the head of fifteen thousand British soldiers and Sepoys with sixty-nine guns, had attacked at Ferozshah an army of between fifty and sixty thousand Sikhs, commanded by Lall Singh, strongly entrenched in the form of a parallelogram, with the village in its centre, defended by upwards of one hundred guns. How terrific had been the contest and how frightful the slaughter! How H.M. 62nd Regiment, after sustaining fearful losses, had been compelled to retire. That the first day's fighting had ended with gloomy prospects for our small force; since night had fallen upon the combatants with the Sikhs still holding a great part of their position, whilst our troops, in close proximity to theirs, bivouacked upon the remainder of the great quadrangle which they had so far succeeded in taking. That our loss amounted to nearly two thousand five hundred in killed and wounded. We heard also how the battle had been renewed the next day, 22nd December, when the Commander-in-Chief and Governor-General once more formed their diminished troops in line for an attack, and that then, to their inexpressible relief, the English gained an almost unexpected victory. I use the word unexpected advisedly; because the Sikhs had every reason to expect a successful issue to the combat, as they had just been reinforced by some forty thousand fresh soldiers under Tej Singh, and unitedly they ought, according to human calculations, to have been able to crush our small array. But, wonderful to relate, they, contrary to what might have been expected, retreated from all their positions, leaving a great many of their guns to be captured. What led them to behave in this surprising manner was, so it was said, the fear that we were going to attack their flank or rear.

But I attribute the retrograde movement of the Sikhs to the treachery of some of their sirdars. For it seems incredible that an army of brave men, who throughout the first day of the battle had courageously maintained nearly the whole of their position, should so unreasonably beat a retreat just after receiving such an accession to their strength! It certainly was a most critical business, for some of our Sepoys were contemplating deserting to the enemy, as I was told by one who overheard their treacherous conversation. This was my first sight of a battle-field, and the horrid scenes that met my view made me feel very melancholy just for the time. We now went after the Sikhs and encamped for about four weeks within a few miles of them, whilst they were fortifying themselves on our side of the Sutlej at Sobraon, about twenty-six miles from Ferozpore. During that time, I used often to see Sir Hugh Gough watching the enemy from the camp watchtower, and a fine old soldier he looked every inch of him. He was one of the best specimens of an old gentleman that I have ever beheld. Highly honoured should I have felt had he condescended to have noticed a regimental Subaltern like myself by asking me the time of day, or making an ordinary remark about the weather. But I never had the honour of a single word from the venerable veteran throughout the whole of this time. It is remarkable how rank is worshipped in the army. No one besides an ensign and a lieutenant knows what a great man a captain is, besides of course the captain himself; and a major or lieutenant-colonel, especially if he is in command of a regiment, is held in great admiration, awe, and respect, as though he were a king; and as for the general of division, I scarcely know how to describe the extraordinary respect paid in military circles to such a magnate. I know this, however, that I stood in such fear and awe of the general, that I felt it really a painful ordeal to pay my respects to the great man. I went to his residence in a state of nervous trepidation, so that it was quite a joyful relief when the general's servant, as sometimes happened, uttered the word "Durwazuh-bund" (The door is closed).* The longing

* This is tantamount to the more untruthful "Not at home," which is the current white lie in society in England.

therefore to obtain those higher ranks in the military profession is most intense; but, alas! such is the unsatisfactory nature of all earthly gratifications, that the attainment of what is so ardently coveted in expectation is rapidly followed, if not actually accompanied, by a blight in the shape of increased cares and anxieties; together with those concomitant infirmities which attend that period in one's existence called the decline of life. Everything here below is evanescent; nothing can satisfy the cravings of the human soul but that peace of God which is the result of a living faith in Christ!

The old veteran I as a youngster so admired at our watchtower on the Sutlej, is no longer living on earth. Life's fitful fever is over with him. And to my mind there is scarcely anything sadder than to hear, as one is continually doing, of the passing away from earth of those who during my Indian service have acquired great renown in that Eastern clime, and as such have been the objects of my admiration. Especially does it pain me so continually to hear, as time passes on, of those old officers who so distinguished themselves during the Indian Mutiny; those whose names at that time were familiar to me as household words, as one by one each in his turn succumbs to the last grim enemy. In this melancholy disorganization of human strength and greatness, how refreshing it is to fall back upon God's word, which assures us that, "there remaineth therefore a rest to the people of God" (Hebrews iv. 9). It is, however, time to return from this digression to the subject in hand. I shall not take upon myself unnecessarily to criticize the generalship of our chief, but give a relation of what I believe to be the facts of the matter. One strange episode of our contact with the enemy was, that between our camp and their position was a post that was held by us during the day. At this post there was a good deal of petty warfare going on. It was a sort of give-and-take affair; whenever they had a chance they fired at us, and *vice versâ*. One day I was on duty there. When it was my turn to watch the enemy, I soon learnt the necessity for caution; for no sooner did I expose my head above the watchtower, than one of the enemy immediately let fly thereat, sending a bullet whizzing close to my skull; when, roused to action, I immediately returned the compliment. The next battle was fought at Budiwal, by a separate force under the command of Sir Harry Smith; who was repulsed with the loss of one hundred and thirty men. But on the 28th January, 1846, Sir H. Smith retrieved this by the decisive victory he gained at Aliwal, when with ten thousand men and thirty-two guns he defeated Runjoor Singh with nineteen thousand men and fifty-six guns. The English loss in killed, wounded, and missing, was five hundred and eighty-nine men. The next blow dealt was the Waterloo of the campaign. On the 9th February we learnt that we were to move out to attack the enemy on the following day; and at dinner we heard that we should be in the thickest of the fight. I prayed during a considerable part of the night, for I well knew that, instead of keeping the solemn vow I had made in my illness at Dinapore, I was living an ungodly life. My prolonged devotional exercises, it is almost needless to say, were of a purely selfish character. Next morning (10th February, 1846), Sir H. Gough, who had before somewhat erred as a Commander from bravery carried to impetuosity, now, in conjunction with Sir Henry Hardinge, led out a splendid force of eighteen thousand British soldiers and Sepoys to attack at least thirty thousand of the best Sikh troops, strongly entrenched in a bend of the river Sutlej, protected by formidable batteries of artillery. A tremendous struggle now ensued. Sir Robert Dick, K.C.B., who commanded a regiment at Waterloo, moved to the assault with his division. My regiment, the 59th N.I., which formed a part thereof,[*]

---

[*] Now the 8th Regiment N.I. It behaved so far respectably during the Mutiny that it was retained in consequence.

emulated the Europeans in cool determination. But so terrible a resistance was encountered, that for a brief space we were checked in our advance; but at last we climbed over their breastworks. General Gilbert charged the centre of the enemy's position with his division, which after being repeatedly driven back, succeeded at last in overcoming all resistance, and entering the entrenchments.

The defences having been carried in every direction, the Sikhs were pressed on all sides, and under this pressure they gave way. But at first they retreated in good order, our brave foes disputing every inch of ground, and I particularly remember the bravery of one lion-hearted Sikh who, for a time scorning to give way, kept on fighting till our line were within about six or eight yards off, when I saw about five or six shots aimed at him, and only then did he turn round, and join the main body of the retreating army; and I hope the brave fellow may have lived to fight on our side twelve years afterwards. This orderly retreat, however, changed its character, and became a disorderly rush to cross the only bridge they had erected across the river. The consequence was that, unable to sustain such a great strain, the bridge broke and precipitated their army into the Sutlej. Now was witnessed a dreadful scene, for our artillery was brought forward, and then deadly discharges were poured into this dense human mass struggling in the water. It was indeed an awful sight to see so many thousands of brave men perishing in the cold waters of the Sutlej, and one that the angels might have wept over, though there was no pity then in the breasts of the victors! Was it cruel? Perhaps it was, but such is war! Happy would it be for the world at large to recognize the fact that war is a great curse, entailing such frightful misery that nothing whatever can justify it, excepting it be strictly in self-defence, such as resisting an invasion, as was the case with us in this instance. The Sikh loss in killed, wounded and drowned, amounted to at least ten thousand men, the greatest part of their loss being occasioned by the breaking of the bridge. Our loss in this action amounted to two thousand three hundred and eighty; Major-General Dick who commanded our division being amongst the killed. It would be untrue were I to say that throughout this fight I felt no fear when I saw men falling all around me, and when the Sikh fire against our advance was so heavy, that it seemed as if balls and bullets filled the air, except just that particular space through which I moved. The fact is that I did not then, and I have never since engaged in any hard fight without having a sense of fear. But a strong sense of duty and a high sense of honour have ever neutralized that fear, or otherwise I should have slunk to the rear. I admire those lines :—

> "The brave man is not he who feels no fear;
> For that were stupid and irrational;
> But he whose noble nature dares the danger
> Nature shrinks from."

The excitement of battle must be experienced to be understood. They are dreamers who think that a hard fight like that of Sobraon at all resembles the manœuvres of soldiers on parade. What then is it like? Why a very hard struggle and a scene of confusion. "Every battle of the warrior," the Prophet Isaiah tells us, "is with confused noise and garments rolled in blood" (Is. ix. 5). I myself saw sights enough to curdle one's blood, sights indelibly impressed on my memory.

Though God had covered my head in the day of battle, yet I forgot to return Him thanks for this great mercy. The fact is, that at that time I did not care to retain God in my thoughts. After the battle we marched upon Lahore, the capital of the Punjaub, and the campaign was ended by the submission of the Sikhs. We annexed a slice of territory called the

Jullunder Doab, and there was a British protectorate of the dismembered Sikh empire, of which Maharajah Dhuleep Sing was the recognized sovereign.

I marched with my regiment after this to Hoshiarpore, in the newly ceded district, where we had to build our houses. But we had not been many months there before we were ordered off, at a very short notice, to form part of a column under the command of Brigadier Wheeler, to put down the insurrection of Shaick Emamodeen in Cashmere. I left everything I did not take with me in my house, which in my absence was broken open and everything of value was taken. This was a serious loss, for which I received no compensation. We advanced to the borders of that beautiful land when Emamodeen gave in. This was in 1846. We were then ordered to Bareilly, which we reached early in January, 1847.

This station in the North-West Provinces,* distant about eight hundred miles from Calcutta, was a desirable cantonment, owing to its particular healthiness and to its being only a hundred miles from that lovely sanatorium, Nynee Tall, with its deliciously cool and remarkably equable climate; its picturesque scenery, set off by the proximity of a beautiful lake, a mile long and a quarter of a mile broad, nestling under the surrounding majestic hills, dotted with the comfortable houses of the Sahib logue; its birds of gaudy plumage, such as the golden pheasant; its shooting, boating and yachting. When I went from Bareilly to this delightful spot, I travelled all night, by Palkee to Rampoor, where during the day I was hospitably entertained free of all cost by the Nawab of that principality, in a comfortable house specially provided for travellers by that open-handed native prince. Starting in the evening I

* Bareilly then abounded with wolves, which were in those days the terror of the natives, whose children they preyed upon. I remember one day the whole station starting off in pursuit of one of these ferocious creatures that in broad daylight had taken off a native child.

reached Kaleedonga, at the foot of the hills, the following morning, and at once rode up to Nynee Tall, a distance of about thirteen miles. I enjoyed myself very much, what with the bathing, shooting, sailing, and pleasant society. Here I made the acquaintance of General Richards, who had served with the Duke of Wellington at the siege of Seringapatam. I also formed the friendship of Captain H. Ramsay, the magistrate of Nynee Tall, now Major-General the Hon. Sir Henry Ramsay, C.B., K.C.S.I., Commissioner of Kumaon. I dined at his house nearly once a week, and then afterwards we used to go together to the house of the Rev. J. H. Budden,* an Independent missionary, where we spent many profitable evenings. Here I renewed my acquaintance with Lieutenant E——, who had been obliged to go to the Invalides after the first Sikh campaign, in which his regiment had been engaged. It is undesirable to mention the cause of his removal from the Service, or to discuss the current rumours of the time on the unpleasant affair.

This visit of mine to Nynee Tall was in 1849. Poor E—— was afterwards drowned in the lake through being capsized in his boat in a sudden squall of wind. But the jaded civilian or the languid military officer requiring a change, either for the good of his health or for recreation, was not restricted in his choice to Nynee Tall, since he might go on a little farther to the well-known and charming hill station of Mussoorie, which, except that it has no lake, is an embodiment of all that is beautiful in verdant mountain scenery. Here may be gathered rhododendrons, orange-flowers, honeysuckles, maidenhair ferns, violets, clematis, and also passion-flowers, and in its vicinity there is a fine waterfall, called the Batta Falls. A good rider may enjoy

---

* I perceive from the last report of the London Missionary Society, dated May 1, 1879, that this gentleman, who has been a missionary for thirty-eight years, is still at the hill station of Almora, which is near Nynee Tall.

himself mightily here; so may a lover of pic-nics, and so may a lady unable to ride by buying a palkee, called here a janpan, for about thirty shillings, and hiring bearers to carry her about. At all events I know that years afterwards I spent a very enjoyable six months here. A little farther to the north there was another hill station, more resorted to than any other, which was quite an accessible sanatorium to Bareilly; this was Simla. To this spot would flock all seekers of appointments. For an officer aspiring to get a civil or military appointment, who desired to go to some place where, by currying favour with the great, he might create an influence for himself sufficient to secure that object, would select Simla, which was, and is, pre-eminently the most fashionable sanatorium in India. Here the place-hunter would stick during the whole period of his leave,* taking every opportunity to ingratiate himself with all who could do him a good turn, as it is to Simla that the Governor-General, Commander-in-Chief, and other magnates annually take their flight to escape the scorching heats of the plains. These great personages draw after them a host of minor swells, too numerous to particularize. Simla,† then, for six months, becomes the head-quarters of the civil and military government of India, and for that time endless festivities and gaieties and frivolities are the order of the day.

Simla has no lake, but the scenery is fine and imposing. These places are now easily reached by rail. The traveller to Simla gets out of the train at Umballa, and goes by Dawk Garee (coach) to Kalka, at the foot of the hills, which he would reach in four hours, provided he has good horses, and if, with the aid of an accompanying elephant, he manages safely to pass a

* Limited to six months on private affairs, from 15th April to 15th October.
† Simla is 1,112 miles from Calcutta, and nearly the same distance from Bombay.

certain rapid torrent in the way that sometimes turns the coach right over. The traveller would then ascend the hill, and if he left Umballa early in the morning, he would, late in the same day, reach Kussowlie, the convalescent depôt. Then he has only to get to rest at the hotel during the night, provided he has prudently secured a room by writing beforehand to the manager. After which, if he does not wish to pay a visit to the Lawrence Orphanage in the vicinity (established for the benefit of the children of deceased European soldiers), he would after breakfast proceed on his way, sleep for the night at the rest bungalow, and leave early the next morning for Simla, which he would reach the same day.

The journey would of course be done much quicker by riding. The road from Kussowlie to Simla is very narrow, with precipices underneath and overhanging high rocks almost detached in some places, and threatening to fall down and crush one. The traveller to Mussoorie would get out of the train at Suharanpore, whence he would travel all night by the Omnibus or Dawk Garee to Rajpore, at the foot of the hills, which he would reach in between ten and eleven hours. Having breakfasted at Rajpore, he would ascend the hill in a janpan borne by bearers, who would convey him to Mussoorie in between two and three hours. There is a fine club and some very good hotels here, besides boarding-houses, so that the traveller ought to have no difficulty in suiting himself. But it is time to return to the subject in hand from this long digression. The second year of my residence at Bareilly (1848) was one of great excitement to us in the North-West Provinces, in consequence of the breaking out of the second Sikh War, which was begun by the murder at Mooltan of two British officers, Mr. Vans Agnew, a civilian, and Lieutenant Anderson, who were both foully murdered by the insurgents at the beginning of the hot season of that year.

The outbreak, which was headed by Dewan Moolraj,

spread rapidly, as most of the old Sikh soldiers eventually joined in this last struggle for the independence of their country. Major-General Whish, who was sent with an army of eight thousand men and a siege train against Mooltan, was forced to raise the siege of that city, in consequence of the defection of Rajah Shere Singh, who with his Sikh army went over to the enemy (14th September, 1848). This was followed by the revolt next month of eight thousand Sikh troops garrisoning Peshawur. This northern insurrection was led by Chuthur Singh, who formed an alliance with Dost Mahomed, the ruler of Afghanistan, whom he engaged to join with him in a joint crusade against us by the offer to the Ameer of Peshawur.

Lord Gough took the field in November, and for a time it seemed very doubtful which side would be victorious. The first engagement at Ramnuggur, on the 22nd November, 1848, was an indecisive one. Ten days afterwards occurred the indecisive action of Sadoolapore. These unsatisfactory actions were succeeded by the sanguinary battle of Chillianwallah on the 13th January, 1849, when Lord Gough attacked Shere Singh strongly posted there with about forty thousand soldiers and sixty guns. This also was an indecisive battle if not worse, for the Sikhs captured four of our guns and H.M. 14th Dragoons galloped to the rear instead of to the front.

Our loss was very severe. H.M. 24th Regiment lost twenty-three officers and over four hundred and fifty-nine men in killed and wounded, and our total loss amounted to nearly two thousand three hundred in killed and wounded. The news of the battle of Chillianwallah created quite a panic in England, and the story goes that the Iron Duke, meeting Sir C. Napier, said to him in his laconic manner, "Either you or I must go out to India." The victor of Waterloo was, however, spared a second trip to India, as Napier, who in military genius was second only to Wellington, consented to go out as Commander-in-Chief. But he arrived in India too late to influence the fortune of the campaign, which was concluded before his arrival.

Happily for the English under Gough, about this time the force under General Whish was free to march to their aid; because the town of Mooltan having been stormed on the 2nd January, Dewan Moolraj had surrendered the citadel on the 21st January, 1849. (Our loss in killed and wounded, during the four weeks' siege, being eleven hundred and twenty.) Being joined by General Whish, Lord Gough's army amounted to twenty-five thousand men, and a hundred guns. With this force, the Commander-in-Chief attacked and obtained a complete and decisive victory over Rajah Shere Singh and sixty thousand men, with fifty-nine guns, at Goojerat on the 21st February, 1849, with the comparatively small loss on our side of seven hundred and seventy-four men in killed and wounded. The remnant of the Sikh army, with Shere Singh their general, surrendered three weeks after to Sir W. Gilbert, commanding the pursuing column, and soon afterwards the Punjaub was annexed to British India by Lord Dalhousie (29th March, 1849). By the treaty entered into with the Maharajah Dhuleep Singh, the British Government bound themselves to pay a pension of not less than four lakhs of rupees,* and Dhuleep Singh renounced for ever all right to the sovereignty of the Punjaub, and surrendered to the Queen that magnificent jewel known as the "Koh-i-Noor" (or mountain of light). This was a happy change for Dhuleep Singh, who was now, in his twelfth year, the ward of the Governor-General. It is unnecessary to say more of the Maharajah, than that he subsequently embraced Christianity, and settled down into the life of an English nobleman.† But though Napier arrived in

* Forty thousand pounds, reckoning the rupee at two shillings.
† Maharajah Dhuleep Singh is a frequent visitor at Court. And, strange to say, his mother, the widow of the renowned Runjeet Singh, after a series of strange and romantic vicissitudes, found a resting-place at last in England, where she died in 1863.

India too late to take any share in the campaign, he came in time to do two things that entitle him to the praise of all good men. This was, that he did his utmost to put down the vice of gambling, and the abominable practice of duelling, by the most stringent measures. He also afforded amusement to Anglo-Indian Society by the most racy orders that were ever issued by any Commander-in-Chief. We marched to Berhampore in the cold season of 1849-50. On reaching which I applied for an exchange into the 42nd Regiment N.I. I did this on account of personal violence that had been offered to me on the line of march, for which I had been unable to procure any redress. I had been struck in the dark when my back was turned, and I could not accuse any one in particular, since I did not know who the offender was. All I could say was this, that I went up to a party of young officers and remonstrated with them for pelting me out of my tent, and ending by saying, "I know why you treat me in this manner, it is because you think me religious." I then turned round and walked away, when as my back was turned some one struck me on the head with a large piece of burning wood. Under such trying circumstances, since I could not obtain a Court of Inquiry, I felt it necessary to change my regiment. This brought me to Barrackpore, where I became intimate with the Baptist missionaries across the river at Serampore. But though I shall not here enlarge upon missionary work, yet I propose to give the next chapter to the discussion of a kindred subject.

CHAPTER II.

Suggestiveness of the Truth of the Bible in Things that may be seen in India—General Remarks on the Folly of Infidelity as contrasted with Christianity—Objections regarding the apparent Discrepancies of the Bible answered—Reply to the Cavils of Scientific Men—The Objections of Infidels cannot stand the Test of a thorough Examination—Actual Experience the most convincing Evidence of the Truth of the Bible—Meeting with the Subject of this Sketch, E. S., at Bareilly — Want of Christian Society at Bareilly — Next-door Neighbour with E. S. at Barrackpore—Description of Barrackpore, and the wretched State of Locomotion in India at this Period—Sketch of Calcutta, and its accessible Health Resort, Darjeeling—Ensign S—— engaged to be Married—The Engagement broken off—His Downward Career—Fires into my Room—Tried by a Court-martial—His Narrow Escape—Does not profit by the Warning—Leaves Barrackpore—Scene presented in his vacant Bungalow—Again tried by a Court-martial and Dismissed the Service—Enlists as a Private Soldier.

DURING my thirty years' Indian service I have frequently met in India with English officers holding infidel opinions. Perhaps this is nothing very strange; but regarded in one particular aspect it should excite some degree of surprise. For, despite the dark pall of heathenism that overspreads that unhappy land like a hideous nightmare, there is yet much which any one with his eyes open may see around him, that tends to foster the belief in the truth of the Bible; such, for instance, as various habits, customs, modes of expression, and the manner of living observed by the natives, which correspond with, and recall to the mind so many familiar things we read of in the sacred volume. These are too numerous to particularize. One, from its apparent irrationality to those unacquainted with Oriental customs, we are tempted to mention. It is taken from the 10th verse of Deuteronomy xi., which speaks of watering the ground with the foot. The sceptical critic might exclaim, what an absurd idea! Yet this is what may now be seen in India. I have myself seen the gardener watering the garden as he went along, here and there, by opening divers tiny embankments holding water, with his supple feet, and thereby setting free the fertilizing liquid to irrigate the garden in such parts as required it. Then what must any observant Englishman think, when he thoughtfully reflects upon the strikingly degraded moral condition of a naturally fine and intelligent race of people (for degraded they are and must be so long as all the respectable classes debase their own wives, mothers and daughters, by condemning them, from feelings of nasty jealousy, to a perpetual imprisonment in the Zenana);* and when he further thinks of a country nineteen hundred miles in length and sixteen hundred miles in breadth, with a population of two hundred million Mussulmen and idolaters being held in subjection by the inhabitants of a Christian and very distant and comparatively small island; and when he still further considers, that the ancestors of these conquered Hindoos were years ago far in advance of their conquerors in civilization!! I repeat the question, what must he think? Can he help arriving at the conviction, if he pursues these reflections to their legitimate issue, that, in illustration of the text (Prov. xiv. 34), "Righteousness exalteth a nation." England owes her elevation in the scale of nations to her pre-eminence as a Protestant country, that has done far more in the way of the translation and dissemination of the Bible, and the evangelization of the world than any other country in Europe; and that, on the other hand, it is idolatry (the same sin that brought such signal judgments upon the Jews of old) to which must be ascribed the present position of the

* The light in which the women of India are regarded by their lords and masters, is best expressed by the Hindoo saying, "If your house is on fire save yourself first, then your cow, and afterwards your wife."

Hindoos as a conquered race. For consider how totally unprecedented in the whole history of the world, is the fact of thirty millions of people holding in subjection two hundred millions of inhabitants of such a vast and distant country as India! In the next place, if he has the curiosity to inquire why the Mussulmen, who form about a quarter of the population of British India, reject Christianity, though they profess to believe in the Old and New Testaments, he will be told, as I have been, that the Bible we have in our possession is a corruption of the original, all the copies of which were destroyed by a wicked king a great many centuries ago. If after hearing this from his Moonshee he will next inquire of the Jews (and there are many of this scattered race in some parts of India), he will find that our Old Testament corresponds exactly with that possessed by the Jew, which is conclusive as to the genuineness of our version, as it is impossible to conceive of any collusion between the Christian and the Jew. Lastly, how can he account for the progress of Christianity in India except by admitting the preeminent power of the Gospel, which induces the Hindoo of high caste voluntarily to submit to what is regarded by his countrymen as the greatest possible disgrace, viz., loss of caste, incurring thereby in some instances very considerable risk of being murdered by his incensed relations, as well as losing his means of livelihood, and not unfrequently suffering, too, the loss of his wife, who would not for the world take a meal with her outcast husband! But it may be objected, are all the conversions genuine? Now, though I am by no means prepared absolutely to affirm this, yet I know, and so might others know, if they cared to investigate the matter, that many are really genuine cases of hearts changed by the wonder-working Grace of God. I have known myself some native Christians that would do honour to any community, and I have no desire to say anything but what is strictly true in the matter.

Therefore, with so many things visible in India that seem like the impresses of things recorded in the Bible, and with so much to be learnt in that Eastern country in evidence of the truth of that Holy Book, it does appear strange in this point of view that there should be found educated gentlemen who, overlooking all this, are so blinded by prejudice as to regard the divine revelation contained in the Holy Scriptures as no better than an idle tale. We propose in these reminiscences to give a sketch of a very singular character, whom I knew as an officer, and whom I met afterwards as a private soldier, whose mysterious death, occurring under strong suspicions of foul play, formed the subject of a police investigation some years ago (as was stated in the newspapers of the time). My purpose is to endeavour to illustrate by the strange incidents of his life (showing such an amazing perversion of natural abilities) the truth of the Scripture which saith, "The fool hath said in his heart, There is no God" (Psalm liii. 1). For, with his capabilities, which were of a very fair standard, the subject of these memoirs might, but for the blighting effects and influence of unbelief, have been at the present time a colonel commanding a regiment, instead of having passed the prime of his life as a private soldier. At the same time, I may observe that it is not my intention to waste my time or that of my reader by raking out of the mire the venomous arguments of infidelity and atheism; venomous of a truth they are, since they are fully bent on the destruction of everything virtuous and holy; in short, of everything worth living and dying for; whilst it may first be observed that these oft-refuted systems of unbelief are so utterly malignant, that they supply nothing in return for what they would take away—neither guidance, inducement, or influence to leading a virtuous and useful life; whilst they afford no support or solace to bear the sorrows and ills of life, and give positively nothing whatever to satisfy the cravings of the human heart after a life of happiness beyond the grave; for the atheist's hopes and fears are confined to this life, as after death annihilation is his expected heaven. What a contrast does this present to the blissful immortality which is the certain and assured inheritance of the lowliest believer in Jesus! The Christian's hopes are based on the perfect atonement of the Lord Jesus Christ, the great sin-bearer, who is the theme of the Divine revelation contained in the Holy Scriptures. These hopes are charmingly expressed in the following beautiful lines to be found in the 1st and 3rd verses of Bonar's hymn:

> 1. I lay my sins on Jesus,
>   The spotless Lamb of God,
> He bears them all and frees us
>   From the accursed load.
> I bring my guilt to Jesus,
>   To wash my crimson stains
> White in His blood most precious,
>   Till not a spot remains.
>
> 3. I rest my soul on Jesus,
>   This weary soul of mine;
> His right hand me embraces,
>   I on His breast recline.
> I love the name of Jesus,
>   Emmanuel, Christ the Lord;
> Like fragrance on the breezes
>   His name abroad is poured.

There are some things hard to be understood in the Bible, some apparent discrepancies which theologians in one or two instances may not have satisfactorily accounted for, owing to the finiteness of the human understanding and to the want of the undiscovered clue requisite to guide us out of the difficulty. But of this we may be quite certain, that it is impossible for the Divine Author of the inspired volume to make a mistake. Nothing can be truer than this. Therefore we must not think of relinquishing our belief in the Bible, or even of treating the sacred Book with a less degree of veneration, because of some difficulties contained therein. In illustration of the principle here laid down, I give the following anecdote, extracted from Canon

Ryle's writings:—" Persons who are conversant with Astronomy, know that before the discovery of the planet Neptune there were difficulties which greatly troubled the most scientific astronomers respecting certain aberrations of the planet Uranus. These aberrations puzzled the minds of astronomers; and some of them suggested that they might possibly prove the whole Newtonian system to be untrue. But just at that time a well-known French astronomer, named Leverrier, read before the Academy of Sciences at Paris a paper, in which he laid down this great axiom,—that it did not become a scientific man to give up a principle because of difficulties which apparently could not be explained. He said in effect, 'We cannot explain the aberrations of Uranus now; but we may be sure that the Newtonian system will be proved to be right, sooner or later. Something may be discovered one day which will prove that these aberrations may be accounted for, and yet the Newtonian system remains true and unshaken.' A few years after, the anxious eyes of astronomers discovered the last great planet Neptune. This planet was shown to be the true cause of all the aberrations of Uranus. And what the French astronomer had laid down as a principle in science was proved to be wise and true." The application of this anecdote is too obvious to require being stated. Our views of things are very restricted, for consider how many things there are in the world of Nature that lie right before us that are incomprehensible, and yet which no one thinks of cavilling about. To give one or two simple illustrations: who can explain the process of the growth of the bones of a child before its birth, or the transformation of an acorn into the mighty oak, or of food into flesh and blood? or who can comprehend the idea of unlimited space, or fathom the inscrutable mystery of an eternity without a beginning or end? or who can comprehend what an infinitesimal atom of matter is? We may of course conceive of its infinite division, but still, every particle must have a top and bottom! We are in fact surrounded with mysteries in the air we breathe, with its varied and wonderful phenomena, its developments of stormy wind and tempest, thunder and lightning, and its strange freaks of fickleness; for, as the Scripture tells us, God thundereth marvellously and doeth great things which we cannot comprehend (Job xxxvi. 5). Then who can understand the secret and wonderful power by which birds fly through the air? Knowing all these things to be beyond our comprehension, is it surprising if there are some things in a Divine Revelation that are imperfectly understood and are yet rightly believed in? What mad folly, therefore, for trifles light as air to reject such a treasure as the Holy Bible, the sufficiency of which is so beautifully expressed by the sorely tried Miss Anne Steele in the following lines:

> " Here may the wretched sons of want
> Exhaustless riches find;
> Riches above what earth can grant,
> And lasting as the mind."

With regard to the cavils of scientific men, our reply is that we admit what science really teaches, but not what it suits them to say it teaches. The so-called scientific facts of yesterday are proved false by the discoveries of to-day, and those of to-day may, in the same way, be refuted by future discoveries. Give us proved scientific facts, and we will accept them; for we deny that science contradicts Scripture. The God of revelation is the God of nature. He cannot contradict himself. The fact is that many men are too ready to accept theories as facts in their eagerness to prove the Scriptures untrue. It is quite absurd for sceptics to speak of the credulity of simple believers in a Divine Revelation; since they themselves are just as credulous concerning their particular crotchets (such for instance as the preposterous Darwinian theory) as those Hindoos who gravely assured me that the tigers, which formerly abounded at the place I was staying at, would invariably stop in mid career of their pursuit of the sacred Brahmin on discerning his holy smell, and turn away, like Cowper's nightingale, "to find a supper somewhere else." Moreover, the objections of infidels, however specious, clever and plausible, cannot stand the test of a searching examination;* but are just like the imaginary figures timid children fancy they see in the dark, which illusion is dispelled by the introduction of a light. Nothing is easier than to cavil at and raise objections to almost any theory that may be propounded by the wisest of men. A child, as every one knows, may ask a question which the greatest philosopher cannot answer. Well would it be for those who have imbibed sceptical opinions, if they would only test their vaunted speculations with the same scrutiny as that which has led them to reject the Bible!

Surely this is but reasonable; for if we Christians are mistaken, then after all we shall not be worse than the infidel; but if, on the other hand, we are not mistaken, what an inexpressibly woful and altogether irretrievable mistake will he have made! Further, it would be well for the sceptic who prides himself on his learning to remember that the greatest minds have reverently received the Bible as a Divine revelation. Two great poets compare the inspiration of the Bible to the sun. Cowper says:

"A glory gilds the sacred page,
Majestic, like the sun;
It gives a light to every age—
It gives, but borrows none."

Watts's comparison is in the following strain:

"'Tis like the sun, a heavenly light
That guides us all the day;
And through the dangers of the night,
A Lamp to lead our way."

* Many years ago, when stationed with my regiment at Chinsurah, I was once considerably staggered when, for the first time, I heard all the principal arguments that are adduced against the Bible, but this only lasted till I was furnished with the right solution of the difficulty, and then I saw that all these sceptical objections were mere sophisms.

The most convincing evidence of the divine origin of the Bible to the believer is that derived from actual personal experience of its truth. But the sceptic naturally objects to all proofs of this sort, because it is quite outside his experience, and beyond his comprehension. The Persian poet Sadi well observes: "It is not the sun's fault that the blind cannot see;" and Spurgeon hits off the same truism in the following proverb of his: "Light is good, but sore eyes do not like it." The great truths of the Bible, to be rightly appreciated, must be believed in, just as food must be partaken of before nourishment can be conveyed to the body. Believers in all ages can heartily assent to what Joshua said to the Israelites: "Ye know in all your hearts and in all your souls, that not one thing hath failed of all the good things which the Lord your God spake concerning you; all are come to pass, and nothing hath failed thereof" (Joshua, xxiii. 14). The accomplished physician, Dr. William Gordon, who had found in Christ a happiness he did not think existed this side the grave, often made use of the following expression: "If I had no other evidence of the truth of Christianity than my own case, it would be sufficient, if all the world were unchristian."

Hoping the reader will not be tired by the length of these general remarks, I shall proceed now with my promised sketch of one who denied both the authority of the Bible, and the existence of any Supreme Being; whose awful profanity in one particular instance is too shocking to be even mentioned. The incidents about to be related are facts. I have recorded nothing but what I either know myself to be true or have good reason to believe to be so. Indeed, I might have added more, but as I did not distinctly remember it, I have thought best to omit the matter.

E. S. was two or three years junior to me as Ensign. His father was a Surgeon in an English Cavalry Regiment, his grandfather was a Presidency Chaplain, and he had one uncle a Colonel, and another a Chaplain, who both lost their lives in the Sepoy Mutiny. I first saw him in 1848, at Bareilly, where we were both stationed. I do not remember anything very distinctly about him at that time; and indeed had no inclination to form any acquaintances of his sort, as I was at that time under serious convictions of my lost state as a sinner, and was in too great anxiety about the salvation of my soul to do anything but look out for some one who could sympathize with my religious aspirations, but I could not meet with one. Now I would not advise others similarly circumstanced to imitate me in the course I thought proper to adopt. I had to make up my mind as to whether I would have worldly society or none at all. This was a serious matter for consideration. But from the fear I entertained that I should be led astray by mixing with worldly people, as had been the case about three years before, when I had been under religious impressions, I therefore determined to shun society, and live a sort of hermit's life, as far as it was actually possible for a regimental subaltern to do so. It was not very long before I felt the ill effects of this, and despite my efforts to obtain relief by studying the native languages, going out shooting, and endeavouring to make a convert of my bearer, and some others, I found that the solitary mode of living affected my health by making me nervous, and I suffered several months from religious melancholy, nor did I obtain peace till some time after I left the station. Now were it possible, if I may use the expression, for me to live over that period again, I should act differently. For solitude in a country like India has its peculiar temptations, which need as much grace to resist as the seducements of worldly company; therefore, and on account of its injurious influence on the health, I should prefer even worldly society to a solitary existence. But I would decidedly absent myself from balls, amateur theatricals, and races. I would not stay long at mess after dinner, and would on no account play billiards for even the most trifling stake. And though I might not feel myself justified in censuring a senior officer at the mess table, yet I would endeavour by a grave countenance to rebuke sin gloried in, and pray for grace to have courage to speak a word in season.

Though I did not form the acquaintance of Ensign S—— at this period, I may cursorily remark that he was a man of remarkably fine physique; he possessed such great bodily strength that he could hold an ordinary-sized man out at arm's length. He was what is termed a griff, when I first saw him at Bareilly. It may here be mentioned that a young officer in those days used to be considered a griff for a whole year, during which time he had often to submit to a good deal of chaffing, and in some instances of practical joking, which in some cases was carried to an iniquitous extent.*

I next met S—— at Barrackpore, where I was stationed from 1850 to the end of 1852. Here we were next-door neighbours, our houses being close to each other. And now, having found peace of soul, through believing in Jesus as my Saviour, I had no objection to forming an acquaintance with him, till at last we

* As in my own case, for example, one of these practical jokes played on me during my griffinage nearly cost me my life. A thoughtless joker one day came up to me and offered me his horse to ride. I objected, saying that I could not ride well. "Nonsense," said Captain W——, who wanted to have a little fun, "the horse is as quiet as a lamb." Assured by this, I essayed to mount the horse, but to my horror I had scarcely got on the animal, which was really a most vicious brute, than it bolted at full speed towards the low-roofed stables. I stretched out my hand to save my head from being dashed to pieces, but a kind Providence here intervened and saved my life, so that I was only knocked flat on the horse's back without any serious injury. Sometimes the practical joking was of a very provoking character, as when I was lying ill at the mess-house of my regiment at Meerut. Some of the officers, merry with wine after dinner, amused themselves by shying empty bottles against my door. The practical joking that was practised on me during my year's probation has left such an impression on my mind that will never, I think, be obliterated.

were on as friendly terms as it was possible for two persons of such opposite dispositions to be.

A friend of his, Lt. H——, an officer of my regiment, employed his leisure time in the kind office of trying to make a better man of him, which had a great deal to do with my going there as often as I did. However, all the kind offices of this friend were in vain; because E. S. was his own enemy, and events soon showed that there was no doing anything for him. We lived at the farthest end of cantonments. At this time Barrackpore was a large military station, and one on the whole much to be desired on account of its pleasant Park and Zoological Gardens, and its proximity to Calcutta, not merely the metropolis of India, but then the general port of embarkation for all residents in the Bengal Presidency; as there was then no railway, as is the case now, to take one all the way to Bombay. The first short line from Calcutta to Hooghly was not then open. When we wanted to go to Calcutta, which was often the case, we either went by boat, which, tide being favourable, could be accomplished in two hours (a distance of fifteen miles), or else in a carriage by land, which was the pleasantest; or with a fast horse one could easily enough ride the whole way. I have mounted outside the Park, and ridden all the way to Lall Bazaar (Calcutta), a distance of fourteen miles, in one hour. But of course no one would think of doing such a thing now that Calcutta is made accessible by railways. Perhaps a short account here of the wretched state of locomotion that then existed in India will not prove unacceptable to the general reader. The three modes of transit in vogue at this period were the following, viz.: 1, Palkee Dawk, whereby the traveller was conveyed in a Palkee,* on the shoulders of palkee bearers, who carry him a certain distance to the tune of a monotonous grunting

* The Palkee resembles a bright-looking coffin with windows, folding-doors and a long pole at each end, in which the occupant can but just manage to sit upright.

sort of chant, which has seemed to my imaginative ears to be very like "Oh! Mrs. Norton, oh! oh! Mrs. Norton, oh! Mrs. Norton!" But this could not be; my imagination must have played me false, as the polite black skins would not think of speaking of such an individual otherwise than as Norton Sahib kee Mem Sahib. There are relays of these sturdy fellows posted all along the way at certain distances to the journey's end; all which has to be arranged beforehand by the person who lays the Dawk. Except in cases of great emergency, or in a few particular places where wild beasts abound so much as to render it necessary to go by day, the journey by Palkee Dawk during the hot weather was invariably made by night, and during the comparatively cooler hours of the morning and evening; for if the traveller rashly ventured to do otherwise it was at the risk of his life. I ran this risk once myself travelling all day in the month of May, when I nearly paid the penalty of my temerity; for though I never faint under any circumstances, yet on this occasion I fell into a senseless state and remained so for about half an hour or more before I recovered consciousness. Avoiding travelling during the heat of the day, the distance accomplished would be fifty or sixty miles, provided you have a generally tidy lot who do not waste their time by squatting whilst they smoke their hubble-bubbles. The principal inconvenience of travelling by Palkee was the being awakened half a dozen times during the night by the clamorous cries of Bukshesh from the importunate bearers, who having finished their course expect a gratuity, which if they do not get, the next set of bearers let you know that they have heard about it. At last, about 8 or 9 A.M., the Dawk bungalow is reached. These houses, built for the accommodation of travellers, are everywhere to be met with.

The traveller is here met by a table butler, who with folded hands makes the most profuse expressions of service; the Sahib has only got to pass the order for anything he wants. The general result of all this palaver is that the Sahib is obliged to content himself with an ill-conditioned fowl, hastily caught and killed, and quickly curried and eaten. The only amusement is the book where travellers are required to insert their names, with the exact time of their arrival and departure, with such remarks as they may think fit to make; which in many instances are decidedly entertaining, and anything but complimentary to the cuisine and cleanliness of the establishment. The accommodation of some of these Government hotels was simply disgraceful. For instance, I have had to put up at one where the table was actually laid with brass spoons, which many years ago may possibly have been plated; whilst at some Dawk bungalows the accommodation and food have reflected the highest credit on the native manager. Ten days of travelling by Palkee Dawk, with such disturbed or almost sleepless nights, was quite enough to knock one up. The way of travelling during the rainy season was also attended with extra difficulties, if not perils, owing to the swollen brooks that had to be crossed, which in April were either dry or only about ankle-deep.

2. Travelling by budgerow was perhaps a more comfortable mode of transit than the one just described; but it was monotonous in the extreme, and the heat was frightful when the voyage was made in the hot weather. There was no mistake about its being a regular voyage, for a trip on the Ganges from Calcutta to an up-country station would occupy as much time as a voyage in a passenger vessel round the Cape to England. An officer with not a large amount of cash at his disposal would, either by himself, or with one or two others, hire a Noah's ark-shaped vessel containing two rooms, a dining-room and a sleeping-room. The crew lived on the top, and whatever noise they chose to make during the night would of course disturb the repose of the Sahib occupying the room below.

Suppose the station to be travelled to from Calcutta was only as far as Cawnpore, yet this would generally occupy the traveller two or three months, though now it may be easily done by rail in two days. Considering the period the voyage would take, supplies had to be taken in accordingly, such as beer and wine, cheese, tins of salmon, &c. &c. The monotony of the voyage was almost unendurable. There was nothing of any interest to attract the voyager, the native craft plying on the river being of the most primitive kind, and the scenery being generally flat and uninteresting, and bathing was out of the question as unsafe.*

This dull state of affairs was only relieved at distant intervals by landing at military and civil stations on the river side, such as Bhagulpore, Monghyr, Dinapore, Benares, Mirzapore and Allahabad. By far the best mode of travelling in those days was by the steamer. Here there was every comfort, good food, and plenty of fellow-passengers. But unfortunately this comfortable means of transit was restricted as to distance, and did not extend beyond Allahabad, which was the terminus of the steamer route. It presented at least one novelty, which was passing through the Sunderbunds— a complete network of the mouths of rivers leading to the sea—which swarmed with huge crocodiles, and which appeared to me such a labyrinth, that it has always puzzled me, though I have been four times through it, how the captain of the steamer could manage always to select the right turning without ever taking the wrong one, with nothing, as it seemed, to guide him throughout this watery wilderness through dense forests abounding with tigers. The

* I used for some time to bathe in a branch of the Ganges, till one day I discovered that I had had a swimming companion in the shape of a crocodile. I need hardly say that I never bathed there again. It may very naturally be asked why the ferocious animal did not seize me when I was swimming about in the water: to this my only reply is, that I can only account for it by attributing my escape to a kind Providence, for I should think the crocodile must have seen me, though I did not observe it till I got out of the water.

steamer generally took about four days in passing through the Sunderbunds, and about three weeks more in reaching Allahabad. What changes have taken place in locomotion in India since those days! First came the intermediate one of coaching. I remember what a wonderful thing it was considered to be able to reach Benares from Calcutta in four days in a Dawk Garee. The same distance now by rail is done in one day. Before I left India, in 1873, there was a railway all the way from Calcutta to Lahore, a distance of about 1,200 miles; and again all the way from Lahore to Bombay, a distance of nearly 1,600 miles. A traveller wishing to avoid the cold of an English winter might with profit take a trip to India, arriving at Calcutta by the beginning of November; then, as soon after his arrival as possible, he should go to Darjeeling for a fortnight, come back to Calcutta and remain there to the end of December, after which he might proceed northwards to Benares and Lucknow, then make the tour of the North-West Provinces. Let him next proceed to Simla or Mussoorie or Nynee Tal, remain there from 1st of April to 30th of October, and then he might make a tour of the Punjaub, after which he should proceed to Jubbulpore and Bombay, and then embark for England by the 1st of March or before, so as to avoid the heat of the Red Sea. The tourist to Bombay should always remember the particular places noted for the manufacture of the different articles he wishes to take home as presents to his friends; such, for instance, as Calcutta for embroidery called chicken-work and fans, &c.; Berhampore for silks and carved ivory work; Bhagulpore also for silks; Agra for fancy work in marble; Delhi for jewellery, &c.; Suharanpore for carvings in wood. The great drawback of Barrackpore then was, that it was a half batta station, where officers drew an inferior rate of pay to those at stations of a specified distance from Calcutta. The "City of Palaces," as Calcutta has been called, situated on the river Gunga (mispronounced by Europeans Ganges) at a distance of about one hundred miles from the sea, containing a considerable European population, is a very busy, bustling, and attractive city, of imposing grandeur, and one decidedly interesting for the eye to gaze upon, with its great mercantile shipping in the river, its wharves, jetties, warehouses, magnificent public buildings, churches, and hotels; its elegant private mansions, its fine fort, lofty monument, and extensive Maidan, suitable for the exercise of large bodies of troops, together with its grand shops, pleasant squares, and tanks of drinking water; its fine public garden, where the band plays on certain evenings in the week; and its Mall, presenting daily in the cool of the evening a brilliant and stirring spectacle, thronged as the roads here are with equestrians, and carriages of all the *élite* of the metropolis. Here may be seen the sahibs riding on horses, driving or being driven about in carriages, military and naval officers, civilians (or burra sahibs), merchants, barristers, doctors, clergymen, and European tradesmen, and clerks, as well as Eurasians (Europeans with more or less of an admixture of Indian blood), and the wealthy natives, and possibly a real native Prince or two. Nor must we omit to mention, in summing up the attractions of the place, the hospitable entertainments so freely dispensed to callers at Government House. Calcutta is just the place for spending a day pleasantly, lounging about at the different places of public resort, such as the Asiatic Museum, or the great booksellers (Thacker and Lepage), Wilson's Hotel, now the Great Eastern, where you can order a grand dinner, or enjoy a very nice tiffin (lunch), consisting of a mutton chop or beef-steak and a bottle of beer, for 3s. 6d., and read the papers to your heart's content, or do shopping at the European shops; or amusement might be derived from a drive to the China Bazaar, which may be dearly bought, as ten to one the visitor would be beguiled into entering some shop by the deceitful assurance of the Baboo, and when once in, it would be well if he escaped purchasing at some cost a little experience of the ways of the natives. Then, in case of the Calcutta resident requiring a change of air, there is, at a distance of about four hundred miles, the attractive hill station of Darjeeling with its magnificent and close view of Kunchinjungie,* and the snowy range. The grandest sight in nature is to be seen here to perfection, and here the constitution that has suffered from the sweltering heats of the plains may renew its strength. This well-known sanatorium is about 7,000 feet above the level of the sea, and possesses a temperature corresponding with that of England, though the rainfall during the rainy season is very heavy.

I hope this description of the great Indian metropolis, so frequently visited by us on pleasure as well as on duty, will not be considered an unwarrantable digression. But I must now really proceed with my story.

Ensign S——'s halcyon days were when, stationed here, he formed an attachment to a very young lady, Miss O——. There seemed a prospect at this time of his leading a steady life. Now that he was about to wed a young and innocent girl, it was hoped that for her sake he would reform and make up his mind to be steady, in justice to the inexperienced girl he was engaged to. We will suppose that he did make an effort to be a steadier and worthier man than he had been. But poor S—— was without ballast, and no domestic bliss, no endearments of a fond wife or innocent prattling of children, were in store for him.

Now may we begin to trace the blighting influences of infidelity. It was left for him to mar his brightest

* Kunchinjungie is a lofty mountain in the Himalayas, 28,000 feet above the sea level. The height to the border of the snow is 18,000 feet, and the peak of snow that never melts is 10,000 feet above that. A good view of Mount Everest, 29,000 feet in altitude, is to be seen a few miles from Darjeeling, at a place called Senchall. The neighbourhood of Darjeeling is now too well known for its tea to need any further description.

prospects. This he did on one occasion, when he quite forgot himself at the lady's house, betraying such egregious folly that the engagement was broken off. This event greatly soured a temper at all times bad enough, and marked the turning-point of the career of this unhappy man; for now he gave the rein to his unbridled passions, and was guilty of such mad acts of folly as would have led to the belief that he was demented, but that his general conversation was sane enough. The first thing he did when he found he could not expect to get Miss O—— for his wife, was to wreak his vengeance on the little pet dog she had given him in their courting days. I did not actually see him do it, but I was credibly informed that he took up his sword and cut the unoffending animal in two. Another act of folly was his fastening a quarrel on myself, one of his few well-wishers. I shall pass this over pretty briefly, having no desire to enlarge on it more than may be thought desirable, since, badly as he behaved to me, I bore him no ill-will, and this I had an opportunity of evincing to him the last time I saw him alive. He took great offence at my having written to him, telling him how much distressed my wife was at his incessant firing from his verandah, and requesting him to desist from a practice which I reminded him was contrary to orders within cantonments. I received a most strange reply, the drift of which I imagined to be an act of violence. But I did not have a visit from him, as I expected. One day, however, he fired into my room with shot, the shot going pretty well through my thick Venetian blinds. Serious injury might have been sustained, as the distance from his verandah could hardly have been more than twenty yards. I was obliged to take military notice of this matter. But S—— was lucky enough to get off scot free. It may seem incredible, but on two occasions S—— came armed into my compound,* creating a dis-

* The field surrounding the house is called a compound.

turbance with my servants, against whom he seemed to have taken a great prejudice. On one of these occasions I happened to be at home, and he was at last persuaded to take his departure. But the other instance was a more serious business. I was then on duty at Fort William, when I was surprised one day by the arrival of one of my servants from Barrackpore, who told me that Ensign S—— had come into the compound, and levelled his gun at one of them, threatening to shoot him, which struck the whole lot of my servants with such terror that they one and all left the house to take care of itself. At last the authorities, lenient as they were to him, were obliged to take notice of his disorderly conduct. He was tried by court-martial for drawing his sword on his adjutant at parade, and on this occasion he had such a narrow escape that one would think he ought to have profited by the warning. But warnings were all in vain, since he heeded them not. He got into trouble for cruelly breaking the arm of one of his servants. At last his regiment was ordered up country, and I breathed more freely when I lost such a troublesome neighbour. When he left I had the curiosity to enter the house he had quitted. The whitewashed walls were studded with pictures of his own drawing; some were of a bloodthirsty nature, such as a life-size sketch of a fierce duel, with a text of Scripture, the meaning of which he had perverted in defence of duelling. And there was one picture so atrociously wicked, that I can only just allude to it to show the frightful depths of wickedness an atheist is capable of, for here on his walls I saw a picture never to be forgotten. This unhappy man had not scrupled to abuse his skill as a draughtsman, by turning into ridicule our Saviour hanging on the cross. Could anything be more awfully wicked? It was not long before he got into trouble again: this time it was for assaulting some native soldiers. For this he was brought before a general court-martial, and dismissed the service. This occurred, I believe, in 1852. One would think he must have bewailed his folly, now that he found himself turned adrift on the world, and thought of the career that might have been before him! But he soon resolved to do that which we cannot think wise in any gentleman to do. It is all very well for a man from the plough or from the working classes to enlist, but for one born and bred a gentleman to take the shilling, is a very different thing. But this ill-advised step was just what he did, and the ex-ensign became a private in an infantry regiment, and served in the rank and file throughout the Crimean War; but he did not avail himself of the opportunity that there presented itself for retrieving his fortunes; if he had done so, he might once more have become an officer. It is not my intention to speak of the British victories gained on that occasion, since I had no personal interest in the war beyond the melancholy one of having lost a brother in it. The only thing that I have been able to learn of this atheist's career during the Crimean War was the very characteristic one, that he is remembered for the opposition he offered to the religious services held by Sergeant W. Mason, the author of an interesting book entitled "A Primitive Methodist in the British Army."

CHAPTER III.

A Season of Trial—Gross Favouritism contrasted with Injustice and Oppression—Dangerous Illness—Slander—Narrow Escape of being Shot at Target Practice—Report the Matter—No Inquiry—Regimental Order thereon—Placed under Arrest on a False Charge—Released by Commander-in-Chief—Misrepresentation—My Vindication approved of by His Excellency—I appeal to the Commander-in-Chief against the Regimental Order, and about the Offence against my Life at Target Practice—Placed under Arrest by Commanding Officer — Brigadier's arbitrary Proceeding—I appeal to the Commander-in-Chief against it—Lord Dalhousie's singular Conduct towards me—Tried by General Court-Martial—Regarded as a Ruined Man—Anecdote—Favourable Results of my Court-Martial —Regimental Order directed to be Cancelled, &c.—Remarks—The Need of a Lawyer to conduct General Courts-Martial—Active and Ungenerous Part taken against me by Lord Dalhousie—Divine Protection—My Triumphant Escape—Systematic Persecution—Arrival at Benares—Description of the Place—Practical Use of Prayer —Dead Set made against me at Benares by my Commanding Officer and the Officers Commanding the Station and Division—I appeal against them to the Commander-in-Chief—My Signal Triumph over them all—My Case noticed very favourably by the Press— Frustration of a Spiteful Design against me—Promoted to Lieutenant—Received Prize of a Thousand Rupees—Join 3rd European Regiment at Chinsurah—Fresh Troubles—Lose my Temper—Severe Punishment—Its Grievous Results—Take my Furlough to England —Nearly Wrecked off the Cape—A Week's Stay at St. Helena— Description thereof—Meet with nice Christian Society there— Arrival in England—Hear of my Brother's Death in the Crimea— Return to India with Recruits—Dangerous Illness—Providential Disappointment at Cawnpore—Arrival at Agra just before the Outbreak of the Mutiny.

WHILST these disastrous events were happening to this perverse young man in whom I had taken such a singular interest, I was myself passing through seas of trouble. These trials were not of my own seeking, but arose from the rotten state of things existing then in the Indian army, showing that an innocent man might have the life nearly driven out of him by constant oppression, whilst another man, protected by favouritism, might do almost anything with impunity. A few instances may here be given of offences unpunished through sheer military partiality. First: It was a well-known fact that in 1849, when I was at Nynee Tall, a duel was fought, and that one of the parties was believed to be mortally wounded, though he finally recovered, and it is also a fact that this offence was hushed up. Still later, when I was stationed at Barrackpore, a duel was fought by two hot-headed young officers at Calcutta, and this, too, was kept secret. Then, before any of these, there was the well-known case of a captain, who, for an irreparable injury done to another officer, was called out by the man he had so foully injured, and shot dead; that is to say, he died from the effects of the wound rather more than a year afterwards, and I never heard that any notice was taken of this sanguinary business. Again, there is now, or was a few years ago, an officer in high civil employ in India who was guilty, many years ago, of the serious offence of beating a Sepoy, and this was, through favouritism, hushed up: I know this because I have heard the officer himself confess it. And I think he added that the man, unable to endure the unredressed injury, went and committed suicide. Again, I myself have seen an officer at mess rise and take another in his arms and throw him in a passion with violence to the ground, and I am quite certain that no official notice was taken of this. I know of another case where a junior officer committed an assault on his senior, and got off with simply a reprimand. I also know of a case where an adjutant on parade used very insubordinate language to his commanding officer without any official notice being taken thereof. The first part of my assertion is borne out by the following narrative:—I had, after four years of hard study, succeeded in passing an examination for high proficiency in Hindee, and the interpreter's examination in Persian, Hindoosthanie, and Hindee. But the hope of deriving any profit thereby was crushed to atoms by the serious collision I came into with the officer commanding my regiment, the brigadier and the general, and this confederacy met with the powerful support of no less a person than the Most Noble the Governor-General of India! "Great men are not always wise" (Job xxxii. 9), and his Lordship was certainly not generous in taking the active part he did against a poor struggling, friendless ensign. And assuredly I must have fallen in the unequal struggle but for God's merciful interposition, since I had not a single friend at the station to stand by me. I shall now state the plain unvarnished facts as they really and truly happened, which I can prove from authenticated court-martial proceedings, and semi-official and official documents in my possession. Simple truth tells its own story best, and the following narrative is strictly in accordance therewith. Though it properly commenced with the year 1852, yet there were not wanting indications of the coming storm before that period. For instance, one day in July, 1851, on parade, when I told my commanding officer I felt unwell, and requested permission to go home, Major Liptrap in reply accused me of feigning sickness, and informed me he would only allow me to leave parade on condition that I went on the sick list. About this time I was attacked with a dangerous illness, which nearly proved fatal. But my escape from the jaws of death produced no relentings in the minds of those who were bent on my ruin. It was also about this time, or not long after, that a great effort was made to blacken my moral and religious character. The facts of the case may thus be shortly told:—

There was a certain lady living near us with whom both myself and my wife maintained a very friendly intercourse, and it so happened that once or twice, or possibly two or three times, I went out riding with her daughter, without a thought of harm, yet on such a trifling circumstance a mighty superstructure of scandal was raised, as that I was doing my best to seduce this innocent young lady. Whereupon the finger of scorn was pointed at me as a canting hypocrite. "Here," said the scandal-monger, "is one of your pretended saints, who, with all his loud professions, can do things quite as bad as any one of us." This vile calumny was based principally on the assertion of a certain officer who declared that he actually saw me taking improper liberties with the lady in question. I need scarcely say that this was pure invention, for at this distance of time I would not allude to such a thing if there had been any truth in it; but so far was this from being the case, that were I on my death-bed to-morrow, I could solemnly declare that there was not the slightest grounds for any such accusation. But the vile story went from mouth to mouth till it ended in Mrs. —— coming one day to me and requesting me, as it had become such a matter of scandal, that I would not again take her daughter out riding. This was, no doubt, mortifying, but two things enabled me to bear it easily: one was conscious rectitude, and the other was that Mrs. —— did me justice by believing me incapable of attempting the villany attributed to me, and this she showed by the continuance of her friendship. As for my calumniator, I treated his slander as beneath contempt. I think this was the best course to pursue, for had I gone to him and denounced the falsehood, there would have been a row, and no good gained. The storm burst on my head with a vengeance in July, 1852. It was on the 29th of that month that I and Ensign T—— went out in the morning with our companies to target practice. To a right understanding of the matter it is necessary to explain the relative position of our companies as they stood on the firing-ground. His company was on the right, mine was on the left.

After the men had fired a certain number of rounds, we went to count the number of balls in the target. He having finished the soonest returned to his company to commence firing; but instead of awaiting my return, he to my surprise commenced firing as I was coming back to the right flank of my company, which was close to his firing flank (as he fired from the left of his company), and as I was about fifteen or sixteen yards in front of the right flank of my company, the danger I was in from the line of fire being so little to the left of my person must be obvious to any one. Strange to say, this he did twice, and perhaps it would not be too much to say that I narrowly escaped with my life, as Sepoys used sometimes to fire very unsteadily. I was naturally filled with indignation at my life being thus wantonly jeopardized, and I took the only proper course I could have adopted, which was to report the affair to the commanding officer. I heard afterwards that Mr. T—— excused himself by preferring a charge of dilatoriness against me, as if tardiness in counting the hits were a sufficient excuse for imperilling an officer's life! But the sacredness of human life, when I happened to be concerned, seems to have been rather an exceptional case; since not long before this, when I complained to Major B—— that Ensign E. S., under his command, had fired into my room, endangering my life, that commanding officer banteringly told me, if I was not shot the next time to complain, and he would notice it! Such a serious complaint as the reckless imperilling one's life, and that on duty, by a brother officer, required serious consideration. But none was ever made, nor were I and Mr. T—— ever confronted together to elicit the facts of the case for the commanding officer's satisfaction, but instead of this, insult was added to injury. For whilst the alleged offence against my life was passed over unnoticed, the following sweeping censure of my conduct appeared in Regimental Orders of the 29th July, 1852: "Ensign White having shown himself quite incompetent to be entrusted with the 6th Company at practice, the target practice of the 6th Company is postponed until further orders. Ensign White is directed not to address official letters on subjects of duty to the Adjutant. A voluminous correspondence cannot be permitted. The letter which has called forth this Order is No. 58. When Ensign White has any question to ask on duty matters he will apply in the first instance to the officer commanding his company, and for anything beyond what that officer can reply to, he will wait personally on the commanding officer at the orderly room. Ensign White is referred to G. O. C. C., dated 27th November, 1837, by which he will learn that correspondence on trivial occasions is not to be countenanced." As an officer and a gentleman, I felt that I could not quietly submit to such a charge of imbecility preferred against me, so long as there was a higher tribunal to appeal to for justice. I therefore requested a Court of Inquiry, but I could not get the authorities to forward my papers. I therefore determined to send an appeal to the Commander-in-Chief, addressed to the Adjutant-General. But before I come to this part of my story I must mention one or two other events that meantime occurred. On the 3rd August I was placed under arrest on the false charge of inciting the Adjutant of my regiment to fight a duel.* But after being kept forty-six days under arrest on this frivolous pretext, I obtained my release on the 18th September, by order of the Commander-in-Chief, who directed an interchange of amends for taunting and reproachful words made use of to each other respectively. His Excellency's decision was also communicated to me on a note I had written to Captain M—— the officer commanding my company; which was to the effect that the Commander-in-Chief thought it very offensive, and directed me to withdraw it. I complied therewith, although I, with good reason,† suspected that His Excellency had condemned me on a one-sided representation

* See evidence of Adjutant himself, "Court-Martial," 1852, pp. 35, 36.
† "Court-Martial Proceedings," 1852, pp. 12, 13.

of the case. I had been punished by a long period of unjustifiable imprisonment or arrest, which means the same thing; since when an officer is placed under arrest it is understood to be under what is called close arrest, which confines him absolutely to his house, till such time as he has liberty to take an hour's exercise in the morning and another in the evening, in solitary roads, as he is strictly prohibited attending any place of public resort.

Any deviation therefrom renders an officer liable to be tried for breaking his arrest and cashiered in consequence. Now, though I expected no compensation for this wrong, yet I was determined that the Commander-in-Chief should see Captain M——'s letter to me, which the authorities at Barrackpore had thought proper to keep back. The fact was that, in obedience to the instructions of my Commanding Officer, I applied to the officer commanding my company for some information I required, but the latter, instead of dealing with the matter in a businesslike manner, indulged me with a long letter full of irrelevant matter, as well as unsolicited and insolent advice. I returned a spirited reply, as any other gentleman would have done, in which I intimated to him that when writing on public matters connected with regimental affairs, all such topics were out of place. This was the note of 3rd August for which I received the reprimand of the Commander-in-Chief. As might have been expected, the military authorities would not forward papers that would have exposed their improper behaviour in exercising a discretionary power as to what should go and what should be kept back, as if His Excellency were not competent to pronounce a decision on a case with all the papers before him!

Under these circumstances I violated the rules of military etiquette by sending an appeal direct to the Commander-in-Chief, addressed to the Adjutant-General. Did His Excellency censure me for this? Certainly not, but, on the contrary, when the suppressed letter forwarded by me was seen, then I was honourably acquitted for what I had been previously reprimanded on judicial evidence. I followed up this success * by sending an appeal to the Commander-in-Chief, dated 28th September, 1852, addressed to the Adjutant-General. In this letter I complained of the great violence done to my character by my commanding officer's most ungenerous and sweeping censure of my conduct in the Regimental Order declaring me to be quite incompetent to take out a company to so simple an exercise as target practice, and I most earnestly and humbly besought His Excellency to afford me the opportunity I coveted of clearing myself from this most painful charge, which, by remaining registered against my name, blighted all my future prospects. I also requested an inquiry into the offence committed against my life by Ensign T—— whilst in the discharge of my duty, that so there might be no occasion for me to prosecute him for the same in a civil court. And I concluded my letter by accusing my Commanding Officer of "cruel oppression."† This letter I sent through the prescribed channel of communication, but it was returned to Major Liptrap by both the Brigadier and the General.‡

Finding that the authorities would not forward my appeal of the 28th of September to head-quarters, I felt necessitated, on the 4th of October, to transmit an exact copy of the same direct to the Adjutant-General, and the very same day the Adjutant came to my quarters to know whether I was going to withdraw my letter of the 28th of September. I at once told him that I had forwarded a copy of it direct to the Adjutant-General. Whereupon the Adjutant carried out his instructions by placing me under arrest.§ One expedient used at this

* See evidence of Major H——, Deputy-Assistant-Adjutant-General, "Court-Martial Proceedings," 1852, p. 28.
† See letter in Appendix III., "Court-Martial Proceedings," pp. 7-10.
‡ See evidence of Commanding Officer and Adjutant, "Court-Martial Proceedings," pp. 10, 29.
§ Evidence of Adjutant, "Court-Martial Proceedings," p. 30.

period to vex me was peculiarly trying, this was the arbitrary treatment of me by my superiors in regard to the impediments thrown in the way of my passing in examinations of the highest character in the native languages, for which I had carefully prepared myself, incurring thereby a great expense, which had to be defrayed from my ensign's pay. Early in August, 1852, I had received a letter from the Secretary of the College of Fort William requiring me to go down to Calcutta for the purpose of being examined in the military prize examination. This, in the event of my being successful, would have given me 1,000 rupees, which was comparatively a mint of money to one only drawing 167 rupees a month! But I now met with a disappointment, being prevented obeying the summons of the Secretary of the College by the vexatious arrest imposed on me on the 3rd of August. On the 12th of September I wrote a moving letter to the Brigadier, requesting he would be pleased so far to mitigate my imprisonment as to allow me to apply for leave of absence for the purpose of being examined in the military prize examination in Hindee and Ordoo at the College of Fort William, as all my hopes of being able to march up the country in the ensuing cold weather depended on my passing in this examination, and of obtaining the money prize assigned to the same; and concluded with an earnest appeal to that officer that he would not withhold from a poor struggling subaltern the opportunity of passing in such a high examination. This application was not granted; perhaps the Brigadier may have been justified in his refusal according to the strict letter of the law, though Colonel M——, the Secretary of the College of Fort William, gave it as his opinion that two days spent entirely in examination could not be said to interfere with military discipline. But whatever excuse may be made for the rejection of my application by the Brigadier, yet unquestionably the next thing he did to disappoint me was altogether unjustifiable, and seemed almost intended to drive me to take some desperate step. For on the 1st of October, when I was not under arrest, and although I had received a summons from the Secretary of the College of Fort William directing my attendance there for the purpose of being examined in the prize examination in Hindee and Ordoo, yet the Brigadier, without assigning any reason for doing so, actually refused me leave to proceed to Calcutta for such a commendable purpose as that of being thus examined.*

I felt that this was going too far, and my grievance was enhanced by the fact that I had not enjoyed a single day's leave during the year, except for the purpose of being examined at the College. Indignant, therefore, at such provoking usage, I sent a letter on the 7th of October, plainly stating these facts, which I concluded by trusting that His Excellency would pardon the irregular way of my forwarding this letter, "as I felt it would be useless my attempting to forward this letter through the prescribed channels, on account of my superiors here being all prejudiced against me." Colonel M——, the Secretary of the College of Fort William, took compassion on my hard case, and interceded for me with Government, that I might be allowed an opportunity of being examined. But, alas! for this kind act that officer received a reprimand from the Governor-General. This I had the bitter mortification of learning in an extraordinary way, inasmuch as a copy of it was sent to me for my information. I call it an extraordinary way, because I subsequently learnt, when belonging to a European regiment, that it was not right to reprimand a sergeant before a private; therefore it is hard to see how it could be proper for Government to inform an ensign of a reprimand given to a colonel!

At last, on the 29th November, 1852, I was brought

* See authenticated copy of rejected application in page 66 of "Court-Martial Proceedings" of 1852.

to a General Court-Martial, charged with "highly un-officer-like conduct." First, in sending the letter of the 28th September, which the charge stated to be "couched in very insubordinate and disrespectful language" with regard to my Commanding Officer, and in which I persisted in agitating matters the final decision on which had been duly conveyed to me. Secondly, in having on the 4th October transmitted a duplicate copy of the above-mentioned letter direct to the Adjutant-General. Thirdly, for the transmission of my letter of the 7th October direct to the Adjutant-General, the assertion therein contained of the authorities at Barrackpore being prejudiced against me, being pronounced by the charge to be both insubordinate and disrespectful.

My position at this period was by no means an enviable one. I had not a single military friend to stand by me. It would no doubt have required much moral courage to have done so. This I freely admit, and therefore I will not find fault because no one was willing to range himself on my side against Commanding Officer, Brigadier, and General. The trading community looked upon me as a ruined man, as they evidently thought that I should be either cashiered or suspended for a long period from rank, pay, and allowances. To give one instance of this not-easily-to-be-forgotten fact. One of the chief English shops, dealers in boots and shoes, etc., having received an order to make me a pair of shoes, refused just at this time to execute the same; and when I sent my servant to inquire why the shoes were not forthcoming, the shopman behaved, as my servant informed me, with the greatest insolence, since he would not give a note to explain the reason of his extraordinary conduct, but instead he returned my pattern shoe, saying at the same time to my man, "Take this to your Sahib; this is my answer." I quite believe this was a substantially true account, because it was verified by my returned pattern shoe and the nonfulfilment of the order. I took no notice of this till two years afterwards, when Mr. —— actually had the coolness to send me a bill for this very pair of shoes, as though he had really supplied me with them! I then seized the opportunity of writing him a reply, couched in such stinging words as must have made him crimson to the roots of his hair. I had a little before this time also given much pain to a most affectionate mother, and to my father, a clergyman of the Church of England, by having informed them that, acting up to my religious convictions, I had submitted to the ordinance of believer's baptism. But notwithstanding the displeasure they very naturally felt at this, they yet deeply sympathized with me at this time, as well as on all other similar occasions. But I must return from this digression to speak of the Court-martial, composed of fifteen officers, who were occupied from 29th November to 4th December in trying the case. I was released from arrest about the middle of January, after I had been kept under this irksome restraint three months and ten days. The wisdom of the course I had adopted was now completely evident, for though I as a matter of course received a reprimand, yet, despite this, I came off with flying colours, since I gained all the chief things I had agitated for, viz.—

1st. The erasure of the obnoxious Order of the 29th July, 1852, which the Commander-in-Chief desired to be at once expunged from the Order Book of the Regiment.*

2nd. Leave to proceed to Calcutta to be examined in the military prize examination, as the Commander-in-Chief, before the promulgation of the sentence, and before my release from arrest, had desired the authorities to allow me to appear before the examiners of Fort William previous to my leaving Barrackpore.† This was doubly gratifying because it was an exculpation of

* "Court-Martial Proceedings," p. 65. See also G. O. C. C., 22nd December, 1852.
† *Vide* authenticated extract of Orders, in my possession.

Colonel M——'s intercession for me that I might be allowed that privilege, for which, as already mentioned, he had received a reprimand from the Most Noble the Governor-General.

3rd. His Excellency directed Ensign T—— to declare that he had no intention of injuring me at ball practice.* This last was the least satisfactory, because even admitting that he had no intention of injuring me, yet at the very least he was at all events blamable for the grossest carelessness, whereby my life was imperilled, and he ought at the least to have received a very severe reprimand. We are too prone to regard it as a divine judgment when any signal calamity befalls one who has deeply wronged us; but we erring creatures should be very careful how we indulge this feeling, lest it should degenerate into a revengeful emotion. Still I cannot help regarding it as a remarkable circumstance that a year after the target-practice affair, Mr. T—— died of cholera at Benares, and a few days afterwards Captain M——, who had taken such a part against me, died likewise of the same terrible disease.

I did not, however, feel much hurt at his getting off so easily, because I was exultant at obtaining such a complete vindication of my character. Though it would be uninteresting to give a regular account of the proceedings of this Court-Martial, yet there is one point that it is desirable to touch upon, as showing the need of an officer possessing sufficient legal acumen to sum up a case with due regard to the evidence, and with some authority to restrain the Court from pronouncing a sentence at variance with the evidence before it, which was done in my case, as may be easily shown. The gravamen of the charge against me consisted of three particulars.

1. Insubordinate language in accusing my Commanding Officer of cruel oppression. Now this language, though insubordinate was proved to be true, it is therefore hard to perceive how I could be guilty of

* "Court-Martial Proceedings," p. 34.

"highly unofficer-like conduct" for speaking the truth. For I maintain that subordination does not mean passive submission to any kind of indignity.

2. That in my letter of the 28th September to the Adjutant-General of the army, I persisted in agitating matters the final decision on which had been duly conveyed to me. It is as plain as daylight that the Court found me guilty of this without any proof, if not in opposition to the clearest evidence before the Court, is obvious from the following considerations :—Because my letter of the 28th September to the Adjutant-General is all about my grievance in regard to the obnoxious Regimental Order, and the offence against my life, with a passing reference to an occurrence in my former regiment, and does not contain a single word about either the affairs of Lieutenant and Adjutant W——, or that of Captain M——, as the letter itself bears witness.* Decisions of the Commander-in-Chief, it is true, had been communicated to me on other matters, but certainly not in the matter of this letter of the 28th September, as specified in the charge.

Not only was it extremely ridiculous to suppose for one instant that I should persist in agitating for an opportunity of clearing myself of the painful charge recorded against me in the Regimental Orders of the 29th July, after I had actually gained the object of my agitation, since the Commander-in-Chief's final decision, according to the evidence of the Brigadier, was an order to Major Liptrap to cancel this very Regimental Order ;† but this imputed offence was not supported by a tittle of evidence, and despite the difficulty of proving a negative, it can be shown without any difficulty that the tenor of the evidence before the Court tended to show that I had not learnt the final decision of the Commander-in-Chief in regard to the grievances mentioned in my letter of the 28th September, previous to

* See authenticated copy of "Court-Martial Proceedings," pp. 7-10.
† *Vide* evidence of the Brigadier, "Court-Martial Proceedings," p. 34.

that date. The fact of the matter is, that the Court appears to have been so completely confused by the multiplicity of decisions, and by the dust thrown in their eyes by the prosecution, that they confounded one thing with the other. The prosecutor, Major Liptrap, on being asked whether he had received any orders to communicate a decision of His Excellency on the matters referred to in my letter of the 28th September, replied that he had, and proceeded to speak of my attendance at his quarters on the 17th September, to have communicated to me an extract from a decision of the Commander-in-Chief, regarding the altercation between myself and the Adjutant, together with His Excellency's directions concerning the note I wrote to the officer commanding my company.* The question being again read to the prosecutor, he still adhered to it, that the decision of the Commander-in-Chief referred to those two matters, and put in the following extract of a letter, No. 1,958, dated 3rd September, 1852, from the Adjutant-General of the army, to the officer commanding the Presidency Division.

1. "Sir W. Gomm considers that Major Liptrap in his recent treatment of Ensign White has not acted judiciously, and that he has displayed much want of consideration to that young officer; the pages of a Regimental Order Book are not the proper place for the appearance of a reprimand, like that of the 29th July, and which besides appears to have been given without confronting Ensigns T—— and White to elicit the actual circumstances that occurred at target practice that morning; had this been done, it seems probable that the whole affair would have been settled amicably."

2. "The note from Ensign White to Brevet-Captain M——, in command of his company, received by the latter on the 3rd ultimo, the Commander-in-Chief thinks very offensive, and accordingly desires that the Ensign be directed to withdraw it, and also to make atonement

* "Court-Martial Proceedings," pp. 10, 11.

to Lieutenant and Adjutant W—— for the virtual imputation of cowardice which he cast upon him at the Commanding Officer's quarters on the 2nd idem.* Lieutenant W—— first, however, affording such explanation of his improperly taunting language to the Ensign on that occasion, as may by you be deemed satisfactory, and which very injudicious language the Major, I am to observe, would have done well to have at once marked with his grave displeasure." The latter paragraph of this letter, with the exception of the last four lines, together with an extract from the Brigade Officer, all about the business of the Adjutant and Captain M——, were, as the prosecutor truly said, made known to me.†

Now there is not a single word about these matters in my letter of the 28th September to the Adjutant-General, and it follows that the first paragraph of the Adjutant-General's letter, which really referred to those matters agitated in my letter of the 28th September, was not read out to me, or the prosecutor would not have particularized the latter paragraph as that which was made known to me, the obvious inference being that consequently the first paragraph was not communicated to me. I could not, therefore, as charged, have persisted in agitating matters after the final decision of which by the Commander-in-Chief had been made known to me. Further, Major Liptrap being again asked what those matters were which had been agitated in my letter of the 28th September, replied that those matters were contained in a letter of a former date which I addressed him through the Adjutant on the 18th, which was returned to him "with this letter No. 140, from Lieutenant and Adjutant W——, to (myself) Ensign White."‡

* It was the 3rd.
† "Court-Martial Proceedings," pp. 11-13.
‡ This letter, which is in my possession, is all about the affairs of Captain M——, and the Commanding Officer's earnest recommendation "that I should abstain from any further agitation of that business."

The Court then in the plainest possible manner put the question: "Ensign White is accused of having in a letter of the 28th September, 1852, agitated matters which he was aware had been under the consideration of the Commander-in-Chief, and the final decision of His Excellency on which had been conveyed to him. The Court wish to know what those matters are?"

"Those matters," replied Major Liptrap, "were relative to Lieutenant and Adjutant W——."

Whereupon "the Court observes, this answer does not appear to refer to any matter alluded to in the letter of the 28th September."*

And as nothing further to the point could be got out of Major Liptrap, that witness resumed his seat as Prosecutor. And yet, incredible as it may appear, the Court found me guilty of highly unofficer-like conduct in having in my letter of the 28th September to the Adjutant-General persisted in agitating matters the final decision of which had been communicated to me on the strength of evidence which, if it proved anything, proved me innocent, and upon the confused evidence of the General, who stated that on or about the 14th September he caused to be conveyed to me orders which he had received from the Commander-in-Chief regarding His Excellency's decision upon my complaints of harsh usage by my Commanding Officer, of my life having been endangered at target practice by Mr. T——, and of the letter received from Captain M——, and that he himself spoke to me on the subject conveying His Excellency's disapproval,† which could not have been the case, or, at all events, it could not have been the final decision set forth in the charge, because the Brigadier (on the 3rd December), in his evidence before the Court, admitted that on my sending an appeal direct to the Commander-in-Chief, His Excellency took a different view of the case, so far as that he

* "Court-Martial Proceedings," pp. 19, 20.   † Ibid. pp. 20, 21.

directed Captain M—— to withdraw his letter, Ensign T—— to declare he had no intention to injure Ensign White at ball practice, and Major Liptrap to cancel a Regimental Order.* Moreover, the General's adverse testimony was not supported by the cautiously-worded and fencing evidence of the Deputy-Assistant-Adjutant-General, who, on being shown my letter of the 28th September to the Adjutant-General, and being asked whether the Commander-in-Chief's decision upon the matters of complaint therein contained, viz., the order issued by Major Liptrap about target practice, and about Ensign T——'s supposed attempt upon my life had been communicated to me, replied that he could not say whether the Commander-in-Chief's decision on the Regimental Order was communicated to me, but that when I wished to forward that letter, or one similar to it, I was told by Brigadier-General S——, in his presence, that it had already been decided on by the Commander-in-Chief, and this he said happened on or before the 27th September.† On being asked by the Judge-Advocate if he could remember, if not the very words yet the substance of what was communicated to me on that occasion by the General, he made a very guarded reply, to the effect that the General returned to me a letter full of my grievances which I wished to be forwarded, and told me that the matter contained therein had already been decided on by the Commander-in-Chief; but the witness in this answer said not a word about the Regimental Order, or the offence against my life. He was therefore asked to look at my letter of the 28th September, and say whether the letter I wished the General to forward, and which the General declined to do because the matter contained in it had already been decided by His Excellency, was similar to this letter? To this critical question the Deputy-Assistant-Adjutant-General returned an indecisive answer, in which he made the following

* "Court-Martial Proceedings," p. 34.　　† Ibid. pp. 22-24.

admission, showing that the letter I wished to be forwarded was not the same as my letter of the 28th September. "I remember," said the witness, "perfectly well at the time Ensign White telling the General that he wished Captain M——'s letter to him to be forwarded to head-quarters, from which I suppose that grievance was included amongst the others, which is not the case in this letter." He was then asked the question point blank. "Can you distinctly recollect if the supposed grievance regarding Ensign T——'s affair and the subject of his conduct having been commented on in Regimental Orders were in the letter which the Brigadier-General would not at first forward?" Witness replied, "I say that all his grievances were included in it, as far as I can remember." Whereupon the President asked the question, "Had the decision of His Excellency the Commander-in-Chief on the matters referred to in Ensign White's first letter been previously communicated to Ensign White?" To which witness replied by referring to the Commander-in-Chief's decision in the case between myself and Lieutenant W——, the Adjutant,[*] a matter unmentioned in my letter of the 28th September; but witness said nothing about the Regimental Order and the alleged offence against my life, of which that letter was full. Nor could this witness be induced by any question, however plainly put, to declare in so many words that His Excellency's decision on these two matters had been made known to me. The real fact of the case which they were so anxious to conceal was this, that the letter I wished the General to forward on the 27th September was my letter to the Adjutant-General of the Army to clear up my misrepresented conduct towards Captain M——, commanding my company, by the production of his suppressed letter to me. This was really the letter which the General refused to forward, telling me that the matters

[*] "Court-Martial Proceedings," pp. 24–26.

which I wished to agitate had already been decided by the Commander-in-Chief.*

Moreover, the General himself appears indirectly to have admitted this, for when, in reference to my attendance at his quarters on the 27th of September, I asked him the following question, "Did you tell me that this affair between myself and Captain M—— was settled by His Excellency?" the General's reply was, "I daresay I did."† I had before been punished on partial evidence on this account, having been reprimanded by the Commander-in-Chief, and directed to withdraw my note to Captain M——. But when I ventured to lay the whole case before the Commander-in-Chief, His Excellency then revised his former decision, since I was not reprimanded for sending my letter direct, instead of through the prescribed channels of communication, but the Commander-in-Chief informed the military authorities at Barrackpore that he considered Captain M——'s letter to me (represented as a letter of advice) to be offensive, and directed its withdrawal.‡

A plain proof this of the underhand dealings of my military superiors at Barrackpore!!! Thus really and truly the case for the prosecution completely broke down, and the adverse finding of the Court showed a complete failure of justice in finding me guilty of what I was as innocent of as the babe unborn!!! And had I been vindictively inclined, I believe I should have had a case for a civil court against my fifteen judges, who I imagine would have been indictable for their illegal sentence. Of course I never dreamt of taking such a step. They may have acted according to their light, albeit a dim one. Lastly, the Court were wrong, so I consider, in finding me guilty of "highly unofficer-like conduct" in having in my letter of 7th October sent direct to the Adjutant-General (complaining of the refusal of the Brigadier to grant me leave to be examined at the

* "Court-Martial Proceedings," p. 31.   † Ibid. p. 22.
‡ Ibid. p. 28.

College of Fort William in the native languages when I was not under arrest) " insubordinately and disrespectfully stated that it would be useless my attempting to forward the letter through the prescribed channels on account of my superiors at Barrackpore being all prejudiced against me." For I maintain on the following grounds that this was not insubordination, except in the extreme technical acceptation of the term, viz.:

1st. Because the Brigadier, in refusing me permission to be examined in the prize examination at the College of Fort William* at a time when I was not under arrest, was doing his utmost in my case to frustrate the object of a Government notification, which had recently been promulgated, encouraging officers to study the native languages by the offer of a reward of a thousand rupees to any officer who should pass two examinations of a prescribed high standard in two native languages. Moreover, the Commander-in-Chief practically did not regard my conduct in this matter as " highly unofficerlike ;" for His Excellency did for me in the matter just what I wanted, inasmuch as he desired the authorities to allow me leave to appear before the examiners of the College of Fort William previous to my corps leaving Barrackpore.† And this at a time when I was under arrest!

2nd. Because it was the truth, borne out by the evidence before the Court, that the military authorities at Barrackpore were all prejudiced against me, as shown by their underhand dealings in the case between myself and Captain M——, by their refusing to forward my papers and the impediments thrown in the way of my being examined. All these things, too, were brought to light whilst I was contending at a considerable disadvantage, for the Court were unwilling to press the General and Brigadier more than they could help.

* " Court-Martial Proceedings," Appendix, last page.
† See authenticated extract of Commander-in-Chief's Instructions, in my possession.

This wretched failure of justice shows the necessity of having a well-trained lawyer to conduct the proceedings of general courts-martial, and one holding some kind of independent position, enabling him to impose some check upon the proceedings, so as to restrain them from the commission of what they might afterwards be held responsible for before a civil tribunal. It is time now to notice the active part the Governor-General of India thought proper to take against a poor friendless ensign. Driven to desperation by oppression, I, in an unfortunate moment, had taken the unwise step of sending a letter to his Lordship, then residing at Government House, Barrackpore, in the hope that he might do something for me, since a word to the General would have been sufficient. But that word was unspoken, and instead of manifesting the slightest generous interest in my behalf, the Most Noble the Governor-General did me an ill turn, for this very letter was with his Lordship's sanction laid before the Court* by the prosecutor, Major Liptrap. Referring thereto in his remarks upon my Court-Martial (22nd of December, 1852), His Excellency the Commander-in-Chief, with a nicer sense of justice than was manifested by the Most Noble the Governor-General, condemned this proceeding as being "quite irrelevant to the charge, and calculated improperly to prejudice (me) Ensign White in the opinion of the Court. An opening address," added His Excellency, "is seldom requisite, but when one is desirable, it should not be made the vehicle for stating matters not put in issue by the charges, into which the Court have no authority to investigate, or the prisoner opportunity to rebut."† It would seem that the Most Noble the Governor-General was piqued by this condemnation of what he had sanctioned, for his Lordship requested His Excellency the Commander-in-Chief to bring me before

---

* "Court-Martial Proceedings," pp. 5, 6.
† See "Court-Martial Proceedings," p. 65; also G. O. C. C., 22nd December, 1852.

a Medical Court, to ascertain whether I was of a right state of mind or not.

I then experienced, what I have done so often since, the truth of those touching words of the Psalmist, "This poor man cried, and the Lord heard him, and saved him out of all his troubles" Psalm (xxxiv. 6); "God is our refuge and strength, a very present help in trouble" (Psalm xlvi. 1). Such verses in those hard times were very sweet to my taste. Truly affliction does not spring from the dust, but accomplishes the object for which it is sent by driving the believer closer to his Saviour. All sorts of things were raked up against me for the consideration of the Medical Committee which in due time assembled at Benares. Whether this was done at the suggestion or by the direction of the Governor-General, I never learnt, but from the interest which he appeared to take in bringing ruin upon my devoted head, the thing does not appear very improbable. This miserable attempt to drive me out of the Service failed, as it deserved to do, in consequence of the Medical Court being composed of upright, conscientious gentlemen,* who did their duty "without fear, partiality, or favour," and I was pronounced to be of a sound state of mind.† This was the Lord's doing: to Him be all the praise! Though I could have no hopes of obtaining a civil appointment as long as the present Governor-General held office, I still worked away to prepare myself for the prize examination, as I had failed to pass when I appeared before the examiners immediately after the trial was over. This may be accounted for by the state of mental excitement I had gone through for about a week. Early in 1853 I applied for six months' leave of absence from Benares to visit Calcutta, for the purpose of trying again to pass. My application was forwarded on, but

* Of whom I have especial cause to remember the names of Drs. Angus and Leckie.
† See Report of Medical Committee, 1853.

my Commanding Officer stabbed me in the dark by a private and confidential report, containing a misrepresentation of my conduct, which I had no opportunity of replying to. The consequence was that I had the mortification to see my leave granted, and at the same time cancelled as a punishment for an imputed offence of which I was quite innocent. It will naturally be asked what was the cause of this mortal hatred which I experienced. My only reply to this question is that I cannot prove the matter, and, therefore, without expressing any opinion of my own, I shall content myself with mentioning what was told me by others. An officer of my own regiment told me in strict confidence that one reason of my being treated as I had been, was on account of my religion; he did not mention what the other reason was. This must not be regarded as any breach of confidence, considering this distance of time, and since I abstain from giving even the initial of the officer's name. I was also told by one of the Serampore missionaries that Captain N—— said to him, "The reason why Ensign White is treated in the way he is, is because he is so good." I know as a recorded fact that Major Liptrap took offence at my having on one occasion sent him a number of verses from the Bible with a recommendation to him to read them.* I may also mention that one of the best friends I had in the regiment told me at Barrackpore that I was worse than a heathen in denying my infant baptism, by being baptized again by the Baptists.

In accordance with the orders previously issued for the annual relief of regiments, I marched with my regiment to be stationed at Benares, where we arrived about the middle of January, 1853. It will be fitting therefore, first of all, to give a description of this renowned metropolis of Hindooism. Benares, with its thousand idol temples and numerous ghauts, is situated on the left bank of the Ganges, four hundred and fifteen miles by

* "Court-Martial Proceedings," p. 39.

road from Calcutta, and contains a population of nearly two hundred thousand souls. The streets are narrow, wherein may be seen roaming at large a lot of lazy but sacred, or rather doubly sacred, bulls, since they are votive offerings to one of the Hindoo trinity, and are branded as the peculiar property of that heathen divinity. It would therefore be perilous to do these lazy oxen harm, or even to do them good by making them do a little work. From remote ages Benares has been known as the "holy city" of the Hindoos, bathing in the waters here being regarded as particularly efficacious in the removal of sin. Here all that is abominable in that noxious superstition flourishes. Having been over the place I will introduce the reader to what meets the eye there. Inside the city are sacred wells, the smell of which is simply abominable, to which the people bring flowers. The sacred bulls are kept in countenance by the thousands of sacred monkeys who have a temple of their own dedicated to Hunooman, the monkey god.* The place also swarms with wild-looking devotees, who appear to be engaged in silent contemplation, looking at no one, and sitting apparently in one unvaried position. But the thing that interested me as much if not more than anything else, was an observatory containing a model of the world, in which the whole mundane system was represented by elaborate configurations. The Brahmin exhibitor came to me for a present, whereupon I told him I would give him one, if he could give me a consistent account of what these figures were intended to represent. But as he could not do

---

* The monkey is a sacred animal in India, and in some parts of the country I have seen regular monkey-trees, heavily laden with these funny creatures, living a life free from alarm, since it would be considered downright sacrilege to harm the smallest of them. And I remember it was most amusing to see how these monkeys would all, both great and small, the mothers with their young ones close in their embraces, follow me about for the sake of a little grain scattered about here and there to allure them on.

this I gave him no present, for which I dare say he bestowed on me an inward curse. There are some turbulent people in the city, as the following incident will show. I was going through the city one day, when I stood to look at a huge figure of Ram, in the act of overcoming his great enemy Rawun, the King of Ceylon, when an impudent fellow started forward, and addressing me, said :—" That," pointing to the prostrate form of Rawun, " is you, and the other (who was pinning him to the ground) is our Ram." Nettled at his uncalled-for impertinence, I instantly smote him with such force in the face as to surprise the rude fellow. But this proof of muscular Christianity is not to be commended. I acted on the sudden impulse, and it was well for me that I escaped maltreatment from the bazaar riff-raff, for on another occasion the sergeant-major of my regiment had a narrow escape of losing his life. I did not see this myself, but he told me about it afterwards, from which it appeared that in righteous indignation he had struck down a naked devotee who was behaving in a manner so abominably, as to be totally unfit to be mentioned. Whereupon he was set upon by the devotee's followers, who were intent on taking his life, and they would have murdered him, had he not succeeded at last in escaping into a house that providentially was near at hand. The British cantonment was Secrole, which is two or three miles from the city.

Major Liptrap hit upon a new plan at Benares to get rid of me. It was this: he used frequently to direct my attendance at his house for all sorts of petty trifles, and when my Commanding Officer got me there (for I always obeyed his arbitrary summons), he said all the most irritating things he could think of, evidently with the design of driving me to make an insubordinate reply; and I firmly believe to this day that he had some one concealed who would be a ready witness to what I might say. I went, therefore, each time in fear and trembling, but I always prayed most earnestly to the Lord to give me grace to enable me to curb my naturally warm temper, and my prayer was answered on every occasion I went there. With this one experience I confute the impious theories of those modern misnamed philosophers, who assert that there is no use in prayer. Can they explain to me by what means I, naturally a hot-tempered man, was enabled always to keep my temper under such a trying ordeal, except by acknowledging the practical use of prayer to the omnipotent Ruler of the universe? Once the provoking things Major Liptrap said to me were almost more than I could bear, and I rose respectfully to take my leave, but he would not suffer me; so I had to remain till he gave me leave to go. It is time now to narrate the dead set made at me by my Commanding Officer, the officer commanding at Benares, and the General commanding the Division, in the case of a native soldier belonging to the company which I commanded. The narrative is given on the authority of a bundle of official letters in my possession. On the 30th May, 1853, I reported to my Commanding Officer (through the Adjutant) the very disrespectful behaviour that morning of my pay-havildar, Sunkatoodeen Sookul, in his having addressed to me such highly offensive words as the following :—" You will never cease being unjust;" and of his disrespectful conduct towards me on other occasions. On the 1st June, in obedience to orders, I attended at the quarters of Major Liptrap, who, in the presence of his regimental staff, entirely took the part of the havildar and found fault with me; he also brought forward the accused non-commissioned officer, who denied my statements. I repeatedly affirmed it to be as I had stated, but Major Liptrap refused to give credence to my statement, saying that the havildar's word was as good as mine; and he, moreover, suffered this lying native to make false complaints against me, the officer commanding his company. I also produced a memo. of further causes of complaint against the pay-havildar, a portion of which I was permitted to read; but it was of no avail, and the end of the disreputable business was that Sunkatoodeen Sookul was allowed to go away unpunished, to my great indignation, as Major Liptrap said to me that "it did not appear at all clear that the pay-havildar made use of those words" which I stated he did. Under such very painful circumstances I felt it necessary immediately to appeal to the officer commanding the station, trusting that he would take such steps as he might see fit for the restoration of good order, which had been so seriously damaged. In my letter to the Brigade Major the same day (1st June), requesting him to lay my case before the officer commanding the station, I laid stress upon this one point: that when my legitimate authority was trampled upon by my Commanding Officer, and when in addition I was exposed to such excessive humiliation and degradation as I had been that morning, it was utterly impossible for me in any degree to check irregularities, and keep up discipline amongst the men I commanded, when my influence over them was so entirely annihilated. I sent this letter in the first instance to the Adjutant of my regiment, requesting him to solicit Major Liptrap to forward it on. This letter with its enclosures was returned to me on the 3rd June, with a very long letter from the Adjutant, containing serious threats of what the Major would do to me in the event of my persisting in wishing to have my papers sent on, and calling me "a contumacious, most troublesome and litigious officer." I was forbidden to write official letters, and informed that in future, when I had anything to communicate to the Commanding Officer, I was to make the subject known in person the day before to the Adjutant, who was directed to report the circumstance, when an hour would be appointed for my attending at the Commanding Officer's quarters, if necessary. This lengthy letter concluded with the following characteristic paragraph:

"In conclusion, I am instructed to acquaint you that unless you can conduct the duties of the company without quarrelling with, and annoying the pay-havildar, Major Liptrap will be compelled to withhold the charge of a company altogether from you." Neither this threat, nor his threatening to report my alleged perverse and disobedient conduct to the authorities, had the power to turn me from my purpose. Ill though I was, and on the sick list, I allowed only one day to elapse, and then (4th June) I sent this curious letter of the Adjutant with my letter of the 1st June to the Brigade Major, and its enclosures under cover of a second letter, dated 4th June, to the Brigade Major, explaining the necessity of my sending the letter direct instead of through the Adjutant. I failed, however, to obtain any justice from the officer commanding the station, as by his directions a severe reprimand was administered to me on the 25th June, and I was ordered not to address the Brigade Major or my Commanding Officer again on that subject. I cannot help thinking that that officer was conscious that his conduct towards me would not bear the light; because when I wrote to the Brigade Major a private note asking if I might be allowed a copy of the reprimand that was read to me, I received the following laconic reply:—

"MY DEAR SIR,

"The Colonel commanding will not permit you to have a copy of the letter read to you yesterday.

"Yours truly,

"D. S. DODGSON."

I now at once resigned the command of my company. I could not do otherwise after being so shamefully distrusted in making a report concerning a native soldier under my command, and at the same time I sent all the above-mentioned papers with an appeal to the Commander-in-Chief, addressed to the Adjutant-General

(D, 25th of June, 1853), which I sent under cover of a letter to the Assistant-Adjutant-General, Dinapore Division, requesting him to solicit the General to forward my papers to head-quarters. All I got by this was another fierce reprimand from the General. It became now a serious question for consideration as to what I ought to do. Was I now to give in, and thus allow my fair name to be bandied about as a dishonoured one after my veracity had been arbitrarily adjudicated to be below that of a native soldier? Was falsehood, screened by power, to win the day? I determined it should not be if by any possibility I could prevent it, especially as my honour as an officer and a gentleman were so concerned. *Magna est veritas, et prævalebit.* I made a last attempt to obtain justice, and that was completely successful. On the 8th of July I sent an appeal to the Commander-in-Chief, addressed direct to the Adjutant-General of the Army, enclosing at the same time all the above-mentioned letters on the subject. Apologizing for the irregularity of sending the letter direct, I urged the particular emergency of my case as my plea for this breach of military etiquette, and I trusted that the circumstances thereof would be considered to justify the step I had taken, under the conviction, as I expressed it, that "truth and innocency in my case must eventually triumph over oppression, even though countenanced by those authorities from whose tribunal I was thus obliged to appeal to one higher." The rest is soon told; I was not brought to a court-martial for thus accusing my Commanding Officer of oppression, and the officers commanding the station and division with countenancing oppression; but on the 8th of August, 1853, I received a letter from the officiating Adjutant of my regiment informing me that the pay-havildar, Sunkatoodeen Sookul, was ordered to be tried by a native district Court-martial on a charge framed against him at army head-quarters in reference to the complaint preferred against him by me. The result may easily be imagined. The Court-martial assembled in due time, and the pay-havildar was found guilty in having been highly disrespectful in using the words to me I charged him with. The matter was taken up by some of the papers. I give an extract from one written by an impartial writer, but I never learnt whom :—

"ENSIGN WHITE'S INTREPIDITY.

"There is a weight in stolid perseverance that will drive it through any difficulties or opposition, so long as they are not actually impenetrable and insuperable, and we have an instance in point, which has just been communicated to us from Benares. Ensign White, of the 42nd Native Infantry at that station, and junior of his rank in the regiment, had occasion to find serious fault with a pay-havildar of the corps, and he accordingly embodies his charges against the non-commissioned officer, and sends them in to the Major commanding the regiment. The Major commanding the regiment examines into the charges and evidence, and the consequence is that he acquaints Ensign White with his having done so, and also with his opinion that the complaints against the pay-havildar were groundless, and that consequently he could take no further notice of the matter. Upon this, Ensign White coolly and quietly collects the papers again, and forwards them to the Brigadier commanding the station. The Brigadier commanding the station also examines into the charges and evidence, and acquaints Ensign White with his having done so, and also with his concurrence in the views and opinions of Ensign White's Commanding Officer, at the same time sending to Ensign White a rather sharp 'wig' for his troublesome and litigious conduct. Ensign White, upon this, quietly collects his papers and charges again, and, with the Brigadier's wig still sticking to his head, sends them off to the General commanding the division. The General commanding the division also examines into the charges and evidence, and acquaints Ensign White with his having done so, and also with his entire concurrence in the views and opinions of the officer commanding the 42nd N.I., and of the Brigadier commanding the station, and concludes by sending Ensign White an enormous 'perruque,' compared to which the Brigadier's present was what military hairdressers would call a very scanty 'scalp.' One would have thought that this would have ended the matter, and that Ensign White of the 42nd N.I., capped in this fashion, and somewhat like the prize fowls one sees with enormous top-knots in the *Illustrated London News*, would have toppled over, and lain helpless on the ground. Not a bit of it. Ensign White calmly collects his papers, and charges again, and without taking any notice whatever of General, Brigadier, or Major, forwards them straight to the Adjutant-General of the Army, for submission to His Excellency the Commander-in-Chief.

"The Commander-in-Chief examines into the charges and evidence, acquaints the General commanding the Benares Division with the fact of his having done so, and also with his entire dissent from the views and opinions of the latter, and of the Brigadier commanding the station, and of the Major commanding the 42nd Regiment of Native Infantry. Here the bore began running up strongly favourable to[*] Ensign White, and the conclusion was that a district Court-martial assembled by order of the Commander-in-Chief, which tried the pay-havildar upon Ensign White's charges, and found him guilty, the General commanding the division approving and confirming the sentence!! We are averse to litigious obstinacy and stubborn perseverance as a system, but it is useful to show that where an officer is in the right he can forward the ends of justice against very great odds, however junior his rank and

[*] The word in the newspaper is "against," but this is an evident misprint for "favourable to."

subaltern his position may be. We think that Ensign White deserves great credit indeed for the unswerving tenacity with which he followed up his point in this instance, and brought a guilty man to justice in the face of all opposition and apparently insuperable difficulties."—*Morning Chronicle*, Nov. 3.

My father and mother at this time were very anxious on my account, as their fears were so great that I must be crushed by contending with such powerful enemies, that they wrote to me, advising me to retire upon the invalid's list. Such advice from those so dear to me affected me so much that I felt quite ill from it, though I had not the slightest idea of adopting such timid councils. I was on out-post duty at Jaunpore at the time the sentence was published.

Major Liptrap now played his last card; he wrote to the officer commanding at Jaunpore, giving him to understand that the havildar had been acquitted. This was of course told me, and it had the effect intended, of making me furiously angry, because the man could only have been acquitted on the assumption of my sworn evidence being untrue. I should have taken some desperate step had it not been over-ruled by a merciful Providence. At last the thought struck me, Why not write first a private note to the Brigade Major? I did so, and then I learnt how I had been deceived, for that officer, whose letter I have before me, wrote to me on the 20th of October, saying, "You are under a mistake with regard to the havildar; he was found guilty of the charge." Soon after this Major Liptrap went on leave, and I never saw him more. He was a man that prospered in the world, and lived to attain a high rank.* A very violent outbreak of cholera occurred this year at Benares during the rainy season, in which two officers of my regiment died. On the 15th

* He retired to England in 1865, and became entitled to his Colonel's off-reckonings in 1866.

of November I was transferred as lieutenant to the 3rd European Regiment, just being raised at Chinsurah. No tongue can tell how delighted I was to escape from one who hated me with such a bitter and remorseless hatred as Major Liptrap did. I was also very glad to leave a place with such unpleasant associations, and where I could not get leave to go to Calcutta to be examined for the prize examination. My transfer to the 3rd European Regiment conferred the great boon of giving me this opportunity of appearing before the examiners, and, though not in order of time, I may dismiss the subject by stating that I passed in due course, and received the prize of a thousand rupees. But I must return from this digression to go on with my reminiscences. As soon as my name appeared in orders I lost no time in hiring a budgerow, in which I and my wife took our voyage to Chinsurah, which is situated on the river Hooghly, about twenty-six miles from Calcutta. I became here very friendly with the missionaries of the Free Church, just as I had been previously friendly with the Baptist missionary, Mr. Heinig, at Benares. I speedily became acquainted with the officers of my regiment. I also formed the acquaintance of the chaplain, an eccentric man, who afterwards committed suicide. The first part of the Indian Railway was opened this year (1854) from Calcutta to Hooghly, a town about a couple of miles from Chinsurah.

Prosperity now made me sinfully careless. I required the rod, and it was wisely sent. Once more I got into hot water with my Commanding Officer. This happened in July, 1854. There is no occasion to say much about this business, since I frankly admit that I was in the wrong on this occasion. The simple fact of the matter is that I lost my temper under what I considered great provocation. When I became sensible of my indiscretion, I offered to withdraw an objectionable note I had written to the Adjutant, and to make an apology for the same. But since I refused to make the very humiliating apology I was required to make, I was tried by a general Court-martial on the 8th of September, 1854, and being found guilty of "conduct unbecoming an officer," in having importunately solicited a few days' leave of absence after it had been repeatedly refused me, and of "unbecoming conduct" in having addressed to Lieutenant C——, the Adjutant of the regiment, "a note couched in very provoking language, and for causing the same to be delivered in public in an offensive manner, I was sentenced to be reprimanded by the Commander-in-Chief, and to be placed one step lower in the list of lieutenants of my regiment. The loss of this step proved a most severe punishment, for not only did I lose my right of seniority to the valuable appointment of Interpreter and Quarter-Master when it afterwards became vacant, but, what was far worse, my promotion to captain was retarded for more than three years, occasioning thereby a loss to me in pay of more than five hundred pounds. The loss of this hard cash proved in future years a regular incubus to me. Certainly, I bought experience at a very dear rate, and it involved consequences of the utmost importance, because my promotion being retarded from 1862 to 1865, prevented my going home as I wished to do in 1863 or in 1864, and by remaining in India I lost my only son, a fine little boy, whose mother died shortly before—the result of an accident going to Darjeeling. And though I was not justified in losing my temper, yet assuredly my punishment was greatly in excess of my offence. Next year, on my father's death, having taken my furlough, I secured my passage by the *Regina*, but I delayed going on board till the very last, and when I went to the vessel, to my utter dismay she was nowhere to be found, and, upon making inquiry, some sailors hinted at the probability of the *Regina* having left for England, which alarmed me so much that for the first and only time in my life I nearly fainted away in the boat I hired to take me on board.

However, recovering myself, I urged the boatmen to take me down the river, and I was at last rewarded for my perseverance by the longed-for sight of my vessel. This was early in June. We had a very stormy passage, and were nearly wrecked in a gale of wind off the Cape of Good Hope. This was either on the 21st or 22nd of August, when for some hours I was every minute expecting the *Regina* to go down, so fearfully was she being struck with a heavy cross sea. We doubled the Cape at last, and then the storm was succeeded by a rather sudden calm. The motion of the vessel became unpleasant in the extreme, for there was no wind to steer by; the consequence was that the ship rolled about frightfully, like a log on the big waves, at the imminent risk of the masts toppling out of her. But by the mercy of the Most High we escaped this second danger, and in due time anchored at St. Helena, a tropical island believed to be of volcanic origin, which is chiefly celebrated for the captivity there of the Great Emperor Napoleon Bonaparte, who, after his defeat at Waterloo, was detained there as a state prisoner till his death in 1821. It is quite a mistake, and conveys a wrong impression, to speak of this island as a rock, as some people do. At all events, I can say from my own experience that I was most agreeably surprised to find it very different from my preconceived notions. I landed at James Town, which is the chief town, and my stay here of a week gave me plenty of time to explore the island, which is by no means extensive, being only about ten miles long and six miles broad. Its mountainous appearance affords the only pretext for its being called the rock on which the great Napoleon spent so many years of his life; for I found some charming country scenery in the highlands of this very salubrious isle. This was in September. I was also delighted to meet with some of the Lord's children here, such as Mr. Bertram, the pastor of the Baptist chapel, and Mr. Janisch, the magistrate, who I believe is now the Governor of the island. This amiable gentleman, who practises the Scriptural precept that all God's children are brethren, received me cordially into his house and entertained me most hospitably. I spent my time chiefly in rambling about from place to place, not forgetting to visit Longwood, where I saw the house in which Napoleon lived and died. I listened to the anecdotes told of this great man, whose captivity was really the happiest event that could have befallen him, since in his exile this mighty world-conqueror was conquered by the love of Christ, and became a true and intelligent Christian. I engaged to give an address[*] concerning my own experience in India at the Baptist chapel; but when the time came for me to fulfil my promise, I must confess that my heart failed me, and I had not the moral courage to go and stand up to speak about myself in a chapel crowded with people to listen to such a novelty as an address from an officer from India.

Instead of putting in an appearance, I sent an excuse, and the people went away disappointed of their expected treat. But Mr. Bertram would not let me off so easily, for the next time I attended service at the chapel, he did a rather extraordinary thing by calling out from the pulpit to me, sitting in one of the pews, asking me to lead the prayers of the congregation, which I accordingly did. At last, after spending a very pleasant week here, the *Regina* weighed anchor, and, homeward bound, we left the island, which, from its cliffy altitude, is not soon lost sight of, since the loftiest mountain rises to a height of 2,700 feet. After a long and dull voyage of five months, I landed at Gravesend, and the first thing I heard of was my brother's death in the Crimea. Early in July, 1856, I left England on

[*] See the interesting account of this in a book called "Remarkable Conversions," published by Nisbet and Co. (1878), pp. 61, 62.

board the *Cambodia*, doing duty with recruits. The principal event of a personal nature was the dangerous illness with which I was seized at the beginning of the voyage. Some time after, the only surgeon we had was taken alarmingly ill with quinsy, and, having no medical man to attend him, his case was a most precarious one, but eventually he did recover. This voyage, unlike the last, was not at all a stormy one. Once we appeared to be getting into a cyclone, but Captain Page backed out of it. We reached Calcutta in exactly four months. From there I went to Allahabad by steamer, doing duty with recruits, and thence I marched up country with them. On arriving at Cawnpore, about the middle of February, 1857, I thought that a splendid opportunity presented itself, as several of the native regiments there were in want of an interpreter, and therefore, as I had passed in such high examinations, I thought that I ought to succeed. I went to one commanding officer after another, but it was of no avail—my strenuous efforts failed entirely. I was greatly disappointed at the time, but how thankful to God I felt afterwards that I was thus saved from being involved in the terrible massacre that occurred there only a few months afterwards. Truly God's ways are the best, and that man is the wisest who with childlike simplicity recognizes the fact at all times and under all circumstances. My dear mother, writing to me from Rochester, on the 16th July, 1857, says, in allusion to my disappointment,—"You felt it very hard not to get the interpretership; had you had your wish, my flesh creeps to think what might have befallen yourself, wife, and babe. I can but say, thank God for His mercies, and may He increase our love to Him a hundredfold." I had some trouble with the recruits I was taking to my regiment before reaching Agra. It is no easy matter to keep always in order a lot of undisciplined hot-blooded young men, especially when they manage to procure a quantity of native liquor, and it is next to impossible to prevent them getting it. I reached Agra early in March, and soon after my rejoining my regiment that horrible storm burst upon us which threatened to engulf all the English in India in destruction, and to subvert British rule by the restoration of Mahomedan supremacy. But this must be reserved for another Chapter.

CHAPTER IV.

Origin and Cause of the Great Sepoy Revolt—Personal Knowledge of this Matter—The Greased Cartridges—Ridiculous Fears of the Sepoys—Their Obstinate Belief in a Lie—Disgraceful Policy of the Indian Government righteously Punished—Remarkable Character of this Divine Retribution—Retrospect of Former Mutinies—Lord Dalhousie's Undignified and Unenergetic Treatment of the Mutinous 38th Regiment in 1852—Circumstances favourable to a General Revolt—Paucity of Europeans for the Defence of an Extended Frontier—Lord Dalhousie's Mischievous and Unpolitic Annexation of Oude—"Right of Lapse"—Its Unfairness—Sattarah, Nagpore, and Jhansi—First Appearance of a Mutinous Spirit at Berhampore and Barrackpore—Premature Outbreak and Massacre at Meerut—Remarkable Inactivity of the European Troops—Mutiny and Massacre at Delhi—Proclamation of King of Delhi—Description of Agra—Taj Mahal—Council of War at Agra—Grand Parade of Troops—Lieutenant-Governor harangues them—Mutiny at Ferozepore—Useless Proclamations of the Governor-General and Commander-in-Chief—Scindiah's devoted Loyalty—Sepoys rise at Alygurh, Etawah, and Mynpoorie—Lieutenant-Governor's Injudicious Manifesto—Cancelled by Earl Canning—Mutiny at Muttra—Intended Rise and Massacre at Agra—Blessing of United Prayers of Earnest Christians—Remarkable Intervention of Divine Providence in our Favour—The Native Regiments at Agra are Disarmed—Organization of a Volunteer Force—The Untrustworthiness of the Agra Police—Mutiny at Gwalior—Our Isolation at Agra—Retirement of the Ladies and Children into the Fort—The North-West Provinces in a Blaze of Revolt—Mutinies at Hansi, Hissar, Nusseerabad, Neemuch, Bareilly, Moradabad, Shahjehanpore—Touching Scene at the Massacre near Aurungabad—Revolt at Futtehgurh—Flight of the English—Mutiny at Cawnpore—Unparalleled Misery of the English besieged in Wheeler's Entrenchments—Dhoondhoo Punt, the Nana Sahib—His Old Grudge against the English—The amazing Treachery of the 6th Regiment N.I. at Allahabad—Sepoys rise at Azimgurh—Outbreak at Benares and Jaunpore—Mutiny at Jhansi—The Ill-used Ranee of Jhansi's Revenge—Atrocious Massacre—Mutinies at Nowgong, Jullundur, Phillour, and Rohnee—Retributive Effects of Wrong-doing in Oude—Sepoys rise at Lucknow, Seetapur, Mohumdee, and Fyzabad—Terrible Sufferings of Mrs. Mills and other Fugitives—Revolts at Sultanpore, Bareitch, and other Stations—All Classes in Oude rise in Insurrection against the usurped Power of the British Government in their Country—Commander-in-Chief dies of Cholera—Mutinies at Indore—Holkar's Noble Reply to the Mutineers—Revolt at Mhow—Sepoys rise in the Vicinity of Agra.

THE sketch which I am about to give of the great

Sepoy Mutiny which set in a blaze of rebellion the North-West Provinces, together with the country down to Allahabad, as well as Oude, Central India and some other parts, and which like wild-fire went the round of the different stations in the Bengal Presidency, is not intended to represent a complete history of that terrific revolt with its ensuing protracted war, as that would be extending my present work beyond its object, which is to give an outline of the leading events of that momentous time much in the same abridged form as that in which I recorded it at the time in my diary, supplemented, however, by some information derived at a later time from books;* except that part relating to Agra, where I was stationed, and which, in consequence of its forming part of my personal reminiscences, I have related at great length. The ostensible and immediate cause of this military outbreak was an infatuated belief on the part of the Hindoo Sepoy,† that the English Government was going to make them lose caste, and so convert them forcibly to Christianity by causing them to use cartridges greased with the fat of the sacred cow, the end of which was to be bitten off. This absurd idea was sedulously fomented by the Mussulmen, who religiously and politically regard us with far more dislike than the Hindoos, and who themselves believed, or pretended to believe, that we had designs against them also, which was to make them use cartridges smeared with hogslard, which is especially detestable to the religious prejudices of the Mahomedans. This was on the occasion of the introduction in 1857 of the Enfield rifle, which required a lubricated cartridge. It appears to have originated with a magazine Lascar at Dum Dum,‡ who one day in January,

---

* Such as the Histories of Kaye, Malleson, Grant, Chambers, Raikes, &c.
† The Hindoos constituted the great majority of the Native army; the Mussulmen represented about a fifth of the whole.
‡ A station about eight miles from Calcutta.

1857, meeting a high-caste Sepoy, asked him for a drink of water from his lota. The Brahmin at once replied with an objection on the score of caste. The Lascar made a taunting rejoinder, that caste was nothing, that high caste and low caste were all the same, as cartridges smeared with beef fat and hogslard were being made for the Sepoys at the Depôts and would be given out for general use throughout the army. The Brahmin carried the story to his comrades, and very soon it became the all-engrossing topic of conversation amongst the Sepoys, so that the story of the greased cartridges was in every mouth before the month was out, and at last the absurd notion that Government was going to deprive them of their caste, and make Christians of them by force, took firm possession of their minds, unshaken by the most solemn assurances and concessions on the part of Government! For although not a round of the greased cartridges had been actually used for practice purposes, and although not one of the large number of the dreaded cartridges (that were then in course of manufacture) had as yet been issued for use to a single Sepoy throughout the Presidency Division, yet as early as 27th January, 1857, in consequence of a representation made by General Hearsay,* a notification was issued from the Adjutant-General's office, Calcutta, granting permission to the Sepoys to grease their own cartridges with whatever lubricating substance they liked, and on the same day orders were telegraphed to various stations that if any greased cartridges had been issued for service they were not to be used.

But this concession had not the desired effect of removing their suspicion. This I (who used to be very familiar with the Sepoys, and who could speak their language nearly as well as my own) can well remember, because in the beginning of March I knew, from conversations with the Hindoo Sepoys, that they were really very anxious about a matter which appeared, according

* Commanding the Presidency Division.

to their notions, to threaten them with loss of caste; and towards the end of this month General Anson, the Commander-in-Chief, addressed the native officers at the Depôt formed for the instruction of the army in the new rifle at Umballa, in a speech wherein His Excellency endeavoured to disabuse them of their unjust suspicion, by informing them that there was not the slightest shadow of truth in the suspicion then prevailing that the object of Government was to subvert their religion by the use of the greased cartridge, and by assuring them on his honour that it never had been, and never would be, the policy of Government to coerce them in their religious feelings, or to interfere with their customs.

It is a singular fact that this explicit, emphatic, and authoritative declaration had not the least effect of undeceiving them of their ridiculous fears. The native officers, it is stated, listened respectfully to the Commander-in-Chief's oration; but when the parade was over they told Lieutenant Martineau, the musketry instructor, that though they themselves did not attribute any such evil design to the Government, yet the truth was, that for one man who disbelieved the story, there were ten thousand who believed it; that, in short, it was universally credited. The Hindoo soldier possesses a child-like credulity in believing any marvellous tale he is told, which he not unfrequently adheres to with all the obstinacy of our James II.

Had the poor deluded Sepoy but been acquainted with the first principles of our holy faith, he would have known how utterly impossible it was for the English Government, or for all the Governments of the whole world by their united power, to force him into a religion which could only be embraced by the personal exercise of faith and love. But this wholesome knowledge was studiously kept from his eyes. We as a nation had been, and were still, actually ashamed of our religion, and selfishly thought that the Hindoo system of theology was best for the Hindoo, whilst at the same time it served our turn best, and so any attempt made to cause the Sepoy to become acquainted with the Christian religion was, as a rule, frowned upon by the authorities. It is a disgraceful fact that the policy of the Indian Government was, and had been for many years, to keep the native soldier in ignorance of the saving truths of the Bible, as though we almost dreaded the idea of his becoming a Christian; and had it been known that I distributed Testaments amongst them, and used my best endeavours to convince them of the truth of the Christian religion, I have no doubt that I should have got into very serious trouble.* But I escaped simply because it was not found out. As a nation we were verily guilty of hiding our light under a bushel, and we reaped the fruit of our cowardice in a fearful ordeal, which ultimately produced a great change for the better. Moreover, previous to the Mutiny, Government was not merely neutral towards Hindooism, but actually favoured it by taking under its protecting care the vested interests of idol temples, and dishonouring God by its notorious connection with idolatry. In consequence of this wickedness we reaped a harvest of the most awful suffering that has ever been endured by man; and it is a very singular circumstance that we were made to suffer from the belief in a lie, which indirectly, at least, arose from our hiding the truth, and that our punishment came from the hands of those very people whose superstition and idolatry we had so sedulously fostered and cherished. Assuredly God's word was verified in our experience — "Them that honour me I will honour, and they that despise me shall be lightly esteemed" (1 Samuel ii. 30). Lightly esteemed the nation certainly was, when the most authoritative and solemn assurances of Government were discredited and treated as so many lies. That the Sepoys

---

* My bearer told me one day that he had been talked to by my Commanding Officer, Major Liptrap, who tried to ascertain from him what I was doing in the way of proselyting the natives.

really and truly believed in the tale of the design against their caste and religion appears to me yet further confirmed by the fact that the Sepoy revolt developed a great amount of religious rancour on the part of those insurgents, as was shown by the blind fury manifested by them towards places of Christian worship; and further by the animosity shown towards their own countrymen professing the Christian religion, who, failing to escape by flight, or concealment, were in some instances, not in all, put to death, when they would not purchase safety by abjuring their religion.* But the Sepoys were ripe for mutiny long before the agitation about the greased cartridges.

We had been sitting for years on the top of a powder magazine, ready to explode at any moment, as shown by a number of public events that had occurred since I entered the Service; besides which, who can tell how many curious incidents were hushed up! Such as the treasonable conversation overheard amongst a party of Sepoys when the battle was going against us at Ferozshuhur† (21st December, 1845). Then the next year, 1846, I saw my own regiment in a mutinous state on being ordered to leave their doles behind them,‡ on being ordered to march to Cashmere against the revolted chieftain, Shaick Imamoddeen. Brigadier Wheeler,§ who commanded the force, on being informed, gave his decision favourable to the wishes of the Sepoys, who got their doles. These matters were of course all hushed up. A mutinous disposition amongst the native soldiery may be traced as far back as the mutiny of two regiments at Vellore in 1806, which resulted in the massacre of above a hundred English soldiers besides civilians, followed by that of the 47th Regiment at Barrackpore in 1824, and still

* This was the case with Wilaiyut Ally, who suffered a martyr's death at Delhi.
† See elsewhere in the account of that battle.
‡ Large iron vessels for drawing water.
§ Afterwards Major-General Wheeler, commanding at Cawnpore in 1857.

later the mutiny of several regiments in the newly acquired Province of Scinde on a question of pay, which occasioned the disbandment of one regiment. But I prefer to give prominence to those outbreaks which occurred during my residence in India. First of all, then, there was the serious mutiny in 1849-50 of several regiments in the Punjaub. This also was on a question of pay; for on the Sikh kingdom becoming a British Province in 1849, the Sepoys serving in the newly annexed country ceased to enjoy the extra allowance of foreign service, and they could not understand why the conquest of the Punjaub should be followed by the reduction of their pay. They therefore (*i.e.*, the Sepoys of three regiments) refused to receive the reduced rates of pay. This outbreak was, however, nipped in the bud.

Some of the recusants were transported for life in 1850, and the disturbance ceased with the punishment of the 66th Regiment N.I., who, having broken into downright mutiny at Govindghur, and having attempted, though in vain, to seize the Fort there, were disbanded, and their place was taken by a regiment of Goorkhas.* But Sir Charles Napier thought that some grounds of dissatisfaction existed. The change which the Sepoys resented was declared by the Chief to be "impolitic and unjust," and, pending a reference to Government, orders were issued for the payment of compensation to the troops on a higher scale than what was sanctioned by the regulations. This was the origin of that memorable contest between the heads of the civil and military Government. Napier may have been wrong in exercising an authority not belonging to his office, which His Excellency justified on the plea of the danger being pressing, and not admitting of delay in action; but not less wrong, and far more irrational, was Dalhousie's denial of the fact of a mutiny having taken place. This his Lordship did in a peppery Minute,

* Styled the 66th Goorkha Light Infantry Regiment, now called the 1st Goorkha Regiment.

which he concluded in the following words :—" I desire to record my entire dissent from the statement that the army has been in mutiny, and the Empire in danger.". Napier held to his opinion with as much tenacity as Dalhousie ; but recognizing the duty of obedience, he adopted the proper course of resigning his post on the 22nd of May, 1850. Lastly, in 1852, the 38th Regiment N.I., stationed at Barrackpore, refused to volunteer to cross the sea to Burmah, and Lord Dalhousie, instead of adopting a dignified and energetic course of action, decreed that this regiment should not be sent to Burmah. These incidents show how ripe the Sepoys were for a revolt. A plausible pretext and a favourable opportunity alone were required to fire the train, and both of these presented themselves in 1857. The former has already been told, and the latter requires to be narrated, which was presented by Lord Dalhousie's annexation of the Punjaub, Pegu,* and Oude, whereby our strategic position was weakened by the far and wide distribution of our European forces to meet the requirements of the newly annexed territories ; the result being that a vastly extended area having to be defended by the same number of Europeans, their strength to act in any emergency was most impolitically diminished. This unwise policy produced an almost complete denudation of European troops between Calcutta and Delhi, the capital of the Moghul Empire, which important station had not a single company of European Infantry or a troop of European Cavalry or Artillery. In the beginning of 1857 there were in the three Presidencies of Bengal, Madras and Bombay, in the service of the Honourable East India Company, two hundred thousand native troops, and thirty-eight thousand Europeans, Queen's and Company's ; of whom there were stationed in Bengal, from Calcutta to the Afghan frontier station of Peshawur) one hundred and

* This Burmese Province, with its three million souls, was annexed in 1852.

eighteen thousand six hundred and sixty-three natives, and twenty-two thousand six hundred and ninety-eight Europeans, making a total of one hundred and forty-one thousand three hundred and sixty-one.* Never, therefore, had the Sepoys a better opportunity of acquiring the mastery than in the revolt of 1857, the difficulties of which were greatly aggravated by the mischievous policy of Lord Dalhousie in annexing Oude with its five millions, in 1856, on account of the misgovernment of its effeminate King, because this high-handed proceeding left a very bad impression on the minds of the Oudeans, so bad indeed that, as we shall see afterwards, they rose with the Sepoys; and secondly, by the injurious effects produced by this annexation in weakening our European strength at an important station like Cawnpore.

Honesty, whatever some politicians may say to the contrary, is the best and safest policy, and had we consulted the wishes of the nobility of Oude by maintaining the quasi independence of that country, there would in all human probability have been no Cawnpore massacre, since H.M. 32nd Foot, instead of being stationed at Lucknow, would have been cantoned at Cawnpore; nor would there have been those horrible massacres in Oude which will be referred to further on. Assuredly the unwarrantable annexation of Oude brought its own punishment. But had we acted towards that wronged kingdom with proper generosity, and more in accordance with the precepts of our holy faith, we should, as I believe, have found a friendly power in the country that proved to be a very hotbed of insurrection, by exciting to a glowing heat the patriotism of the great landholders who felt it their duty to stand by their King.† But nations like individuals not unfrequently reap as they sow.

* See return prepared by East India Company, showing the strength of their forces in India at the commencement of the Mutiny.
† This, for instance, was strikingly shown as late as November, 1858,

I base my assertion of what may have been the case on what happened in the Mahratta state of Gwalior, which being conquered by the English in 1843, might by the law of conquest have been annexed to British India. But Lord Ellenborough wisely forbore to do so, and by his generous treatment of this fallen state he bound its Maharajah (Scindiah) by a tie of gratitude, so that in our time of need he became our most staunch ally, risking his kingdom if not his life in our cause.*

Well would it had been for us, indeed, if Dalhousie had profited by the example of Christian forbearance set by Ellenborough. The difficulties of our position were further, though in a much minor degree, increased by Lord Dalhousie's grasping policy in substituting "the right of lapse" for the dearly-prized right of adoption. According to this innovation native states, on the occasion of their sovereigns dying without legitimate male heirs, were annexed to British rule on the assumption of our being the paramount power in India. On this principle Dalhousie annexed the Principality of Sattarah in 1849, which was followed by the annexation of Nagpore in 1854. The Principality of Jhansi, in Bundelcund, was also annexed by his Lordship in 1854, in spite of the protestation of the deceased Rajah's widow, who, after brooding over her wrongs for three years, took a fearful revenge in 1857, as will be seen farther on when we come to speak of the dreadful mutiny and massacre at that place. The first appearance of a mutinous spirit manifested itself in the 19th Regiment Native Infantry at Berhampore, about a hundred and twenty miles from Calcutta. This was on the 27th of February, 1857, and on the last

when the revolt was quite suppressed, in the case of that pre-eminent chieftain, Beni Madho, who in reply to the proclamation sent to him by Lord Clyde, stated that he felt it his duty to stand by his King, and that he would not surrender.

* I can say, from general report at the time, that Scindiah's services in 1857 were invaluable to us at Agra, which is distant about seventy miles from his capital, Gwalior.

day of the following month, the 19th was disbanded at Barrackpore. The scene now changes to that military station in the vicinity of Calcutta. There was no European regiment cantoned here. The native regiments stationed here at this time were the 2nd, 34th, 43rd,* and 70th† Regiments Native Infantry. On the 29th of March, 1857, occurred the mutiny of the 34th Regiment Native Infantry, on which day Mungal Pandy, a Sepoy of that regiment, fired at the Sergeant-Major, and fought a desperate hand-to-hand battle with Lieutenant Baugh, the Adjutant, within a few yards of the quarter-guard of the 34th Regiment, where a Jemadar and twenty men were on duty. The conduct of the mutineer appeared to meet with the approval of the Sepoys of the regiment, for, with the solitary exception of the Adjutant's orderly, none of the Sepoys moved to the assistance of Lieutenant Baugh, and some of the soldiers of the guard even struck that wounded officer on the ground, and threatened to shoot Shaick Pultoo, the only man who interfered in behalf of Baugh. Finally, General Hearsay, accompanied by his sons, rode to the quarter-guard, and ordered them to confine Mungal Pandy, who was hung on the 8th of April; and on the 22nd of April, Issurey Pandy, the Jemadar who had behaved so abominably as commanding the quarter-guard 34th Regiment Native Infantry, was also hung, and the regiment (*i.e.*, the seven companies at Barrackpore) were afterwards disbanded. The officer commanding the 34th Regiment Native Infantry was Colonel S. G. Wheeler (with whom I was well acquainted), a thoroughly devoted Christian; he was remarkably grave in his manner, and the desire of his whole soul was to be instrumental in bringing the natives to the knowledge of Christ as their Saviour. He was taken to task for preaching to the Sepoys, and on his retirement afterwards he followed the bent of his mind without let or hindrance. The rest of the

* Now the 6th Regiment N.I.   † At present the 11th Regiment N.I.

regiments at Barrackpore, though no doubt tarred with the same brush as the 34th N.I., were allowed to remain as they were, and were not disarmed till the 14th of June. The mutiny of the Bengal Army in right earnest, with its attendant massacres and insurrections of the turbulent classes of the people, did not commence till the month of May, and then it began with three native regiments at Meerut,* where one would naturally think that it must have been suppressed immediately, considering the powerful force of Europeans stationed there, which comprised Her Majesty's 6th Carabineers, 60th Rifles, and a large force of Artillery. On the 24th of April the 3rd Bengal Cavalry Regiment was drawn up on parade for instruction in the recent changes introduced into the platoon exercise, wherein, from deference to the national prejudices, the ends of the cartridges were to be torn instead of bitten off. Out of ninety troopers to whom the ammunition was tendered eighty-five refused to take it. Pursuant to the instructions of the Commander-in-Chief, the recusants were tried by a native general Court-martial, which sentenced them to ten years' imprisonment with hard labour. The sentence, which was confirmed by the General commanding the division, who commuted the sentence of eleven young troopers to five years, was read out to the prisoners at a general parade on the 9th of May, when their uniform being stripped off, and fetters fixed to their ankles, they were marched off to the gaol, two miles distant, in the sole custody of a native guard.

On Sunday evening, 10th May, the troopers of the 3rd Cavalry with yells rushed to the gaol and liberated their imprisoned comrades. The Sepoys of the 11th and 20th Regiments N.I. at the same time rose in revolt. Colonel Finnis, commanding the 11th, who went into their midst to remonstrate with them, was shot dead. The mutineers were at once joined by a

* Meerut is distant 906 miles from Calcutta.

host of budmashes,* and, half mad with excitement, they began to slaughter every white man, woman, and child they met with, and this they appear to have done without let or hindrance. It may well be asked, But what were the two thousand English soldiers in cantonments doing to prevent these atrocities? To this the melancholy answer must in truth be returned, that they did nothing worth mentioning; though but for General Hewitt's wretched incapacity the mutiny would have been promptly stamped out in the blood of the mutineers. As it was, the Christian people in some parts of Meerut were abandoned to indiscriminate slaughter as though there had not been a single English soldier at the station! The horrors of incendiarism and murder which that night witnessed were almost indescribable. This fearful affair was productive, however, of one most beneficial result, that it unmasked the atrocious designs of the enemy, and put us on the alert. For the fact is, that the outbreak at Meerut was premature, and consequently spoilt the execution of the preconcerted plan for a simultaneous Sepoy revolt all over the country, which was fixed for Sunday, 31st May, 1857. This interruption of the design to murder the English everywhere on a fixed day was a merciful interposition of Divine Providence, which saved British rule in India!! The Meerut mutineers arrived at Delhi † next day (11th May). They shot Mr. Simon Fraser, the Commissioner, and Captain Douglas, commanding the palace guards, and then they butchered the station chaplain, Rev. W. Jennings, and his daughter. There was now a general and indiscriminate massacre of Europeans, attended by the plunder of their property, and firing of their houses. The Church was an especial object of the fury of the insurgents. The native regiments, the 38th, 54th, and 74th, all fraternized with the Meerut mutineers, and murdered several of their officers; the rest escaped to

* The worst classes amongst the native community.
† Delhi is distant forty miles from Meerut.

Meerut and Umballa. This tragic scene was wound up by the proclamation of the titular King of Delhi as King of India.

From information obtained through natives I greatly fear that the most dreadful outrages were committed on this occasion, which cannot of course be substantiated, since "dead men tell no tales." Such was the commencement of the great Sepoy revolt. But I must now return to Agra, which being the station I was cantoned at with my regiment, is the standpoint from which I myself viewed, and have consequently given a corresponding sketch, to be found in the following pages, treating of the stirring events that occurred in those fearfully exciting times, many of which are indelibly branded on my memory. Agra, which is 796 miles from Calcutta, and 130 miles distant from Meerut, was the seat of the Government of the North-Western Provinces. The Lieutenant-Governor, Mr. John Colvin, resided here. The native town, which is a large and important one, is commanded by the red sandstone Fort situated on the right bank of the river Jumna. This fortress, which is about three miles from the civil lines, and rather over a mile from cantonments, was constructed by the Emperor Ackbar, and has inside the imperial palace and audience hall, the pearl mosque of pure white marble, and Ackbar's throne. But what has given world-renown to Agra is the surpassing grandeur of one of its monuments, the Taj Mahal, situated on the same side of the Jumna as the fort and city, which was erected in the reign of our Charles I. by the Emperor Shah Jehan, as a tribute of affection to the memory of his favourite Empress. Some idea may be formed of the vastness of the work when it is considered that it took some twenty thousand men nearly twenty years to finish it. The "Taj" stands by itself on the banks of the river, like a fairy palace in the wilderness, with its superb avenue of cypresses. It is difficult to give any description that would convey a correct impression of this marvellous monument of Oriental architecture. I have seen nothing to compare to it in Paris, or in my travels through Holland, Belgium, Germany, Switzerland, Italy, or anywhere in England. This costly tomb, constructed of pure white marble, wrought with matchless skill into one poetic design, relieved by mosaic work formed of precious stones, is certainly the most magnificent mausoleum ever made by man.

On the Taj side of the Jumna was the military station, which was in the Meerut Division. There were cantoned here at this period my regiment, the 3rd Europeans,* Captain D'Oyley's troop of European Artillery, and the 44th and 67th Regiments Native Infantry, commanded by Brigadier Polwhele. The civil station, with its Government House, Offices, College, Roman Catholic Cathedral, &c., was beyond the city. Great was the excitement amongst us on hearing of the mutiny at Meerut, the news of which reached Agra on the 11th May by a telegraphic message from Meerut; and this feeling was further increased to fever heat by the tidings of the horrible massacre at Delhi, which reached us on the 13th May. Mr. Colvin, the Lieutenant-Governor, who had received reports from which he was led to suppose that the mutineers after sacking Delhi were marching on Agra, held a council of war on the 13th May, which was attended by the leading civilians, Mr E. A. Reade, Mr. G. Harvey, Mr. H. B. Harrington, the Honourable Mr. Drummond, Mr. W. Muir, Mr. C. Raikes, and Mr. C. Thornhill, and the principal military authorities, Brigadier Polwhele, Colonel Fraser, Chief Engineer, and others. At this grand consultation it was determined that a general parade should be held the following morning for the purpose of haranguing the troops. It was also resolved that a body of Europeans and Eurasian militia should be raised, and that an attempt should be made to quiet the minds of the

* Now Her Majesty's 107th Foot.

community by a system of patrolling. Next day (14th May) there was a grand parade of all the troops at Agra. Mr. Colvin first addressed my regiment in a speech in which he spoke with warmth of the cruel murder of the Delhi chaplain's daughter. The Lieutenant-Governor next spoke to the native regiments in Hindoosthanie, when, after expressing his confidence in their loyalty, he desired any man who wished either to leave his regiment, or had any complaint to make, to step forward. Whereupon the Sepoys set up an equivocal kind of shout, by which they may have intended to signify their satisfaction, as no man responded to Mr. Colvin's invitation to come to the front; or it may have proceeded from a defiant feeling of indifference. Under these circumstances no decisive measure was adopted towards those regiments, who were allowed to retain their arms as usual. The same day that this was going on at Agra there occurred the mutiny of the 45th Regiment N.I. at Ferozepore. The mutineers burnt the bungalows of their officers in cantonments, as well as the Protestant and Roman Catholic churches. Happily, the families of the officers were safe in the barracks, and no murders of Europeans were perpetrated, and the mutinous 45th Regiment was pursued and scattered over the country. The following day, 15th May, our telegraphic communication with Calcutta was stopped. Soon afterwards we began roughing it by having a picquet duty to sleep out all night on the ground, with the canopy of the skies for our bed-curtains. The Governor-General and Commander-in-Chief tried to stop the progress of the mutiny; the first did so by a proclamation of the 16th May, warning the native soldiers that the tales told about Government meditating any injury to their caste were malicious falsehoods, and declaring to the people that the Government of India had invariably treated the religious feelings of all its subjects "with careful respect," and that it would never cease to do so, and the latter made a like attempt by an address to the army on the 19th May, informing them of his determination that the new rifle cartridge should be discontinued, and that in future balled ammunition should be made up by each regiment for its own use, and solemnly assuring them that no interference with their caste or religion was ever contemplated, and pledging his honour that none should ever be exercised. But it was too late now to make any attempt at conciliations. Things had gone too far to expect anything from concessions. The result was that the attempt was attended with as little success as would be the effort to stop a train at express speed by putting a shilling on the line. We were now destined to have no peace for a long time to come. Now was shown the wisdom of Lord Ellenborough's enlightened policy towards the Maharajah Scindiah of Gwalior, who now testified his grateful loyalty to Government by the offer of his own body-guard to our Lieutenant-Governor.

On the 21st May tidings reached us at Agra that the head-quarters wing of the 9th Regiment N.I. had mutinied the previous day at Alygurh, a station which is distant fifty miles from Agra, and eighty from Meerut. This was followed by the mutiny of the detachments of the regiment stationed at Etawah and Mynpoorie.* News of these events caused considerable perturbation amongst our people. Places of refuge, such as the Government House, Post Office, Agra Bank, and some other places, were about this time appointed, where, if danger threatened, the Christian community might resort to. On the 25th of May our Lieutenant-Governor issued the following manifesto:—

"Soldiers engaged in the late disturbance who are desirous of going to their own homes, and who give up their arms at the nearest Government civil or military post, and retire quietly, shall be permitted to do so unmolested. Many faithful soldiers have been driven into resistance to Government only because they were in the

* Etawah is distant 73 miles, and Mynpoorie 70 miles, from Agra.

ranks, and could not escape from them, and because they really thought their feelings of religion and honour injured by the measures of Government. This feeling was wholly a mistake, but it acted on men's minds. A proclamation of the Government now issued is perfectly explicit, and will remove all doubts on these points. Every evil-minded instigator in the disturbance, and those guilty of heinous crimes against private persons, shall be punished. All who appear in arms after this notification shall be treated as open enemies."

This ill-judged proclamation was properly cancelled by Earl Canning, on the ground of its affording an escape to all, even the most guilty of the mutineers. His Lordship issued a proclamation in its stead, offering pardon on wiser terms. The officers of the 44th and 67th Regiments N.I. for the most part clung to the belief that their men would not mutiny, but the number of incendiary fires at night showed that they meant mischief; and there would have been a mutiny, and a dreadful massacre at Agra on Sunday, the 31st of May, but for an overruling Providence, which completely disarranged their meditated treachery which was to take effect in the morning, by way of following up the mutiny of the three companies of their regiments at Muttra, an outpost station about thirty-five miles from Agra.

Those companies, according to their arrangements, mutinied at Muttra on the 30th of May, when one officer, Lieutenant Boulton, was shot dead, and another, Lieutenant Gibbon, was wounded. The Sepoys then seized the treasure, and proceeded to Delhi. Agra's safety on this, as on other occasions, was due to the prayers of a praying band of the Lord's children there; for prayer moves the Hand that moves the world. This holy brotherhood was not confined to any particular section of the Christian Church, but embraced, for instance, Baptists, Church-of-England people, American Presbyterians, and others. But there was no jarring here between Church and Dissent, for, pressed by one common danger, they who had always regarded each other as one in Christ were now more than ever one to each other. I expect that my attributing such power to prayer will cause a sneer to rise on the face of some, but I laugh to scorn those pretended philosophers who maintain that there is no use in prayer. Let the thoughtful reader mark how deliverance was sent to ward off the wholesale destruction we were threatened with. The news of the mutiny at Muttra was brought by camel express to Agra very late in the evening of the same day. This timely information saved us. There could be no hesitation now, so it was resolved to take the initiative by disarming the two native regiments next morning. The Adjutant galloped round at dead of night to the houses of all the officers of the 3rd Europeans, warning them to repair at once to the barracks. It was about midnight when he came to my quarters. The night was passed under arms. Early next morning, Sunday, the 31st of May, we marched to the parade. I noticed on this occasion that the Commanding Officer gave no order to the men to load, which was a great mistake, and might have been attended with very serious consequences. We found the two native regiments drawn up either in close or quarter-distance column of companies, I forget which of the two it was. On the one side the conspirators were confronted by my regiment (3rd Europeans), and on the other by Captain D'Oyley's troop of European Artillery, in case they should think of offering resistance to being disarmed. Brigadier Polwhele spoke to the Sepoys, and the command was given to pile arms. The Sepoys at first hesitated for a brief space, but at last perceiving that they had lost their opportunity, and seeing that their design of attacking us when unprepared was completely disconcerted by finding us thoroughly ready and quite on the alert, they then, though with great reluctance and gloomy looks, obeyed the order to pile their arms, which were soon afterwards placed on carts and conveyed to the Fort by myself and another officer with a party of my regiment. Had any one called out "Deen, Deen," at the critical time when the Sepoys hesitated to surrender their arms, then, as many of their muskets were afterwards found to be loaded, I feel sure that they would have fired a volley into us, which might have told with fearful effect at such close quarters. The disarmed Sepoys were then dismissed to their homes on leave, though no doubt most of them found their way to Delhi. Fuller effect was now given to the carrying out of the resolution formed at the Council of War on the 13th of May, for the organization of a volunteer force of horse and foot, and clerks in public offices, tradesmen and civilians responded to the call.

About this time I noticed a change in the demeanour of the native population; and as for our police, the Agra police were a villanous lot of traitors, although they were trusted in by Mr. Drummond, the magistrate. In June the country around Agra was in a most disturbed state. Disastrous news was daily brought to our Lieutenant-Governor, and we watched with great anxiety the progress of events at Scindiah's capital, Gwalior, which is but seventy miles distant from Agra. There was stationed at Gwalior, and the outpost stations of Siprée and Augur, the force known as the Gwalior Contingent, which consisted of rather more than 8,000 soldiers, commanded by English officers, with four field batteries, comprising four 24-pounder howitzers, two 18-pounders, and twenty 9-pounders, twenty-six in all. We had not long to wait for the impending *dénouement*, as intelligence of the Gwalior mutiny reached Agra on the 15th of June. The dreaded event had occurred the previous day, on Sunday, the 14th of June, on which evening the Sepoys rose and shot down their officers in the prevailing darkness. Major Hawkins and Captain Stewart of the Artillery, Majors Blake and Sheriff of the Infantry, fell beneath the fire of the mutineers.

These ferocious men relentlessly executed their murderous work. Mrs. Stewart and her boy were shot dead. Strange to say, these savages spared her little girl.* Doctor Kirke, the superintending surgeon, was killed before his wife.

Mr. Coopland, the chaplain, six sergeants, and some others, were also murdered. But a number of officers, with several ladies and their children, under the cover of darkness, managed to escape either to the Residency or to the Maharajah's palace. Thence, being provided with carriage, they went on to Agra, where they arrived on the 19th June, and were received with all the kindness due to suffering humanity. It is but fair to the Maharajah Scindiah to say that he was greatly grieved at these terrible events, which he was powerless to prevent. Towards the end of June we were completely isolated; the ladies and children retired into the Fort, and the officers slept at night in the soldiers' barracks for safety. I think I was about the last, if not the very last, officer to spend the night unguarded in my house, so that I was remonstrated with for my imprudence; and I remember being told by a brother officer that he expected I should pay the penalty of my rashness with my life. The provinces under the Lieutenant-Governor's rule were aptly described as "in a blaze of ravage and riot." The British Empire in Oude and the North-West Provinces appeared to be fast tottering to its fall, as station after station followed the example set at Delhi, till the whole of those parts became one vast hotbed of rebellion, leaving to isolated bands of Englishmen little more than the ground they occupied when they stood heroically at bay against overwhelming hordes crying for their blood. An abridged summary of the different mutinies we heard of in June will now be given, which will be narrated with a little variation, and in several instances with further particu-

* I think this must have been the little Charlotte Stewart I used to see in the Fort.

lars than as it was recorded in my diary at the time. I may at the outset observe, that though I had a good many relations in the civil and military employ of the Government, I only lost one, my cousin, Lieutenant G. Mills, who was murdered by the mutineers of the Mehidpore Contingent. On the 28th May occurred the mutiny of the Hurriana Light Infantry and 4th Irregular Cavalry at Hansi and Hissar, which was attended by an indiscriminate massacre of Europeans. And on the same day (28th May) the 15th and 30th Regiments N.I., with a native battery of Artillery mutinied at Nusseerabad in Rajpootana. The 1st Bombay Cavalry being ordered to charge the mutineers turned threes about when within a few yards of the battery, and left their officers to be slaughtered, two of whom were killed and two severely wounded. The 72nd Regiment N.I., 7th Gwalior Contingent, and a wing of the 1st Light Cavalry mutinied at Neemuch on the 3rd June. No officers lost their lives, but the wife of a sergeant and her three children were murdered. The Bareilly Brigade, consisting of the 18th and 68th Regiments N.I., with the 8th Regiment Irregular Cavalry, and a native battery of Artillery rose in revolt at Bareilly, the capital of Rohilcund, on the 31st May. They shot dead Brigadier Sibbald, and every white face they could meet with. Major Pearson and four other officers were killed by villagers in their attempt to escape by flight. Two judges, Mr. G. D. Raikes and Mr. D. Robertson, Mr. Wyatt, Deputy Collector, Doctors Hay and Buck, with three other civilians, together with all the women and children who had not left for Nynee Tall, were murdered, most of them by the express orders of the newly proclaimed Viceroy of Rohilcund, Khan Bahadur Khan. Three days afterwards the 29th N.I. mutinied at Moradabad, which is about fifty miles distant from Bareilly. The Sepoys here, content with seizing the Government treasure, spared the lives of their officers, who with their families and the civilians escaped to Meerut and Nynee Tall in safety. On Sunday, 31st May, the 28th Regiment N.I. arose at Shahjehanpore, distant forty-seven miles from Bareilly. This was my cousin's regiment; but happily he was not with it. One party of Sepoys attacked the English at church, whilst another fired the bungalows in cantonments. Mr. M. Ricket, the magistrate and collector, the commanding officer, Captain James, and the surgeon, Dr. Bowling, were shot dead. The chaplain and a clerk were also both killed. The rest of the officers escaped to Mohumdee in Oude, where they arrived in a wretched condition two days afterwards. But on the mutiny of the Sepoys at Mohumdee, on the 4th June, the poor fugitives next day once more sought safety in flight. But when a mile from Aurungabad they were attacked by the Sepoys. Resistance and escape were both impossible. "We all collected under a tree," says Captain Orr, the sole survivor of the dreadful tale; "the poor ladies all joined in prayer, and coolly and undauntedly met their fate." Let us cling to the hope that this baptism of suffering was used by the Holy Ghost as a means of bringing to the saving knowledge of the Lord Jesus Christ such of these sufferers who may not hitherto have thought much of those things that belong to the everlasting well-being of the soul, especially since the narrator of the sad story gives us to understand that it was in the attitude of prayer these dear English ladies undauntedly awaited their fate; for saving faith has the distinguishing quality of robbing death of its sting. With the exception of a drummer boy, every one of the Shahjehanpore party perished: viz., Mr. Jenkins, C. S., twelve commissioned officers, a quartermaster-sergeant, a band-master, eight ladies, and four children. Mr. Thomason, the deputy commissioner, a lieutenant on the veteran establishment, and some clerks, were also slaughtered. On the 18th June the 10th Regiment N.I. mutinied at Futtehgurh, a station in the Agra Division, distant about twenty-five miles from Shahjehanpore. A fortnight before the outbreak about one hundred and seventy non-combatants started off in boats for Cawnpore. Finally, however, only one hundred and twenty-six continued their ill-fated journey.* Of the rest, one party with Mr. Probyn accepted the hospitality of Hurdeo Bukhsh, a landholder at Dhurumpore, and another party of about forty returned to Futtehgurh on the 13th June.

The 10th Regiment on revolting tendered their allegiance to the Nawab of Furruckabad, who had declared against us, and the English to the number of one hundred retired within the Fort, though we at Agra did not in June learn the melancholy fate of our countrymen besieged here, yet as there will be no occasion to refer to the Futtehgurh mutiny, the following brief account is given, though out of place. After a gallant defence the English evacuated the Fort on the 4th July, and under cover of night they attempted to drop down the river in three boats, commanded respectively by Colonel Smith, Colonel Goldie, and Major Robertson. Colonel Goldie's boat, however, had to be abandoned, and its occupants shifted to Colonel Smith's boat. Major Robertson's boat having grounded on a sandbank was attacked by the Sepoys, who opened fire on our people. Major Robertson and many others were wounded; many of the ladies in their desperation threw themselves into the river, many were drowned, and many were killed, whilst very nearly all the rest were taken prisoners, and blown from guns by the orders of the infamous Nawab, who inaugurated his accession to power by the slaughter of some forty Europeans captured in various parts of his district. Mr. Jones, and Mr. Fisher, the chaplain, escaped for the time by swimming to Colonel Smith's boat. Major Robertson found shelter in a village, where he died; and Mr. Churcher some months afterwards succeeded in reaching Cawnpore, when reoccupied by the

* This was the party that fell into the hands of the Nana Sahib, and shared the fate of the English massacred at Cawnpore in July.

English after the defeat of the Nana. Colonel Smith's boatload of fugitives were all massacred near Cawnpore, between the 10th and 15th July, by orders of the Nana Sahib, with the single exception of Mr. Jones, who joined Mr. and Mrs. Probyn and escaped with them to Cawnpore on the 1st September.* We heard of the mutiny at Cawnpore of the 2nd Light Cavalry and the 1st, 53rd, and 56th Regiments N.I. on the 4th June, and General Wheeler being besieged in his entrenchments, where nearly a thousand souls, including 450 men,† found themselves in an indefensible position. During the siege, which lasted from 6th June to 27th June, the misery of the garrison was unparalleled, being unsheltered from the furnace heat of a June sun, which was intensified by the absence of all privacy, which violated the decencies of life in a manner shocking to feminine modesty. I shall have occasion to refer to the massacre farther on in my narrative. But I shall say a few words about Dhoondhoo Punt, the Nana Sahib, whom the Sepoys acknowledged for their leader. He was at this time thirty-three years of age, and had an old grudge against the English, dating from the death of Badgee Rao, the last of the Mahratta Peishwas, who died at Bithoor, near Cawnpore, in 1851. This ex-Peishwa, who was in receipt of an annual pension of eight laks of rupees from the British Government, had adopted Dhoondhoo Punt as his son, to succeed him in the title and pension of the Peishwa. But Government had refused to recognize this adoption. The Nana Sahib memorialized the Home Government; but it was all in vain: for the Honourable East India Company decided that the pension of his adopted father was not hereditary, and that he had no claim whatever to it. The Nana's time for retaliating had now come; he had the

---

* Cawnpore is distant eighty miles from Futtehgurh.
† Of whom only about three hundred were regular soldiers—sixty Artillerymen, sixty of 84th Regiment, seventy-four 32nd Regiment, and sixty-five Madras Fusileers.

English at his mercy, and he was determined to have his revenge, as will be seen farther on in its proper place in our narrative. We heard this month the harrowing particulars of the singularly atrocious mutiny of the 6th Regiment N.I. at Allahabad, which showed an amazing amount of treachery, and was a remarkable instance of the sad infatuation that prevailed in trusting the deceitful Pandies. This regiment was believed by Colonel Simpson and the other officers of the regiment to be loyal to the backbone, and so indeed they would have been if their protestations of fidelity had been genuine. They had, moreover, demanded to be led against the rebels at Delhi. For this they received the thanks of the Governor-General at an evening parade on the 6th June. But after being thus praised for their loyalty, they rose in revolt about 9 P.M. of the same day. Captain Plunkett, riding to the mess that evening with Colonel Simpson, spoke with delight of the pride he felt at the noble conduct of the regiment. A numerous party of officers sat around the mess-table, congratulating themselves on the distinction for fidelity which their regiment had just gained. In the midst of this false security the bugle call sounding the alarm was heard, and the faithful 6th was found to have actually revolted! Colonel Simpson succeeded in escaping into the Fort; but Captain Plunkett, Adjutant Steward, Quarter-Master Hawes, and Ensigns Pringle and Munro were shot down on parade, and nine boy Ensigns who had just joined to do duty with the regiment were murdered in cold blood: Fort Adjutant Birch, and Inness of the Engineers were also killed. Pearson and Woodgate, Cadets, were taken prisoners, and escaped by twice swimming across the river. I heard afterwards the story of the escape of one of these officers from his own lips. He told me that he was seized by a party of Sepoys, when just as they were going to kill him they were diverted from their purpose by hearing a cry raised that the rest of the regiment was rushing to plunder the treasury, and being eager to secure their share of the loot, they left their prisoner to hasten there for that purpose.

Directly their backs were turned the released officer ran for his life, and succeeded in getting into the Fort. Simultaneously the city of Allahabad* broke into rebellion. The houses of the Christian inhabitants were plundered and burnt, and every European or Eurasian found outside the Fort mercilessly put to death with every possible aggravation of cruelty. The Fort was secured by Lieutenant Brasyer, who with a party of Sikhs, supported by a few invalid European Artillery and a handful of volunteers, disarmed and expelled the Company of the 6th garrisoning the Fort. On the 3rd June the 17th Regiment N.I. mutinied at Azimgurh, and murdered their Quarter-Master, Lieutenant Hutchinson, and their Quarter-Master-Sergeant. The outbreak at Benares occurred on the 4th June, when the Brigadier attempted to disarm the 37th Regiment N.I., who resisted, and being joined by the Loodiana Regiment of Sikhs, and 13th Irregular Cavalry, a fight ensued between them and two hundred and fifty Europeans under the gallant Colonel Neil, who put them all to flight with severe loss. But notwithstanding this triumph of the English a detachment of the Loodiana Regiment of Sikhs mutinied the very next day (5th June) at the outpost station of Jaunpore, when they shot Lieutenant Mara, the officer commanding them, and Mr. Cuppage, the joint magistrate, and plundered the station. A few days afterwards Government caused martial law to be proclaimed in the divisions of Benares and Allahabad. The Sepoys at Jhansi,† consisting of a wing of the 12th Regiment N.I., and a wing of the 14th Irregular Cavalry, revolted on the 6th of June, and having killed all the

* Allahabad is about 500 miles from Calcutta by the public high road.
† Jhansi, the capital of the province of that name, is 142 miles south of Agra.

officers in cantonments they could lay their hands on, they marched towards the Fort overlooking the town, which was held by Captain A. Skene, the Commissioner, and a handful of English, who for a short time made a resolute defence, and even drove back the rebels. The insurrection here was headed by the ill-used Ranee of Jhansi, who had been panting for revenge during the past three years. She was at this period a well-favoured woman of about twenty-nine, and was determined to avenge the wrong inflicted upon her by Lord Dalhousie in 1854, when he annexed her country in the manner already related.

The day after the mutiny (7th June) was a day of grievous humiliation to the English besieged in the town fort; since they were reduced to the necessity of imploring the help of this injured woman.

The pitiless Ranee sent the English messengers to the mutineers, who murdered them. On the following day (8th June) Captain Skene capitulated on the promise made on oath by the insurgent leaders that their lives should be spared. But on quitting the Fort they were all, to the number of nearly sixty, treacherously put to death. Not a man, woman or child survived that day's horrid butchery. The day afterwards (9th June) the other wing of the 12th Regiment N.I. and the remaining wing of the 14th Irregular Cavalry mutinied at Nowgong. The officers, accompanied by the European community, managed, after a fortnight of extraordinary suffering, to escape to Nagode and Banda, excepting Lieutenant Townshend, who was shot dead in an encounter with bandits, and Major Kirke with three other officers and a lady, who died from exposure to the sun and fatigue. On the 7th June the 30th and 61st Regiments N.I., with the 6th Regiment Light Cavalry and Artillery, mutinied at Julunder, and next day (8th June) the 3rd Regiment N.I. mutinied at Phillour. The 5th Irregular Cavalry mutinied at Rohnee in Deoghur (Eastern Bengal) on the 12th June, and murdered their Adjutant, Sir Norman Leslie, and severely wounded Major Macdonald, their Commanding Officer, and Surgeon Grant.

We also at Agra heard this month of the terrible retribution that had overtaken us for our wrong-doing in annexing Oude the previous year; for the whole country revolted as the Sepoy regiments mutinied. Lucknow, the capital, set the example of revolt.

There were stationed there at this time H.M. 32nd Foot, about 700 strong, commanded by Colonel J. Inglis; a company of European Artillery, the 7th Regiment Native Cavalry, the 13th, 48th, and 71st Regiments N.I. There were also at Lucknow or its immediate vicinity two regiments of Oude Irregular Infantry, a regiment of Military Police, one regiment Oude Irregular Cavalry, and two batteries of Native Artillery. The numerical strength of the Sepoys was ten times greater than that of the Europeans. Sir Henry Lawrence had in the beginning of May disarmed one regiment, the 7th Oude Irregulars, and on the 12th of May he held a grand durbar, at which he made an impressive speech, and rewarded with presents certain loyal soldiers for their fidelity. Notwithstanding all Sir Henry's efforts to maintain peace, the regiments rose at Lucknow on the 30th May. It began with the 13th and 71st Regiments N.I. Brigadier Handscombe was shot dead by the latter regiment. The 48th Regiment N.I. were sullen, being not active in the mutiny, whilst refusing to act against the mutineers, to whom they afterwards deserted in great numbers; and about a week afterwards a detachment of this regiment, with one of the 7th Cavalry, mutinied and murdered their officers, Captains Burmister and Staples.

Rather more than three hundred Sepoys from these regiments ranged themselves on the side of the English. Next day, Sunday, 31st May, the Europeans, with the faithful remnant of the three native regiments, attacked the mutineers, who were drawn up on the racecourse near the lines of the 7th Native Cavalry. On our guns opening upon them they soon took to flight. Out of the four regiments only four hundred and thirty-seven men remained true to their salt. When it was known that the soldiery had revolted in the capital, their brethren at the out-stations rose at once, and all classes with them; the 41st Regiment N.I., with the 9th and 10th Oude Irregulars, mutinied at Seetapore on the 3rd June. Colonel Birch, the Commanding Officer of the 41st N.I., was shot dead. Mr. Christian, the Commissioner, with his wife and child, and Mr. and Mrs. Thornhill were murdered, as were Lieutenants Graves and Snell, with their wives and children. The same fate befell Lieutenants Dorin, Small, and Greene, and Dr. Hill and some others.

Sir Mountstuart Jackson, with his sister,* Mr. and Miss Birch, and Mrs. Doran effected their escape from Seetapore. Of the other fugitives, some reached Lucknow, whilst another party found shelter in a village till they were rescued. The Sepoys at Mohumdee rose in revolt on the 4th June. The Europeans took to flight, and next day shared the fate of the Shahjehanpore fugitives massacred near Aurungabad. On the 8th June the 22nd Regiment, a horse battery of Native Artillery, the 6th Oude Infantry, and a squadron of the 15th Irregular Cavalry mutinied at Fyzabad. The Sepoys permitted the departure of the English unmolested; but scarcely had they left Fyzabad in four boats, on the 8th of June, when the 22nd Regiment despatched a messenger to the 17th Regiment, then on the Gogra, begging them to intercept the boats, and slay all the white people in them. These barbarous instructions were obeyed, and the two first boats were intercepted at Begumgunje. Resistance was impossible. Colonel

* Sir M. Jackson was murdered in cold blood several months afterwards by the mutineers, but his sister, who was kept in miserable captivity, was, after passing through incredible suffering, rescued on the 19th March, 1858.

Goldney, the Commissioner, was shot dead on the spot, and all who remained in these boats perished. One party, however, made a desperate attempt to escape across country. They lost two of their number, who were drowned in trying to cross a stream. Being joined afterwards by the occupants of the fourth boat, they were so hotly pursued, that they lost six more of their party, Lieutenants Lindsay, Thomas, English, Ritchie, and Cautley, who with Sergeant Edwards were all killed. The only survivor was Sergeant Busher, who eventually reached Ghazeepore in safety. The occupants of the third boat, under Colonel O'Brien, through Divine mercy succeeded in making their escape to Dinapore in safety. Mrs. Mills (whose husband, Major Mills of the Artillery, was murdered in the second boat) remained for a while with her three children at Fyzabad; but, starting afterwards, she crossed the Gogras into the Gorruckpore district, where she wandered from village to village for eight or ten days, enduring terrible sufferings. She, however, got at last to Gorruckpore.

Colonel Lennox and his family, who had not left with the others in the boats, managed through the assistance of a friendly native to reach Gorruckpore. There was also another party who had not started with the boats, consisting of Captain Reid, Deputy-Commissioner, Captain A. Orr, Captain Thurburn, and Mr. Bradford. These fugitives reached Shahgunge on the 11th June, when being joined by their wives and children and by some others, they continued their flight, and after suffering dreadfully from hunger and exposure to the scorching rays of the sun, they reached Gorruckpore on the 21st June. On the 9th June the 8th Regiment, Oude Irregulars, and a corps of Military Police mutinied at Sultanpore. Colonel Fisher, and his second in command, Captain Gibbings, were shot dead, and the rest of the officers escaped to Benares; but the civilians were put to death. The ladies happily were two days before sent towards Allahabad. On the 10th June the Sepoys mutinied at Bareitch, when Lieutenant Clarke and Mr. Cunliffe, the Deputy-Commissioner, were shot, and Mr. Jordan, Assistant-Commissioner, was killed a few days afterwards. There were also other mutinies in Oude, that were happily attended with no massacres, such as the mutinies of the Sepoys at Salone, Sikrora, Gonda, and Durriabad on the 9th and 10th of June. Moreover, a great revolution was accomplished in Oude before the middle of June, as the Talookdars reoccupied the villages they had been dispossessed of, and all classes joined in the insurrection against what they rightly regarded as the usurped power of the British Government in their country. In June we at Agra received some intelligence of these terrible mutinies, which by the light of later information I have now described with far more accuracy and particulars than were known at the time. We also heard of the death of General Anson, Commander-in-Chief, who died of cholera at Kurnal on the 27th May, and was succeeded in the command of the Delhi Field Force by Sir Henry Barnard.[*] Things were certainly drawing to a crisis in the very beginning of July. On the 1st of that month the mutinous troops of Holkar attacked the civil station of Indore, the capital of Holkar's dominions, when they murdered thirty-nine English and Eurasian men, women, and children, pillaged the Government Treasury, and demolished all the public and private buildings. Colonel Travers and the rest of the fugitive party succeeded in making good their escape. The rebels reminded Holkar of his distinguished ancestor, Jeswunt Rao Holkar, and urged him to make common cause with them, and march to Delhi. But Holkar refused to comply with their request, and is stated to have made the following noble reply:—" The strength of my forefathers has departed, and I do not consider

[*] Sir H. Barnard also died of cholera on the 5th July, and was succeeded by General Reid, who within a fortnight was forced, from ill-health, to relinquish the command to Brigadier A. Wilson.

rapine, and the murder of innocent beings, as part of any religion." On the same day (1st July), the 23rd Regiment N.I., and the right wing 1st Light Cavalry, rose in revolt at Mhow, distant thirteen miles from Indore, and shot dead Colonel Platt and Adjutant Fagan, whilst Major Harris of the Cavalry was cut to pieces by his own men. But these dastardly miscreants took to flight when Captain Hungerford opened fire upon them with the guns of his horse battery. On the same day (1st July) the main body of the 1st Cavalry Regiment of the Gwalior Contingent mutinied at Hatras, distant about twenty miles from Agra, whereupon Captain Alexander and the other officers rode into Agra, and the following day (2nd July) a detachment of the 2nd Cavalry Gwalior Contingent, and a battery of Artillery, mutinied at a place seven miles from Hatras; their Commanding Officers, Captains Burton and Pearson, and the other officers also escaped to Agra.

CHAPTER V.

Imperilled Condition of Agra—Mutiny of the Kotah Contingent—Fight with the Neemuch Brigade at Shahgunj—Description of the Battle—Our Defeat with terrific Loss, and Retirement into the Fort—Great Dismay there—Remarkable Saying of the Lieutenant-Governor—Awful Conflagration and Massacre at Agra—Terrible Disorder Outside the Fort—Hardships—Devoted Attention paid to the Wounded—Life Inside the Fort—Adoption of Precautionary Measures—Causes for expecting an Attack—Our Native Christians rise in Public Estimation—A Melancholy Day—Arrival of the News of the Cawnpore Tragedy—Successive Arrivals of Messengers with Gloomy Tidings—State of Affairs before Delhi—Desperate Condition of the Besiegers—Particulars of the Cawnpore Massacre—Wonderful Escape of Lieutenants Thomson and Delafosse—Subsequent atrocious Massacre of the Women and Children—The Mythical Story of Miss Wheeler—Gloomy Forebodings—Sir Henry Lawrence's Defeat, and Death—Sir Henry's dying Words—Sir John Lawrence's View of the Situation—Natives expect our Ruin—God the Source of all Comfort to the Christian in such Seasons of Gloom—Execution of Martial Law at Agra—Energetic Course adopted in the Punjaub—Disarming of Regiments at Mean Meer (Lahore) and Peshawur—Mutineers blown from Guns—Mutiny at Jhelum—Mutineers fight with a Wing of H.M. 24th Foot—Severe Loss of the Latter—Subsequent Destruction of these Mutineers—Mutiny at Sealcote—Destruction of these Mutineers—Eminent Service rendered by the Punjaub Officials—Despatch of Sikh Troops from the Punjaub to Delhi—Arrival of Nicholson—Victory of Nujufgurh—Havelock's Victories—Futtehpore and Aong—Defeat of the Nana Sahib—Reoccupation of Cawnpore—Havelock's Advance into Oude—His Victories—The grievous Necessity to Fall Back—Brigadier Neil's stern Justice—Havelock defeats the Nana at Bithoor—A Native Regiment crosses Bayonets with British Soldiers—Havelock's precarious Position at Cawnpore—Koonwur Singh's Insurrection—Wake's Defence of Arrah—Defeat of Captain Dunbar by Dinapore Mutineers—Major Eyre defeats Dinapore Mutineers—Relief of Arrah—Mutiny of the 27th Bombay N.I.—Mutinous Conduct of 8th Madras Native Cavalry—Mutiny at Segowlie—Sepoys of Ramgurh Battalion and Jodhpore Legion rise—Despatch of a Force from Agra—A Miserable Night in Command of the Advance Guard—Battle near Alygurh—Sent in to Agra with Sick and Wounded—Personal Violence offered me by a Junior Officer—Unjust Adjudication of the Case by my Commanding Officer—I appeal against this to Commander-in-Chief—Placed under Arrest—Extreme Injustice of this Proceeding—Deprived of the Means of Grace for nearly Five Months—Religious Consolations—Impartial Testimony of an Officer of my Regiment—Sympathy of the Editor of the *Mofussilite*—Death of Mr. Colvin—News from the Punjaub—Annihilation of the mutinous 51st Regiment N.I.—Arrival of Siege Train at Delhi—Preparations for the Assault—The hazardous Nature of the Undertaking—Hear at Agra of the Capture of Delhi.

WITH the fabric of Government falling to pieces all over the North-Western Provinces, and mutiny and insurrection drawing nearer and nearer to us every day, it soon became evident that we at Agra should ere long be struggling in the breakers ourselves—that we should, in fact, very shortly have to sustain an attack, if not from the Gwalior Contingent, at least from the Neemuch mutineers, who were daily drawing nearer to Agra. It is time now to notice the mutiny of the Kotah Contingent, which was brought into cantonments on the 2nd July, on which day it became known that the rebel army was at Futtehpore Sikri, which is twenty-three miles from Agra. The troops despatched by Scindiah to our assistance, it should be remembered, were no longer at the station, having been sent to keep order in the neighbouring district. The folly of trusting in the staunchness of the Kotah Contingent was made manifest two days later. I happened on that day (4th July) to be in the barracks, when an officer of the Contingent galloped up in hot haste to where I was sitting, and after a hurried communication of the startling news that the Kotah Contingent had mutinied, inquired for the Commanding Officer; but finding from me that he was not there, he rode off in search of him, whilst I immediately ran from barrack to barrack warning the men to be ready to turn out at a moment's notice. At last the Colonel and the rest of the officers arrived, and then a part of my regiment was sent out in pursuit of the mutineers, who, having shot dead their Sergeant-Major, had decamped to join the Neemuch brigade. The Kotah Contingent, however, had got too much start of us, so our men had to return. But Captain Prender-

BATTLE OF SHAHGUNJ.

gast, with a party of volunteers, was rather more successful, inasmuch as they succeeded in cutting off a few stragglers, and capturing some of their camels and ammunition. Next day, Sunday, 5th July, instead of going to church and chapel we fought the sanguinary battle of Shahgunj or Sussiah, about three miles from cantonments. The enemy's force consisted of the 72nd Regiment N.I., 7th Regiment Gwalior Contingent, the Kotah Contingent, two troops of the 1st Light Cavalry, four troops of the Mehidpore Horse, and one troop of Horse Artillery. Their guns were placed half on one flank and half upon the other, and were screened by rising ground and thickly planted trees. Their Infantry were posted inside the village as well as behind it, and their Cavalry was massed in rear of both flanks. The force which Brigadier Polwhele led out to the attack was composed of about five hundred men of my regiment with Captain D'Oyley's troop of Artillery, consisting of about seventy European soldiers and fifty native drivers, and nearly sixty Mounted Militia, making a total of six hundred and eighty, who were in good spirits and eager for the fray. The enemy outnumbered us by at least seven to one. I should have been left behind with the detachment of the regiment kept back as a reserve to hold the Fort; but in order to be present at the battle I got myself transferred to one of the companies going out.* We advanced in line with one half battery under Captain D'Oyley on our right, and the other under Lieutenant Pearson on our left. The more prudent plan would have been to have endeavoured by manœuvring to have drawn them out of their strong position, and so have got them to fight a fair battle with their vastly superior numbers on the open field. But this was not attempted. The battle

* Although I was an officer of more than twelve years' standing in the Service, yet my position on parade at this period was, as senior subaltern, in rear of my company; but throughout the Mutiny campaigns from '57 to '59 I invariably led a company in every engagement.

commenced by the mutineers opening fire upon our troops as they were advancing to the assault. Brigadier Polwhele ordered us to lie down whilst our guns answered the fire of those opposed to us. But the enemy were too well posted under cover for us to do them any serious injury. I took particular notice of the effect produced by the fire of our guns, as the balls in quick succession struck the mud walls of the village, which appeared to me as harmless as beating carpets, and which was just what it reminded me of; so that I believe the only one gun that did the enemy any damage was the howitzer.

This waste of precious time gave the enemy the victory, which we, humanly speaking, should have gained if we had at once charged the mutineers with the bayonet. This was the right moment for hurling us at the enemy, but the Brigadier, instead of doing so, trusted in his guns to silence the enemy's artillery, and for two hours we witnessed an artillery duel. This was a fatal mistake, which was taken advantage of by the enemy's gunners, who, having got our range, exploded two of our ammunition waggons, blowing up our artillery men; they also dismounted one of our guns, and ignited its carriage. At last Captain D'Oyley was mortally wounded by a grape-shot. "I am done for," said poor D'Oyley; "put a stone upon my grave and write that I died fighting my guns." One of his subalterns, Lieutenant Lamb, was also mortally wounded by a grape-shot. Finally, when the artillery ammunition was all expended, and when the right time had consequently passed, an advance of the 3rd Europeans was ordered. Two columns were then thrown forward, one commanded by Major G. P. Thomas of the 3rd, and the other, of which the company I led formed a part, was commanded by Colonel Fraser of the Engineers. After an obstinate defence the village was carried. But we suffered a very severe loss from the enemy's guns, and the fire of marksmen from the house-tops, as well as from the obstinate resistance made inside the village. I passed by poor Major Thomas lying mortally wounded* in one of the lanes. The enemy, driven out of the village, still held a covered position. This was a critical moment, and I believe, that had we improved our success by charging them once more, they would have given way; for it is said that their artillery were limbered up for flight. Undoubtedly the risk would have been great, for failure would have involved the loss of all our guns, and of every unmounted man besides. At all events a retreat was ordered in consequence of the artillery ammunition being all expended. But I must stop here to notice the gallant charge made by our sixty Mounted Militia, composed of members of the civil service, clerks, our frozen-out military gardeners,† and some equestrians of a wandering circus from France. This mere handful of men had the boldness to charge the enemy's cavalry. Of course they were far too few to make any impression except this, that Englishmen, when once their blood is up, are too plucky to count the numbers of their enemy! They returned with the loss of the head man of the circus, Monsieur Jordon, who was killed, and six others were mortally wounded in the hand-to-hand combat that ensued. The enemy, as might have been expected, pertinaciously harassed our retreat, which was conducted in good order in the direction of the Fort instead of to the cantonments from which we had started. Their artillery galloped ahead and pitched into us repeatedly, which was extremely unpleasant. The enemy's cavalry set up a ringing cheer, as though they were going to charge right down upon us. The thought that then passed rapidly through my mind was that it would be all up with us if they did so, because I knew that our men could not have formed square to resist cavalry.

* Major Thomas died afterwards in hospital.
† Officers whose regiments had mutinied or been disarmed were sometimes so called.

Happily, the stalwart mutineer troopers had not the courage to come near us, since they were checked by a volley which we delivered within musket range,* which made many a horse riderless. The rebel cavalry, notwithstanding this repulse, rode after us to within a mile of the Fort, and they once more charged, but were again repelled as before, merely by our musketry fire. I differ entirely from the following opinion expressed by Mr. Kaye in his book, viz., that throughout that four-mile march the column was never really in danger; for I maintain that we were in great danger; because, in the first place, if the six troops of rebel cavalry had charged right through, which they might have done, as I am sure we could not have formed square, then they would have had us at their mercy, and not a man, at least of the infantry, would have escaped, and our guns would also have been captured. Fortunately, or rather providentially, the rebel cavalry were wanting, not in discipline, but in courage, or they would have done this. Secondly, there was very considerable danger to be apprehended from the treacherous Agra Military Police, that they, in conjunction with the Mussulmen citizens of Agra, would have interposed between us and the Fort, and so have cut off our retreat. The beaten army reached the Fort as the day was closing. I felt quite done up, having had nothing to eat or drink since breakfast, and after marching so many miles under a July sun. Our loss was frightful; my regiment lost 100 men at the very least in killed and wounded, and the total loss of the whole force under that heading amounted to quite 150 out of 680 men engaged. Great was the dismay of our people inside the Fort when the terrible reality of the retreat became known to them; their hearts, indeed, failed them through fear. Our enforced retirement into the Fort was the very thing which was particularly dreaded by Mr. Colvin,

* We had not the Enfield rifle then; we were armed with the old musket.

our Lieutenant-Governor, a well-meaning man, who gave all his energies to the public service. "The wrath of God is upon us," he had exclaimed, "if we retire into the Fort."* The same evening that we entered the Fort after the unsuccessful maiden fight of my regiment, the houses in cantonments and the civil lines were set fire to by the budmashes. The sight of this mighty conflagration, which raged over a space of some six miles, was a most melancholy spectacle, and one never to be forgotten. But sadder still was the fact that Mr. Hubbard, Professor of Literature, Agra College, Major Jacobs, and thirty other men, women, and children, principally Eurasians, who had declined to betake themselves to the shelter of the Fort, relying, I suppose, on the expectation that we should defeat the mutineers, and return to cantonments, were all barbarously massacred. One of these unfortunates, Major Jacobs, however, defended himself with great desperation, till at last he fell, overpowered by numbers. My dear old mother in England had seen in large letters in the *Times*, "Horrible Massacre at Agra," and was terribly alarmed, thinking we might have been involved in it, and wrote to us the following melancholy lines:—

"My most tenderly beloved children: as I write I feel that I may be writing to those that are passed away from human sight; and that I may not even have the satisfaction to hear how they passed. This silence is as the grave. A day or two before the mail came in (I suffered sadly after the horrors of Cawnpore, where seven of the Lindsays were massacred—those three lovely girls, son and mother; you may remember that sweet Miss Lindsay) came "Horrible Massacre at Agra," in large characters in the *Times*. Every night and day I thought of your little darling and your poor wife in her present state. My only relief was in prayer, and in reading God's word, and in feeling that you

* Raikes' "Notes on the Revolt in N.W.P.," p. 57.

loved and trusted in your Saviour, and that he would never leave nor forsake you ; but that as your day so should your strength be. It would be impossible to describe the state of horror and excitement in England. I am thankful to say much that is right is being done. Prayers in the church, private prayer urged by our bishops, large prayer meetings held over the country, and subscriptions for the sufferers. It is most right that, as a nation, we should humble ourselves for our shortcomings towards India in the way of preaching a Saviour to them. I rejoice to think I have seen you, my darling, and should I never see you more, may I be enabled to say, 'Not my will, but thine be done:' 'The Lord gave and the Lord hath taken away ; blessed be the Name of the Lord.' What should I suffer if I felt that you were living without God in the world. But now I trust that through the gate of death you would enter into eternal life. I cannot write on any common subject. I suppose, should you ever receive this, things will be in a better state. Great fears for Lucknow, and alarm that the native police at Agra have not been disbanded. With more love than I can tell to self, wife, and little babe, believe me now and ever till death your most affectionate mother,

"E. WHITE."

The day after the battle (6th of July) a party of volunteers went out, who, having buried the dead, brought back the dismounted gun that had been left behind. Nevertheless, disorder was rampant outside the Fort for a day or two after our defeat, and the King of Delhi was proclaimed in the city. Plundering went on unchecked for the time. I have reason to remember this, since I lost all my tents, as well as a box full of baby's clothes, which was a serious loss to me in the low state of my finances. At first few servants made their appearance, and we had to draw our own water from the wells inside the Fort, and for some days we were dependent on the commissariat for our butcher's meat, which was unprocurable in the ordinary way. With regard to the allotting of quarters in the Fort, all I have to say is this, that whatever desirable quarters others may have possessed, this is certain, that those assigned for my residence were not such as the most contented man would like to live in. The exceeding wretchedness of this accommodation will, I should think, be apparent when I inform my reader that I and my wife, with our little girl, had to share a horrid close ammunition store-room with poor Mrs. Hawkins* and her children; that this cell was without any kind of aperture to let in a breath of air, except, of course, the entrance folding-door, which had to be closed at night every time it rained (which was frequently the case), in order that I might get some shelter from the rain by placing my bed close up to the closed door, as decency forbade my sleeping inside, and even then half of my bed used regularly to get wet, so that it was a great mercy, and most surprising, that I escaped getting rheumatic fever. The ladies inside were, perhaps, even more to be pitied, as they must have been quite half-stifled by the close suffocating heat. Happily, this miserable state of things did not last long; for about a fortnight afterwards Mrs. Hawkins removed; and oh the joy that I felt at having no longer to sleep out in the pattering rain! There are, of course, comparative degrees of happiness; but the flight of the wildest imagination could never have carried me so far as to think that the exclusive possession of such a hole as this should ever afford me joy. But so it was, and it became not long afterwards the birthplace of my second daughter. Extensive quarters were assigned for a lot of nuns, school-girls, priests and monks, with a bishop at their head. Our wounded in hospital were devotedly ministered to by our Protestant ladies. I went amongst

* The widow of the Major Hawkins killed in the Gwalior mutiny on the 14th June.

the poor men to try to cheer them with my sympathy, and I well remember one case that particularly arrested my attention, and excited my admiration; it was that of one of our poor artillerymen who had been blown up by the explosion of a tumbril on the 5th of July, and who now exhibited a marvellous example of composed fortitude. I was so struck with his quiet demeanour, that I could not have thought he was suffering such agony, till on my asking him the question he told me such was really the case. About the 8th of July a military demonstration was made by marching with some artillery and infantry through the city. This produced a reaction. People flocked to the Fort with provisions, and a bazaar was established on a space of ground just outside the Fort, which became a flourishing market, where we could purchase everything required to satisfy our daily wants. Servants also came pouring in, to the delight of masters, who felt, after all, that they could not get on without the much-abused black man. The services of the well-known army contractor, Jotee Pershaud, were invaluable in the business of victualling the garrison.

I must not also forget to notice that we had in the Fort two newspaper printing establishments belonging to the *Delhi Gazette* and its rival paper the *Mofussilite*. From these newspapers I derived my information of those events of the outside world, which I at once recorded in my diary. A commencement was now made to the strengthening of the defences of the fortress; numerous guns were mounted on the ramparts. The powder magazines were covered with mud to protect them against the chances of being shelled. For it must be remembered that at this time the Gwalior Contingent, with numerous field guns and a heavy battering train, was within seventy miles of Agra, and that its leaders were continually boasting they would attack us. Watch and ward was kept by a Captain and his subaltern in a small dilapidated tent. I never found out why they could not supply us with a proper tent instead of one with holes in it, that were so large that I felt it necessary to keep my cap on all day long to prevent a sunstroke. The different components of the garrison were told off and warned, so that every man might be at his appointed post as soon as an alarm should be given. The native Christians naturally rose more in public estimation, inasmuch as for weal or woe they were one with us. We had about 350, of whom about 270 were adult males. The fourth day of our entry into the Fort was a memorable one for the gloomy tidings which in rapid succession were brought in by messenger after messenger. One came with news that the Sikhs and Goorkhas had turned against us at the eleventh hour. Another came with the tidings that our army was on the retreat from Delhi. The portentous nature of such a disaster as this would prove was quite enough to strike us with awe; and though this information afterwards turned out to be false, yet there was so much truth underlying it, that the reality was only a shade or two better than what was reported to us that day. For despite the defeats inflicted on the mutineers on the 30th and 31st May near Ghazeeoddeen Nuggur, and on the 8th June at Budleeka Serai,* and the repulse of the grand attack of the Delhi mutineers on the 23rd June, the centenary of Plassy, yet still but very little progress was made in June by the Delhi Field Force towards the reduction of the rebellious city. Indeed the army of retribution was so pressed in its turn, that the besiegers found themselves besieged instead of besieging, and but for indomitable English pluck the siege would have been raised. The third piece of news was but too true, for we then heard of the massacre at Cawnpore of General Wheeler and the survivors of the siege there.† These

* Colonel Chester, Adjutant-General of the Army, was killed at this battle.
† The numbers who left the entrenchment are stated to have been four hundred and fifty.

having capitulated on the strength of a safe passage to Allahabad being guaranteed to them by the Nana Sahib, quitted the entrenchments on the 27th June, and had just embarked that day at the ghaut in budgerows, for the purpose of proceeding to Allahabad, when a signal having been given by sounding a bugle, two or three guns that had been previously concealed were brought forward, and a murderous fire of grape-shot and musket balls was opened upon the crowded boats from both sides of the river. Many were burnt to death through some of the boats being set on fire. A number of women with children in their arms sprang into the current, and many of both sexes reached the shore. The men were all killed by the Nana's orders, and the women and children, wounded and half-drowned, to the number of 125, were confined all together in one room in the Nana Sahib's camp, where they were a prey to grief and horror, and subjected to every foul indignity. Sir Hugh Wheeler, who had fought with Lord Lake before Delhi in 1804, and who by nature was particularly considerate towards the prejudices of the Sepoys, was by them cut down as he was on the point of embarking, though many of the Sepoys, so it is said, wished to spare his life. There were, however, four persons who escaped almost by a miracle, one would think. These were Lieutenants Mowbray Thomson[*] and Delafosse,[†] who with Private Murphy and Gunner Sullivan actually managed to escape by swimming down the river to Moorar Row, where they were received by a friendly Rajah, and finally reached Allahabad. The crowning horror of the Cawnpore tragedy was the last massacre on the 15th July, when more than two hundred women and children, consisting of the Cawnpore captives and fugitives from Futtehgurh, who were confined in a bungalow near the Assembly Rooms, were all

[*] Now Colonel Mowbray Thomson, holding political employment, being in charge of ex-King of Oude, according to Army List of 1878.
[†] Now Colonel H. G. Delafosse, C.B., commanding 101st Royal Bengal Fusileers.

inhumanly murdered by Mussulman butchers. These stony-hearted ruffians went in amongst our helpless ladies and poor children, and slaughtered them like a flock of sheep, and next day (16th July) they were thrown into an adjacent well.* The sight that met Havelock's victorious soldiers as they entered is too heartrending to describe, and is enough to call up tears even at this distance of time, and therefore I prefer to draw a veil over these last culminating horrors, which we did not hear of till the very end of July. One interesting incident, that was credited at the time, turned out to be little better than a fabrication. I allude to the story that was told of the heroism of General Wheeler's daughter, who was said to have shot five Sepoys with a revolver, and then to have saved her honour by throwing herself down a well, which is narrated in Chambers's "History of the Indian Revolt." The true facts of the case I have gathered from a correspondent to one of the Indian newspapers, who felt such a deep interest in the fate of Miss Wheeler that he took the trouble to trace the matter out in the most thorough manner, when he found that that unfortunate young lady became the prize of a trooper, who carried her about with him till at last he took her to his home, when Miss Wheeler's arrival there provoked the jealousy of the man's wife to such a degree, that the trooper, to procure peace at home, murdered the woman he had so foully wronged. Divine vengeance did not, however, suffer this vile creature to live long after. The trooper perished on the battle-field. From this digression I must return to that particularly melancholy day, the fourth of our entry into the Fort, to mention the last piece of unpleasant news, which was, that the enemy were undermining the Fort to blow us all up.

This was, however, soon afterwards found to be in-

* I saw the well years afterwards, when it became known as the "Memorial Well."

correct. But on this day I had very gloomy forebodings as to the future, and every thoughtful man amongst us must at this period have felt it very doubtful as to the possibility of our being able to hold on till succour should come to our aid. We all knew that a large army would be sent out sufficiently strong to rescue all surviving beleaguered bands of Englishmen at Lucknow, and through the North-West Provinces, or to avenge their fall if they came too late. But could the tremendous strain be kept up till such time as the regiments should arrive from England? this was the question.*
And it must be remembered that, apart from the difficulties and delays of the Commissariat Department, even when they did arrive, they would still have to march several hundreds of miles after disembarking at Calcutta; for Raneegunj at this period was the Railway terminus, and it was only 120 miles from Calcutta, and Lucknow was about 620 miles from Calcutta, and much more from Bombay; whilst Agra was 796 miles, and Delhi 900 miles from Calcutta, and nearly the same distances from Bombay.

It is well known what difficulty was experienced in June in sending a few hundred men up country, since prompt movement of troops by land on a requisite scale was found to be impossible. A railway to Cawnpore, distant 628 miles from Calcutta, would in all human probability have averted the terrible catastrophe of the 27th June, for H.M. 64th Foot arrived in Calcutta on the 3rd June, and was followed soon afterwards by the 35th Foot and 78th Highlanders and other regiments. Nor was the apprehension of our being finally overwhelmed, and sharing the fate that had happened, as we had just heard, to our countrymen at Cawnpore, at all lessened by the sad news about a week later from Lucknow, which was that Sir Henry Lawrence had been defeated at Chinhut with great loss,

* By the end of the year nearly 40,000 men were sent off to the scene of the Mutiny.

that the English were besieged in the Residency at Lucknow, and that Sir Henry had died on the 4th July, from a wound inflicted by a shell on the 2nd July. The death of this benevolent, kind-hearted and good man was a great loss.* His last counsel was "No surrender!" "Let every man," he said, "die at his post; but never make terms. God help the poor women and children!" And he desired that on his tomb should be engraven the words, "Here lies Henry Lawrence, who tried to do his duty." That I may not be accused of being a croaker, and of exaggerating the dangers that really existed, I shall here quote the trustworthy testimony of no less a person than Sir John Lawrence, then Chief Commissioner of the Punjaub (the late Lord Lawrence), which is to be found in Mr. Raikes' book,† and is as follows.

"I assure you," wrote Sir John from Lahore on the 21st October, 1857, "when I look back on the last four months I am lost in astonishment that any of us are alive. But for the mercy of God we must have been ruined. Had the Sikhs joined against us, nothing, humanly speaking, could have saved us. No man could have hoped, much less foreseen, that they would have withstood the temptation to avenge their loss of national independence."

That the natives expected that we should be turned out of the country was, I think, evidenced by the criterion of the money market; as I perfectly remember that at this period, and for long afterwards, the native money-changers gave eighteen instead of sixteen annas, the proper change for the rupee. The reason for this was that the natives believed that the copper currency would suffer deterioration in the event of native rule being substituted for that of British. Under such circumstances of gloom, unrelieved by any reasonable hope of extra-

* Sir Henry Lawrence was succeeded by Major Banks, who also was killed on the 22nd July.
† Mr. C. Raikes' "Notes on the Revolt," p. 74.

neous help for a long time to come, what a consolation it was to the Christian believer (and there were many such in the Fort) to take refuge in God, and then to feel that there was One at hand who cared for and loved him, and who would make all things work together for his good.

The irreligious and the sceptic having at such times nothing to fall back upon, have cause to fear, but it is not so with the pious Christian. "He shall not be afraid of evil tidings: his heart is fixed, trusting in the Lord" (Psalm cxii. 7).

Happily, though surrounded by enemies, we were not called upon to sustain a siege, which in the over-crowded state of the Fort would have entailed fearful suffering. For in July, within the Fort and entrenchments, we had full three thousand five hundred European and Eurasian men, women, and children, besides which we had two thousand three hundred native Christians, Hindoos, and Mussulmen.

Military law having been proclaimed at Agra in June, we had under its provisions a pretty good number of Courts-martial. I never sat on any of them except as an unpaid Interpreter. Many rebels were hanged on gallows outside the Fort. I have myself seen as many as six or seven hanging on one occasion. July passed with no prospect of Delhi being soon taken; since the Delhi Field Force continued to be the besieged rather than the besieging party, being harassed by constant attacks from the mutineers. Moreover, not less than one hundred officers had been killed in action, or had died of wounds, or sunstroke, or cholera, or were on the sick list, and eleven hundred sick and wounded had to be tended; for at the close of that month (July) General Wilson forwarded to Government a report showing that out of eight thousand and thirty-four soldiers under his command, he had eleven hundred and sixteen non-effective from sickness and wounds received in action. Some consolation was derived by the news we received from the Punjaub of the energetic course adopted towards secret traitors and open mutineers, which it is necessary just to notice *en passant;* and to do this we must go back to the 13th May, when Brigadier S. Corbett, with H.M. 81st Foot and two troops of European Horse Artillery, disarmed the 16th, 26th, and 49th Regiments, N.I., and the 8th Light Cavalry at Mean Meer, six miles from Lahore;* and this prompt measure was not enforced a bit too soon; since it was afterwards discovered that those regiments had plotted the massacre of every European there and at Lahore.

Nine days after this, on the 22nd May, the 24th, 27th, and 51st Regiments N.I., and the 5th Light Cavalry were disarmed at Peshawur,† where they were watched by H.M. 70th Foot and 87th Fusileers, and some European Artillery stationed there under the command of Brigadier Sidney Cotton, commanding the frontier force. This was a master-stroke of policy, and exercised a beneficial influence in maintaining peace in the Punjaub. One regiment, the 21st N.I.,‡ was exempted from the disarming process. We also heard with much satisfaction of the wholesome severity exercised at Peshawur, where forty Sepoys of the 55th Regiment N.I. were blown from guns, on the 10th June. This regiment having mutinied at Murdan on the 20th May, was vigorously pursued, and satisfactorily accounted for, nearly three hundred being killed in their flight, or captured, and the rest escaped to the hills, where they had a wretched time of it. Then we heard in July of the mutiny of the 14th Regiment N.I., at Jhelum in the Punjaub, on the 7th July, on which occasion they fought a battle with a wing of H.M. 24th Foot, under Colonel C. Ellice, some artillery, and a party of Lind's Mooltanee Horse. The mutineers fought under cover, and the English were repulsed. The detachment of H.M. 24th Foot suffered very

---

* Lahore is 1,240 miles from Calcutta.
† Peshawur is 1,540 miles from Calcutta.
‡ Now the 1st Regiment N.I.

severely, having lost five officers, and seventy-four men in killed and wounded. The mutinous 14th then decamped, but very few managed in the end to escape, as most were either drowned, cut to pieces by their pursuers, or captured and blown from guns. On the same day that the 14th N.I. mutinied at Jhelum, my cousin, Major A. Mills' regiment, the 58th Regiment N.I., was disarmed at Rawul Pindee. We also received intelligence of the mutiny of the 46th Regiment N.I. and a wing of the 9th Native Cavalry, on the 9th July, at Sealcote in the Punjaub, when the Brigadier and three other officers, together with a Scotch Missionary with his wife and child were all murdered. That fine fellow, Brigadier-General Nicholson, was, however, on the track of the murderers. He was in command of a movable column, composed of H.M. 52nd Foot, a troop of European Artillery, with a horse battery and a wing of the 9th Native Cavalry. Nicholson had a fortnight before disarmed the 33rd and 35th Regiments N.I.; he now (9th July) disarmed my old regiment, the 59th N.I., and on hearing of the mutiny at Sealcote, he at once disarmed the wing of the 9th Cavalry he had with him. On the 12th July Nicholson fought the Sealcote mutineers at Trimmoo ghaut, where he defeated them with great loss, and routed them again with great slaughter on the 16th July. This lot of mutineers was also very satisfactorily accounted for, as they were almost entirely cut up. And on the 29th July the disarmed 26th Regiment N.I. mutinied at Lahore, and having killed Major Spencer, took to flight; but they were so pertinaciously pursued by the Punjaub police and the new levies, that hardly a man survived. We did not, however, hear of the mutiny of the 26th N.I. till the next month (August). August came and passed without Delhi being taken; but this month there was a perceptible improvement in our position. Things then began to look a little more hopeful; because, though around the horizon were black portentous clouds, yet there was one bit of blue sky visible to the north of us, and another to the south. For the Punjaub officials had been straining every nerve to hurl every available European and Sikh soldier against Delhi, and the tact displayed in inducing our former enemies the Sikhs to cast in their lot with us, when they might have seized the opportunity to seek the recovery of the independence of their country, was indeed a masterpiece of skilful manœuvring. Sir John Lawrence and his able assistants were not the men to let the grass grow under their feet. As early as the 9th June one regiment arrived at Delhi from the Punjaub; this was the Corps of Guides* under Captain Daly. And between the 26th June and 3rd July there arrived at Delhi from the Punjaub, the head-quarters H.M. 8th Foot, the head-quarters 61st Foot, Coke's Rifles (1st P.N.I.), a squadron of Punjaub Cavalry and some artillery, making our effective strength there six thousand six hundred men of all arms. But in August we heard of the arrival at Delhi of the movable column under Brigadier-General Nicholson. This force consisted of H.M. 52nd Foot, a wing of H.M. 61st Foot, 2nd Punjaub Infantry, the Kumaon battalion 4th Sikh Infantry, two hundred and fifty Mooltanee Horse, and some artillery. Nicholson was a tower of strength by himself, and, flushed with victory, he was eager for a new exploit. The enemy's attempt to intercept our siege train coming from Ferozepore afforded him the opportunity he wanted. So Nicholson engaged the Neemuch Brigade at Nujufgurh on the 25th August, and after a well-contested and sanguinary battle, he gained a signal victory, killing eight hundred of the Sepoys, and capturing thirteen of their guns. We also heard in August, or at the end of July, of Brigadier H. Havelock's victorious progress in his advance with his small army towards Lucknow, of his victory at Futtehpore on the 12th July, when he cap-

---

* This regiment had marched from Peshawur to Delhi, about six hundred miles, in twenty-two days.

tured twelve of their guns, of his defeating the enemy at Aong on the 15th July, and of his brilliant victory over the Nana on the 16th July, followed by the reoccupation of Cawnpore, when the English found they had come too late to rescue the women and children they had hoped to save. After accomplishing so much, Havelock reminded his soldiers that their work was only begun. "Your comrades at Lucknow," said the General, "are in peril. Agra is besieged; Delhi is still the focus of mutiny and rebellion. You must make great sacrifices if you would obtain great results. Three cities have to be saved, two strong places to be disblockaded." Havelock wrote to us that he hoped to come soon: in the meantime, added he, "let Agra be as Jelalabad." News reached us also in August of Havelock's crossing the Ganges into Oude, of his victories at Onao, and Busheerutgunj on the 29th July, of his falling back, and his fresh start for Lucknow on the 4th August with about fourteen hundred men of the 1st Madras Fusileers, H.M. 84th Foot, and 78th Highlanders, with two heavy 24-pounders, two 24-pounder howitzers, and Captain Maude's battery of guns, and of his defeating the enemy once more at Busheerutgunj on the 5th of August. It must here be stated that it was only by means of spies and secret messengers that news was procurable of passing events. All these successes of the English General availed nothing towards the accomplishment of the ardently longed-for relief of Lucknow, since Havelock felt compelled, after inflicting another defeat upon the enemy at Busheerutgunj, to recross the Ganges to Cawnpore (13th August), where he had to stay for more than a month before he could make a fresh start for the Oudean capital. This retrograde movement was grievous to all. It was depressing to the British soldier, and gave much pain to the General ordering it, as being prejudicial to British prestige, and for fear lest it might seal the fate of the beleaguered Lucknow garrison. This, however, was necessary; because Havelock found that there were thirty thousand rebels with fifty guns between him and his destination, and his rear was threatened by a powerful force under the Nana, and in addition to this cholera had broken out in his camp. I heard this month (August) with pleasure of Brigadier-General Neil's execution of stern justice upon the Cawnpore murderers, when left in command there; how he compelled the guilty Hindoos, at least the chief rebels, or ringleaders, to lose their caste before being hung, by forcing them to sweep clean a certain part of the blood-stained floor, which was described by an eye-witness as being several inches deep in blood. "My object," wrote Neil, "is to inflict a fearful punishment, for a revolting, cowardly, barbarous deed, and to strike terror into these rebels. The first I caught was a Subadar, or native officer, a high-caste Brahmin, who tried to resist my order[*] to clean up the very blood he had helped to shed; but I made the Provost-Marshal do his duty, and a few lashes compelled the miscreant to accomplish his task. When done, he was taken out, immediately hanged, and after death buried in a ditch at the roadside. No one who has witnessed the scenes of murder, mutilation, and massacre, can ever listen to the word 'mercy' as applied to these fiends."

Neil's wholesome severity, I may here remark, met with universal applause. It is much to be regretted that the two rival Generals at Cawnpore did not like each other, and one cannot read without pain about the account of the ill-feeling that existed between two such fine characters as Havelock and Neil, which is given in Colonel Malleson's valuable history. No doubt the blame was not all on one side, and it only shows that the best of men are far from being perfect.

Whilst awaiting reinforcements at Cawnpore, Havelock, on the 16th of August, marched with a small force against the Nana, who was at the head of four thou-

[*] Of the 25th July.

sand rebels at Bithoor, and defeated that arch-fiend of the Mutiny. On this occasion the Sepoys of my old regiment, the 42nd N.I.,* actually crossed bayonets with our men, and did not yield till sixty of them had fallen. Havelock returned next day to Cawnpore; and now it seemed doubtful whether even this place would not have to be abandoned, since, finding he had around him about thirty-seven thousand of the enemy, including five thousand of the Gwalior Contingent, which threatened Cawnpore from Calpie, and that his army was reduced to about 700 effective soldiers, Havelock wrote word to the newly-arrived Commander-in-Chief, Sir Colin Campbell, on the 21st of August, that if reinforcements arrived soon he would, notwithstanding the threatening aspect of affairs, continue to hold Cawnpore, but that otherwise he should be forced to retire on Allahabad.

Havelock's failure, through no fault of his own, to execute the programme arranged for the succour of our besieged and sorely-pressed countrymen at Lucknow, tended, at least to a considerable extent, to throw the victories of his miniature army into the shade, which were still further neutralized by news of a dismal nature that reached us from other quarters; foremost of which was the formidable insurrection in Behar, headed by Rajah Koonwur Singh, and the terrible defeat inflicted on a force of three hundred and fifty soldiers of H.M. 10th and 37th Foot and sixty-five Sikhs, under the command of Captain Dunbar, by the Dinapore mutineers. These regiments, viz., the 7th, 8th, and 40th Regiments N I., having revolted at Dinapore† on the 25th of July, left for Arrah, a small civil station about twenty-four miles from Dinapore. Here they were joined by Rajah Koonwur Singh, at the head of three or four thousand armed men. Having plundered the treasury, they proceeded to attack Mr. Boyle's house, a detached two-storied

* The 42nd Regiment N.I. mutinied at Saugur on the 7th July.
† Dinapore is 376 miles from Calcutta.

building held by Mr. Wake, the collector, who, with fifty Sikhs and fifteen European civilians, and a Mahomedan deputy-collector, with uncommon gallantry defended the place against two thousand Sepoys and several thousand insurgents for a whole week, though there was not a single military man amongst them to aid them with his professional skill. The force under Captain Dunbar, after some delay, left Dinapore by steamer on the 29th of July in pursuit of the Dinapore mutineers. After going some distance, the Commanding Officer disembarked his men at Beharee ghaut, whence he pushed on across country to rescue Mr. Wake's garrison. After marching ten or eleven miles, the English suddenly fell into an ambuscade, at or near midnight (29th of July). They were mowed down in the darkness by successive vollies of musketry from an invisible foe. Captain Dunbar with more than half his men were killed on the spot, and on the retreat, which became a disorderly flight, to the steamer. It was a mournful party that returned to Dinapore on the evening of the 30th of July. Out of fifteen officers twelve were killed or wounded. The total loss was a hundred and seventy officers and men killed, and a hundred and twenty wounded, being a grand total of two hundred and ninety out of four hundred and fifteen engaged. This was a most miserable business altogether, and would have sealed the fate of Wake's heroic band, but for the skill and gallantry of Major Vincent Eyre, who, with 150 men of H.M. 5th Fusileers, 40 artillerymen with three guns, and about 20 volunteers, having on the 2nd of August inflicted a signal defeat on the Dinapore mutineers and Koonwur Singh's followers, accomplished the relief of Arrah next day. This success the Major improved soon afterwards by defeating Koonwur Singh and taking the fort of Jugdespore, that chieftain's stronghold. Then in August we heard at Agra that the 27th Regiment Bombay Native Infantry* had

* Eventually nearly all these mutineers were destroyed.

mutinied at Kolapore (1st of August) and murdered three of their officers. This was indeed bad news, as it was feared that it was but the precursor of the revolt of the whole native army in that Presidency; and ere long the existence of a great Mussulman conspiracy was detected at Poonah, Belgaum, Dharwar, Sattara, and other places. Some uneasiness was caused this month by the declaration of the troopers of the 8th Madras Native Cavalry, who being ordered to march to Madras and embark for Calcutta, stopped on their march, and declared that they would not go forth "to war against their countrymen."

For this act of insubordination this turbulent regiment was disarmed. Moreover, in August we still heard of more mutinies, such as that of the 12th Irregular Cavalry, which rose in revolt at Segowlie on the 25th July, and murdered their Commanding Officer, Major Holmes, with his wife, together with the other Europeans residing there; the Ramgurh Infantry, which mutinied on the 30th July, when *en route* to Hazareebagh, and marched back to Ranchee breathing hostile imprecations against the Europeans. Captain Dalton, Commissioner of Chota Nagpore, and the rest of the officials (amongst whom I had a brother-in-law) quitted the station, which being thus abandoned was plundered by the rebels; and on the 5th August the Sepoys of the Ramgurh Battalion stationed at Purulia and Chybasa rose in revolt. The Jodhpore Legion also mutinied at Erinpoora on the 22nd August. Despite all this, and though no actual progress was made towards taking Delhi,* yet still, judging from such news as actually reached us in August, there was on the whole an improvement in the general posture of affairs. The storm had somewhat abated. We had recovered our spirits and were ready to retrieve the disaster of Sussia.

* For General Wilson, in a letter dated 20th August, stated that the force under his command was then being besieged by the mutineers. See Colonel Malleson's "Hist. Indian Mutiny," vol. ii. p. 3.

Colonel Cotton was now commanding at Agra in room of Brigadier Polwhele, who had been removed from the command. A force under the command of Major Montgomerie was now sent to Alygurh against Ghousa Khan, who had proclaimed himself Subadar of the King of Delhi. This miniature army consisted of three companies of my regiment, a hundred and fifty strong, with four officers; two 9-pounders, and a 24-pounder howitzer, manned by about thirty European artillerymen; and thirty militia. We left Agra late on the evening of the 20th August. I commanded a party of my regiment composing the advance guard, mounted on elephants. The only appliance for keeping our seat was by holding on to the rope bound round the enormous quadruped. The instructions which I received were short and simple. I was, in case of coming in contact with the enemy, to dismount my men, and form them up to resist any attack that might be made, till the main body should come up. The night, which passed without any encounter, was the most miserable one that I have ever spent; for soon after starting I was attacked with ophthalmia. I kept my seat on the elephant as long as I could; but at last I felt it so very difficult to hold on by the rope with the pain I was in, that I dismounted and marched on foot at the head of the advance party on elephants. And oh! the agony I endured every time I strained my eyes in the darkness to keep clear of the elephants! It was indeed a wretched time, never to be forgotten by me.

The long night, however, passed at last, and next day it was proposed to send me back to Agra, but against this I earnestly protested, feeling sure that I should be murdered on the way. So I was allowed to stay and get on as best I might. One eye at least was like a ball of fire, and the surgeon used to make me lie down whilst he dropped some horrid burning stuff into it. Having been joined by a troop of sixty or seventy native horsemen raised by Thakoor Govind Singh, we attacked the enemy in the vicinity of Alygurh on the 24th August. I commanded a company in this action, though my eyes were painful, and I could not see very well. Ghousa Khan's army was said to be about four thousand men; but this may have been somewhat exaggerated; but at all events we were a mere handful to them. They were composed of undisciplined armed insurgents, and a detachment of the 3rd Cavalry. The battle raged furiously for some time; the militia cavalry under Lieutenant De Kantzow* behaved, it is stated, with conspicuous bravery. I shall, however, record just what met my limited vision, which was a body of fifty or sixty Ghazees sweeping right down on my company. On they dashed, sword in hand, inflamed by religious fanaticism, and rendered insensible to fear by having freely partaken of the soothing bhang. On they rushed just like so many mad dogs. I had only about thirty men with me to the front, and one of these ran out a considerable distance in advance, apparently desirous of distinguishing himself by driving them back by his single-handed prowess; but the poor man paid dearly for his undisciplined act of valour, for he was cut to pieces in a few moments by the sharp swords of the Ghazees, and this appeared to have had a bad effect on my men. I purposed fighting the Ghazees then and there with the bayonet; but the soldiers, entirely of their own accord, and positively without any order from me, went to the right about, and ran to a sufficient distance to enable them to load and fire upon the Ghazees, most if not all of whom were killed, as it appeared to me.

We now formed up near a gun, which fired with much precision and exhilarating effect, by means of which, in conjunction with our musketry fire, the rebels were driven back. I believe the two other companies

* This young officer received the Queen's gracious approbation, and an autograph letter of thanks from Earl Canning for "admirable services" rendered by him at imminent peril of his life at Mynpoorie during and subsequent to the mutiny of the Sepoys at that station.

of my regiment maintained a successful fight with the enemy; but I could not see what they did. The enemy, so it is stated, left three hundred dead on the field, which was rather more than the total force of the victors. Still, if the truth is to be told, this action, though to a certain extent successful, must be regarded as an indecisive one, because we retreated the same day towards Agra. I was sent on in advance with the sick and wounded, and as soon as I reached Agra I was besieged by the quidnuncs anxious to know all about the battle; and then, instead of keeping a quiet tongue in my head, I indiscreetly blurted out the whole truth about my company going to the right about when I wanted to engage the enemy with the bayonet. This got me into grievous trouble, and brought me once more into collision with my military superiors, as I shall now proceed to show. A desperate quarrel was fastened upon me on the 9th September by a junior officer, who so far forgot himself as to offer personal violence to me when I replied with becoming indignation to his unjust imputations and insulting language; for this he was very properly placed under arrest by the senior officer present, Lieutenant F. Stephenson, the Interpreter and Quarter-Master of the Regiment, who made the following report of the matter for the Commanding Officer's information, which I give below verbatim therefrom, merely substituting Lieutenant O—— for the name of the offender:

"About half-past seven I came out of my room and took my chair in front of my quarters. Lieutenants White, Blake, and O—— were sitting there; there appeared to have been some disagreement between Lieutenants White and O——, which I did not hear. I heard Lieutenant O—— say to Lieutenant White, 'The best thing you can do is to hold your tongue, and shut up;' to which Lieutenant White replied, 'You choop ro.'* Lieutenant O—— immediately arose,

* The Hindoosthanie for "be silent."

and pushed Lieutenant White and his chair over together, upon which I placed Lieutenant O—— under arrest.*

"I have the honour to be,
"Sir,
"Your most obedient Servant,

"F. STEPHENSON,
"Lieutenant 3rd European Regiment.

"To Lieutenant R. Thompson,
"Adjutant 3rd European Regiment."

Two days afterwards (12th of September) we both had to attend the Commanding Officer's quarters, when Colonel Riddle admonished Lieutenant O—— for the unruly temper he displayed, but which I understood him to say he would not call using violence towards me.

But at the same time I, too, was admonished, without rhyme or reason, for the inclination which my Commanding Officer was pleased to say I had manifested to disobey orders; though how I had done so I cannot for the life of me perceive. I at once expressed my intention of complaining to the Commander-in-Chief against this adjudication of the matter, whereupon Colonel Riddle admitted that I had a right to complain to the Commander-in-Chief if I liked. I then went home, and the same day sent off a letter through the prescribed channel to the address of the Adjutant-General of the Army, complaining of the recent harsh treatment of me by my Commanding Officer, and appealed in particular to the Commander-in-Chief against my Commanding Officer's adjudication of this case, wherein I had been so grossly insulted by a junior officer. For writing this letter, which was couched in moderate and guarded language, I was placed under arrest by direction of

* See letter in my possession.

Colonel Cotton, commanding at Agra; and I was furnished by the Adjutant with a true copy of the Fort Adjutant's letter directing this unjust proceeding. This strange letter, dated 15th of September, 1857, was to the following effect:—

"The Commanding Officer regrets that he has not the power of at once bringing Lieutenant White to a Court-martial, but will take the earliest opportunity of bringing his conduct to the notice of His Excellency the Commander-in-Chief, with a view to his being tried by a General Court-martial for his litigious and unofficer-like behaviour. You will be good enough to furnish Lieutenant White with a copy of this letter.*

"I have the honour to be,
"Sir,
"Your most obedient Servant,
"W. PATTON, Captain.

"To Fort Adjutant Lieutenant-Colonel Riddle,
"Commanding 3rd European Regiment."

Thus was I denied my undoubted right of appeal to the highest military authority, and I was threatened with a Court-martial and charged with unofficer-like behaviour when I was quite innocent of any offence. But the best proof of my innocence was that I was never tried on this charge; but after having been kept under arrest for five months, I was released by order of the Commander-in-Chief, without receiving the slightest reprimand from His Excellency!!!†

I was this time completely at the mercy of these two men, the officer commanding my regiment, and Colonel

---

* See letters in my possession.
† See General Order of Commander-in-Chief, dated Camp, Cawnpore, 10th February, 1858, in my possession.

Cotton, commanding the station, and they made me feel their power in a manner I can never forget; for I was kept under close arrest for four whole days, during which time I was kept in the sultry month of September a prisoner in the horrid hole (already described) which was assigned to me for my residence. I dared not step outside my hovel lest I should be charged with breaking my arrest, as the punishment for this would be cashiering. I bore it, however, as best I could, and at the end of four days the severity of my arrest was greatly mitigated by being allowed to take morning and evening exercise for an hour each time. One thing more was done which appeared to me to savour of a persecuting spirit, which was that my application to attend divine service was refused; so at Agra I was for nearly five months deprived of the means of grace!!! They doubtless thought this would make me feel, and they were not mistaken; but they could not withhold from me the consolations of the God of all Grace. He sympathizes with his oppressed children in their forsaken condition. I think I am right in saying that a private soldier, irrespective of the nature of his offence, is invariably marched to attend divine service. If I am correct in this assertion, then it is obvious that I was in this particular treated with singular malevolence! My brother officers appeared afraid or unwilling to show me any countenance, for fear, I suppose, of displeasing the Commanding Officer. But I have by me a letter from my dear old mother, written some years afterwards, telling me that an officer of the late 3rd European Regiment had spoken of me to a friend of the family, telling him "how much I had been persecuted." One pleasing circumstance deserves here to be mentioned. There was one gentleman friendly with those against me whose kindness was at this time particularly refreshing. This was no other than the editor of the *Moffussilite*,[*] who, though almost a perfect stranger to me, felt so grieved to see me so

[*] A leading newspaper in the North-West.

ill-treated, that he paid me a visit of sympathy, telling me, though he heard all about me from the other side, that he saw there was a dead set being made against me, and he commiserated me for the trouble I was in. But it is time to speak of the great public events that occurred during this month; and first of all must be mentioned the death of our poor dispirited, worn-out Lieutenant-Governor, Mr. John Colvin, who died in the Fort on the 9th September. The news that reached us this month from the Punjaub continued favourable.

The disarmed 51st Regiment N.I., having mutinied at Peshawur on the 28th August, were annihilated; since upwards of a hundred were shot dead on the spot, a hundred and fifty more were cut down in the pursuit, and nearly four hundred were brought in prisoners; whilst those who escaped to the hills were reduced to bondage by the hill men. The tidings that reached us from Delhi about this period were decidedly of a more hopeful character, and denoted an improvement in the state of affairs at the great focus of rebellion; inasmuch as our siege train drawn by elephants arrived at Delhi on the 4th September. It consisted of sixty pieces, fifteen of which were 24-pounders, twenty 18-pounders, and the remainder howitzers and mortars of various sizes; and we heard of the arrival of the last reinforcement, which raised the Delhi Field Force to nearly ten thousand men fit for duty. Three men, Brigadier Neville Chamberlain, Adjutant-General, Colonel Baird Smith, Chief Engineer, and Brigadier-General John Nicholson, were working indefatigably to complete arrangements for the assault of Delhi. As for the General in command of the army, he expressed a written opinion of his hopelessness of being able to take the place till relieved from a force from below. That the attempt would be very hazardous was quite obvious to any one with a grain of sense in his head. For, in addition to the terrible mortality, and the besieged state of the besiegers, which has already been noticed, it must also be considered that Delhi, a city seven miles in circumference, filled with an immense fanatical Mussulman population, was moreover garrisoned by forty thousand Sepoys; it had also a hundred and fourteen pieces of heavy artillery mounted on the walls, and the fort itself had been made very strong by perfect flanking defences, and a glacis so as to prevent our guns breaking the walls lower than eight feet from the top. General Wilson, however, at last resolved to undertake the tremendous responsibility of assaulting the imperial city; though, when the final reinforcements reached Delhi on the 6th September, they only raised our effective force to 9,866 men—British soldiers, Sikhs, and Goorkhas. Besides which there were on our side between two and three thousand men belonging to the Cashmere, Jheend and Puttiala Contingents. On or about the 20th September[*] we heard the joyful news of the assault and capture of a considerable part of Delhi, and a week afterwards official intelligence was received of the complete success of the British arms, and the capture of the King. An account of this important event, by which the neck of the Mutiny was completely broken, will be given in the next chapter.

[*] From a native source of information we heard, on the 18th September, of our troops getting into Delhi; and on the 21st September we got news of the capture of the magazine, with its vast stores and upwards of a hundred guns.

CHAPTER VI.

Description of the Assault and Capture of Delhi—Death of Nicholson—Capture of the King—Captain Hodson shoots three Princes—Colonel Greathed's Pursuit of the Mutineers—Brigadier Showers' Successes—Mutiny of Regiments after the Escalade of Delhi—Nagode, Jubbulpore, Chittagong, Dacca, and Julpigoree — Havelock's Victorious Advance to Lucknow—Sir James Outram—His Grand Chivalry—Commander-in-Chief's Remarkable Order thereon—Outram's Bravery—Sore Peril of the Besieged—Relief of Lucknow—Great Mortality of the Garrison—Surprising Loyalty of the Faithful Sepoys—Battle of Agra—Strange Refusal of Permission to go out to the Battle with my Regiment—Complete Defeat of Mutineers—Lady Nurses—Their Devotedness—Troubled State of Rajpootana—Repulse of Colonel Lawrence—Murder of Major Burton—Defeat of Captain Tucker—English still Besieged at Lucknow—Arrival of Sir Colin Campbell at Cawnpore—Advance of Commander-in-Chief—Captain Peel and the Naval Brigade—Warlike Operations—Desperate Fighting at the Secunder Bagh—Second Relief of Lucknow Accomplished—Withdrawal of Noncombatants from Lucknow—Death of Havelock—Defeat of General Windham at Cawnpore—Arrival of the Commander-in-Chief—He defeats the Enemy—Their Defeat again by Grant—Pious Despatch of the Victor—Defeat of Jodhpore Legion—Seaton's Victories of Gungeree and Puttialee—Tried by Court-Martial—Injustice of the whole Proceeding—Cruel Sentence—Remarkable Circumstances following it—Condition of Affairs at Agra—Departure of Siege Train—Leave Agra with my Regiment—Letter from Head-Quarters—Commander-in-Chief declines to confirm Sentence of Court—Hard Usage and extreme Unfairness—Appeal to Commander-in Chief—Authorities refuse to forward it—I Trust in the Lord—Lord Clyde comes to Gwalior in 1859—My Interview with him—Its Happy Results—Continuation of the Narrative of the Events of 1858—Reoccupation of Futtygurh—Advance of Commander-in-Chief to Lucknow—Outram repels repeated Attacks—Jung Bahadur's Diversion in our Favour—Brigadier Franks' Victories at Chandah, Humeerpore, and Sooltanpore—Sir Hope Grant takes Meeangunje by Storm—Great Strength of the Enemy at Lucknow—Huzrut Muhul, the Begum—Operations against Lucknow—Storming of Queen's Palace and Imambara—Unexpected Capture of Kaiser Bagh—Immense Loot—Outram's March through the City—Conquest of Lucknow—Escape of the Rebels—Excessive Caution of Commander-in-Chief—Remarks on the Character of Outram.

IN narrating this memorable event it should here be mentioned that General Wilson's directions to his men were to spare the women and children, but to give no quarter to the mutineers. Our batteries opened fire on the guilty city the morning of the 13th September, and by the evening two practical breaches, one in the Moree bastion, and the other in the water bastion, being made, it was determined to make the assault the next day. Four columns were told off for this purpose. The first, commanded by Brigadier-General Nicholson of the Bengal army, consisted of a thousand men, viz., three hundred men of the 75th Foot, under Lieutenant-Colonel Herbert, two hundred and fifty men of the 1st Bengal Fusileers,* led by Major Jacob, and four hundred and fifty men of the 2nd Punjaub Infantry, under Captain Green. This column was to storm the breach near the Cashmere bastion, and escalade the face of the work. The second column, commanded by Brigadier W. Jones of H.M. 61st Regiment, consisting of eight hundred and fifty men, viz., two hundred and fifty men of H.M. 8th Foot, led by Lieutenant-Colonel Greathed, two hundred and fifty men of 2nd Fusileers,† under Captain Boyd, and three hundred and fifty men of 4th Sikh Infantry, under Captain Rothney, was to storm the water bastion. The third column, commanded by Colonel Campbell of H.M. 52nd Foot, was to attack the Cashmere gate. It consisted of nine hundred and fifty men, viz., two hundred men of H.M. 52nd Foot, led by Major Vigors, two hundred and fifty men of Kemaon Battalion, under Captain Ramsay, and five hundred of 1st Punjaub Infantry, led by Lieutenant Nicholson. Major C. Reid of the Bengal army commanded the fourth column, consisting of eight hundred and sixty men, composed of the Sirmoor Goorkhas,‡ the Guides, with some European and Native pickets; and to this force was added one thousand two hundred men belonging to the Cashmere Contingent. This column was to attack and clear the suburbs of Puharunpore and Kishengunje, and to enter the city by the Lahore gate. The Reserve, commanded by Brigadier Longfield of H.M. 8th Foot, was composed of fifteen

* Now H.M. 101st Royal Bengal Fusileers.
† Now H.M. 104th Bengal Fusileers.
‡ Now the Prince of Wales's Own Goorkhas.

DEATH OF NICHOLSON.

hundred men, viz., two hundred and fifty men of H.M. 61st Foot, led by Lieutenant-Colonel Deacon; four hundred and fifty men of 4th Punjaub Infantry, under Captain Wilde; three hundred men of Belooch Battalion, under Lieutenant-Colonel Farquhar, and three hundred Jheend auxiliaries, under Lieutenant-Colonel Dunsford. To these were afterwards added two hundred men of H.M. 60th Rifles, under Lieutenant-Colonel Jones of that regiment. The Cavalry, under Brigadier Hope Grant, were to guard the lines. Before daybreak on the morning of the 14th September the troops were drawn up ready for the terrible struggle, and soon afterwards the columns rushed forward to the assault. The first by desperate courage gained the breach; its leader, Brigadier-General Nicholson, was the first to mount the wall. The second, under Brigadier Jones, about the same time gained the breach at the water gate, and cleared the ramparts as far as the Caubul gate. Nicholson led his men along a narrow lane to attack the Lahore gate* and bastion in the face of a terrific storm of grape and musketry; but he encountered so obstinate a resistance, that he could not dislodge the enemy from a position that was impregnable without the aid of artillery. Here Major Jacob of the 1st Fusileers was mortally wounded, and several other officers belonging to that regiment were struck down. Nicholson himself was also mortally wounded,† and his brigade was obliged to retire to the Caubul gate.

But it is time now to notice the proceedings of the explosion party. Lieutenants Home and Salkeld, with Sergeants Carmichael, Smith and Burgess, Bugler Hawthorne, and some Native Sappers were entrusted with the very dangerous task of blowing in the Cashmere gate with powder bags. In accomplishing this duty in broad daylight, Lieutenant Salkeld was mortally

---

* This gate leads to the Chandnee Choke, the principal street of the city.
† Nicholson died on the 23rd September, in his thirty-fifth year.

wounded, Sergeants Carmichael and Burgess were killed, also a Sikh havildar and a soldier. Though only one-half of the massive gate was driven in by the explosion, yet it was sufficiently shattered to admit the third column, which, led by Colonel Campbell, carried the Cashmere gate. Things were not, however, going on so well with the fourth column, under Major Reid, who found himself confronted by about fifteen thousand men. Reid himself was shot down, and his column afterwards retreated. The reserve column, under Brigadier Longfield, followed the third column through the Cashmere gate, and cleared the College Gardens. The result of the day's fighting was that the first and second columns held the line of walls from the vicinity of the Cashmere gate to the Caubul gate; the third column and the reserve held the Cashmere gate, St. James's Church, Skinner's house, the College Gardens, the water bastion, and one or two other buildings; whilst the fourth column, being defeated, had retired to the camp on the ridge. But even this partial success was not accomplished without very heavy loss; since sixty-six European officers and eleven hundred and four men were killed and wounded in the assault, and Delhi was not taken, as the great suburb of Kishengunje was still in possession of the mutineers, and the Lahore bastion with numerous strongholds were still held in force by them. Sir Hope Grant tells us in his book,* that the General did not seem thoroughly satisfied with the assault. We learn also, from Colonel Malleson, that "the General's first thought had been to withdraw the assaulting columns to the position they had so long held on the ridge," and that "from this fatal determination General Wilson was saved by the splendid obstinacy of Baird Smith, aided by the soldierly-like instincts of Neville Chamberlain."† Kaye says that the half-success of

* See Grant's "History of the Sepoy War."
† Malleson's "History of the Indian Mutiny," vol. ii. p. 55.

the enterprise was extremely disheartening to General Wilson, and that when he put the critical question as to what was to be done, he asked Colonel Baird Smith, the Chief Engineer, whether he thought we could hold what we had taken, whereupon the Colonel decisively replied, "We must do so."[*] And the same writer, speaking of the cloud that hung over us, truly observed, that at that time "the destinies of the English in India trembled in the balance." The enemy meantime, it should be borne in mind, were keeping up a vigorous fire from the Selimgurh and the magazine upon the positions held by the English. Despite everything, however, the English, with bull-dog tenacity, held on to their grip of Delhi, and their perseverance met with its due reward, as the morning of the 16th dawned with brightening prospects for the besiegers; for during the night and early morning Kishengunje, being evacuated by the enemy, was at once occupied by our men. Then our Engineers and Artillery officers exerted themselves to the utmost in bombarding the great buildings of Delhi; and a breach having been effected in the magazine, that important position, with its vast stores and one hundred and seventy guns and howitzers, was taken the same day (16th September). Moreover, the rebels began now to lose heart, since a considerable number of Sepoys commenced streaming out of Delhi this day. The advance of our troops on the following day (17th September) was slow and difficult. Some progress was made, but our soldiers were repulsed in endeavouring to advance towards the palace. Next day (18th September) an attempt made by Colonel Greathed to take the Lahore gate failed, from the refusal of the European soldiers to follow their officers. Notwithstanding this, our advance was this day pushed farther on; as our soldiers took the Delhi Bank, Major Abbott's house, and the house of Khan Mahomed Khan, and our posts were

[*] See Sir J. Kaye's "History of the Sepoy War."

brought near to the palace, and Chandnee Choke. On this day, too, the English, supplied with great mortars from the captured magazine, bombarded the magnificent palace of the great Moghuls,* which the old King evacuated the same day (18th), finding it too hot for him. Further success was achieved by the besiegers on the 19th. The Burun bastion, which commanded the Lahore gate, was evacuated by the enemy, and occupied by our troops on the night of the 19th. The enemy, now thoroughly cowed, were hurrying out of Delhi as fast as they could. Early the following morning (20th of September), the 60th Rifles took the Lahore bastion at a rush, and expelled the enemy. Major Brind afterwards carried the Jumma Musjid, and the same day the palace was taken, the British flag hoisted, and Delhi evacuated by the rebels. Bukht Khan, Commander-in-Chief of the mutineers, quitted the city on the night of the 19th of September, taking with him his best soldiers. General Wilson at once took up his quarters in the palace. We are told by Kaye that when, on the 20th of September, Delhi fell into our hands, it was little more than a vast solitude!† Our losses throughout had been enormous, considering the number of men engaged therein; since it appears, from an official return, that from the commencement of operations in the neighbourhood of Delhi, 30th of May, to its capture, 20th of September, we lost in killed and wounded three thousand eight hundred officers and men. But, in addition to these, many died from disease and exposure to the sun. Having received permission to promise the aged sovereign his life, Captain Hodson, on the 21st of September, with fifty of his troopers, galloped after the King, who had fled to Hoomayoon's tomb, a few miles to the south of the city.

The royal fugitive, perceiving that he had played out

---

* A full description of the palace of the great Moghuls will be found farther on, in an account of my visit to Delhi.
† See Sir J. Kaye's "History of the Sepoy War."

his game and had lost the stakes, agreed to give himself up to Hodson, on receiving a promise from that officer that his life would be spared. On receiving this message, Captain Hodson gave the required promise, whereupon the King came forth and surrendered himself to Hodson, who received from the fallen monarch the sword of the last of the Moghul Emperors.* Having brought his royal captive to Delhi, Hodson started next day (22nd September) with a hundred troopers in search of two of the King's sons and a grandson, who were believed to be the chief exciters of the Delhi atrocities, and who he was informed were hiding in Hoomayoon's tomb. Hodson was successful in finding the three villainous Princes, who surrendered to him; and having first upbraided them for their shameful conduct towards our poor countrymen and countrywomen, Hodson shot them all three with his own hand when within a mile of Delhi, and ordered their corpses to be exposed to public view in front of the Kotwallie. Though I saw nothing at the time objectionable in Hodson's killing these Princes, yet now, after the lapse of so many years, when time has removed those prejudicial heats which so blind the judgment at such times of excitement, I cannot but think, on calm reflection, that the conduct of that gallant officer was very blamable. The slaughtered Shahzaduhs, who are described by Sir Hope Grant as "fearful villains,"† deserved to die for their barbarity to our women and children; but since they voluntarily surrendered themselves to his mercy, they ought not to have been put to death without being first tried.

Two days afterwards (24th September) a column, under Lieutenant-Colonel E. Greathed, commanding H.M. 8th Foot, left Delhi in pursuit of the mutineers. It consisted of Captain Remington's and Captain

* Several months afterwards the King was tried by a military court, and found guilty of the massacre of the British in Delhi. But Earl Canning spared his forfeited life, and sentenced him to be transported to Burmah.
† See Sir Hope Grant's "History of the Sepoy War."

Blunt's troops of Horse Artillery, and Major Bourchier's Battery, with one hundred and eighty European and sixty Native Artillery; two hundred Native Sappers; three hundred men of the 9th Lancers; four hundred Sikh Cavalry; four hundred and fifty men of H.M. 8th and 75th Regiments; and one thousand two hundred men of 1st and 4th Regiments Punjaub Infantry, making a total of two thousand seven hundred and ninety men and eighteen guns; whilst another column was despatched nine days afterwards under Brigadier Showers to settle accounts with the rebels in the Rewaree district, which expedition was most successful, since Brigadier Showers took four forts, seventy guns, and £80,000, and compelled the surrender of two Princes. The capture of Delhi, it may here be remarked, was accomplished by the troops under General Wilson without the aid of any of the reinforcements despatched from England on hearing of the outbreak at Meerut and Delhi. The effect of this grand success was visible at Agra, as, for instance, to the best of my remembrance, the money-changers about this time resumed their ordinary practice of giving sixteen instead of eighteen annas for the rupee, which showed that the natives had now confidence in the stability of the English Government. It is, however, rather remarkable that some regiments mutinied after the entry of our troops into Delhi, as the 50th Regiment, which revolted at Nagode on the 16th of September; the 52nd N.I., which rose at Jubbulpore on the 18th of September; two companies of the 32nd Regiment N.I., which mutinied at Deogurh on the 9th of October; three companies of the 34th Regiment N.I., stationed at Chittagong, which had remained true to their salt for six months after the outbreak at Meerut, revolted on the 18th November; they were defeated by the Silhet Light Infantry Battalion, commanded by Major the Honourable R. B. Byng, who lost his life in the engagement. The Chittagong mutineers soon afterwards, however, met with repeated defeats in rapid succession, whereby they lost more than two hundred men, and the greater portion of the few that remained, blocked up in a hilly country, perished miserably. On the 22nd of November a detachment of the 73rd Regiment N.I., consisting of about two hundred and fifty Sepoys, mutinied at Dacca on an attempt being made to disarm them by Lieutenant Lewis with eighty-five sailors and two guns. They were defeated in the battle that ensued, forty-one were killed on the spot, and eight were brought in desperately wounded, and a few more were drowned or shot in attempting to cross the river. Our small party lost eighteen in killed and wounded. Lastly, on the 4th and 5th of December, the detachment of the 11th Irregular Cavalry stationed at Mudareegunje and Julpigoree, mutinied, and went off spreading alarm through the district. But it is time now to return to Agra. Not many days after hearing the good news from Delhi we were made further joyful by hearing of the first relief of Lucknow by Havelock, on the 25th of September. To Major-General Sir James Outram, the well-known Indian Bayard, had been assigned the honour of accomplishing this glorious enterprise; since he had in August been appointed to the command of the troops in supercession of Havelock. But, on arriving at Cawnpore on the 16th of September, the first act of the most noble Outram was to leave to Havelock the glory of relieving Lucknow; for on the very day of his arrival he published an order waiving his rank in favour of Havelock, and notifying his intention of accompanying the force in his civil capacity as Chief Commissioner of Oude, and tendering his military services to Havelock as a volunteer! Well might Sir Colin Campbell, when announcing to the army this transcendent act of chivalry, make use of the following stirring language in reference to the self-sacrificing order he was called upon to confirm :—" With such a reputation as Major-General Sir James Outram has won for himself, he can well afford to share glory and honour with others. But that does not lessen the value of the sacrifice he has made with such disinterested generosity in favour of Brigadier-General Havelock, C.B., commanding the Field Force in Oude. Concurring, as the Commander-in-Chief does, in everything stated in the just eulogy of the latter by Sir James Outram, His Excellency takes this opportunity of publicly testifying to the army his admiration for an act of self-sacrifice and generosity on a point which, of all others, is dear to a real soldier." This was no exaggerated praise, nor was it by this single act that Outram was entitled to the epithet of the Indian Bayard; for his career was all of a piece; he was as an officer and a gentleman *sans peur et sans reproche*.

On the arrival at Cawnpore of the long-expected reinforcements, consisting of seventeen hundred Europeans from the 5th and 90th Queen's Regiments, the force at Havelock's disposal amounted to three thousand one hundred and seventy-nine men, viz. :—

European Infantry	2,388
Volunteer Cavalry	109
Artillery	282
Sikh Infantry	341
Irregular Cavalry	59
Total	3,179

This force was divided into the following three brigades :—

1st Brigade.—5th Fusileers, 84th Foot, two companies 64th Foot, and 1st Madras Fusileers. Commanded by Brigadier-General Neil.

2nd Brigade.—78th Highlanders, 90th Light Infantry and Sikh Regiment of Ferozpore. Commanded by Brigadier Hamilton.

3rd Brigade.—Captain Maude's Battery, Captain Oliphant's Battery, and Major Eyre's Battery. Commanded by Major Couper.

Besides these there were the volunteers, with Outram at their head, and a troop of Irregular Cavalry. On the 19th of September the English army crossed the Ganges by a bridge of boats, being feebly opposed by the enemy on the opposite bank, and on the 21st of September Havelock defeated the rebels at Mungulwar, on which occasion Sir James Outram greatly distinguished himself, by charging the enemy's battery, sword in hand, at the head of his handful of volunteers, and capturing the regimental colour of the 1st Regiment N.I. Driving the enemy before him, Havelock defeated ten thousand rebels at Alum Bagh, about six miles from Lucknow, on the 23rd of September. Having halted a day at Alum Bagh, the relieving army moved forward to accomplish their grand enterprise. It was indubitably a most hazardous undertaking, with only three thousand men to attack fifty thousand rebels under cover, and it would have been justly regarded as rash had it not been for the extreme necessity of attempting at any risk the rescue of our countrymen and countrywomen, who had been besieged for nearly three months by a horde of ruffianly rebels thirsting for their lives, and were in sore peril. Moreover, as far back as a month ago, Havelock was aware of the great danger the garrison was in from the daily attacks and mining of the enemy, who were within a few yards of their defences, as he had been apprised of this state of things from a letter received on the 23rd of August, from Colonel Inglis, the Brigadier commanding there, which letter contained this pressing reminder. "If you hope to save this force," wrote Inglis, "no time must be lost in pushing forward." Under such circumstances what might not be accomplished by Englishmen, who had seen the room, ankle-deep in blood, where hundreds of their countrywomen had been foully murdered, and had seen the well where they had been ignominiously thrown down, and when, moreover, these same men were commanded by a General who, combining skill, courage, and piety, enjoyed their complete confidence! We may depend upon it that the pious Havelock, for one at least, made it a matter of earnest prayer, and that he was in consequence divinely guided. After leaving the sick and wounded and baggage behind under a guard at Alum Bagh, our men, moved with compassion for those in sore peril and distress, advanced to meet the hated foe, Outram leading with the first brigade, and Havelock with the second. Our brave soldiers drove the enemy from a succession of gardens and walled enclosures, and crossed by the Char Bagh bridge. From thence they pushed on towards the Residency, a distance of two miles. But when they got opposite the Kaiser Bagh they suffered severely from the enemy's cannonade and musketry fire. Still they pushed on, fighting their way desperately through the streets, in the course of which the gallant Neil was shot dead. At last the Residency was reached, and the first relief of Lucknow was accomplished. The enthusiastic welcome that then met their brave deliverers from the overjoyed garrison must be left to the reader's imagination, it being well nigh indescribable. On that night Havelock and Outram (who had been wounded) clasped hands with Inglis. The entire losses of accomplishing this gallant enterprise, including the heavy loss suffered by the rear-guard next day (26th September), in forcing its way through, amounted to seven hundred and two officers and men in killed and wounded. Some idea may be formed of the terrible sufferings of the helpless women and children, and the losses of the brave defenders, in the space of only three months, when we find from Colonel Malleson's valuable history[*] that, "when the siege began the number of ladies amounted to sixty-eight, and of children sixty-six. Of the former, seven ladies, and of the latter twenty-three, succumbed to the want of suitable food, to the fire of the enemy, and to privations. We also learn from the same authority that

[*] See Malleson's "History of the Sepoy Mutiny," vol. i. p. 487.

of the nine hundred and twenty-seven Europeans, one hundred and forty were killed, or died of their wounds, and one hundred and ninety were wounded. Of the seven hundred and sixty-five natives, seventy-two were killed, and one hundred and thirty-one were wounded, and a few of them deserted. The fidelity and gallantry of the loyal remnants of the 13th, 48th, and 71st Regiments N.I. were deserving of great praise. They were chiefly posted at the Balie Guard, and were so near the enemy as to be exposed to great temptation to desert, and thereby sacrifice the beleaguered Europeans; but they nobly turned a deaf ear to every persuasion, promise, or threat made to seduce them from their allegiance. A few years afterwards, when I met the survivors, who then formed the 16th Regiment N.I. (the Lucknow Regiment), and were stationed in Fort William, I much wished to commit to writing the personal history of these men, which I thought would make a very interesting book; but they showed such an unmistakable dislike to having their fidelity thus placed on record, that I was obliged to give it up. About a week after hearing of Havelock's relief of Lucknow, we were threatened by a large force of some ten thousand rebels with thirteen guns, who were marching in our direction from Dholpore; they consisted of the Mhow mutineers (*i.e.* the 23rd Regiment N.I. and 1st Light Cavalry), the Indore rebels, and a considerable force of fugitive Sepoys from Delhi, under Prince Ferozshah, and they now determined to attack Agra, expecting only to have to cope with the 3rd Europeans, a troop of Artillery, and the Agra Militia. I had been for some time in a bad state of health (and no wonder); but when I heard, on the evening of the 9th October, that my regiment was under orders to leave the Fort next day to engage the enemy, I felt naturally most desirous to accompany it. I therefore wrote a public letter, making an earnest request that there might be a suspension of my arrest, that so I might be allowed to accompany my regiment. Early next morning (10th October), the Adjutant told me that Lieutenant-Colonel Riddell would not let me go out into action with my regiment; but at the same time he informed me that he was directed by the Commanding Officer to call my attention to the fact of my being on the sick list. Thinking that if this objection were removed I might still be allowed to go out, I immediately called in the doctor, who, about 8 A.M., took me off the sick list. A little before the commencement of the fight in cantonments about to be described, I sent my servant to the Adjutant's quarters to inquire whether he had received the surgeon's certificate, which I hoped would be the means of facilitating my wishes. Soon afterwards my man returned, telling me that the Adjutant, instead of giving him a reply, got angry with him, and told him to go to hell. Unable to gather anything from this, I went about 11 A.M. to the parade, where I found my regiment nearly ready to go out, and I at once asked the Commanding Officer for permission to accompany the regiment; but when I heard from him that Colonel Cotton would not give me leave to do so, I manifested my sense of military subordination by going back quietly to my quarters, though I felt exceedingly disappointed and deeply aggrieved. Very soon afterwards I was filled with unfeigned amazement at learning that, for the public spirit I had manifested on the occasion, an extra charge, that of breaking my arrest, was preferred against me! But I must now return to notice the doings in our behalf of Colonel Greathed's column, who, having overtaken and defeated a body of fugitive mutineers at Bolundshuhur, and having cut up a large body of rebels at Alygurh, came now to our relief on the morning of the 10th October by long forced marches, in consequence of an express sent to him by Colonel Fraser; the Chief Commissioner urging him to come to our help, and was having a fight with the enemy, which had just begun, when I asked Lieutenant-Colonel Riddell's permission to be allowed to accompany my regiment to the battle then raging in cantonments. The men had marched forty-four miles in twenty-eight hours,* and were encamped on the parade ground. They were weary and exhausted after their exertions, and were for the most part lying on the ground like thoroughly tired soldiers enjoying a rest after their long weary march, and were totally unconscious of the presence of the enemy,† who were close to them, screened from their view by the high standing crops; when suddenly, a little before 11 A.M., ere the camp was pitched, the sound of cannon was heard, and round shot came pouring into camp from three directions, and the enemy's cavalry charged our artillery, and sabred the gunners of one gun. It was a complete surprise, but it was only a momentary one. Nothing tries good troops so much as a surprise like this, which was enough to have caused a panic. But our brave soldiers soon showed the good stuff they were made of; that admirable regiment the 9th Lancers were soon in the saddle, and one squadron of that regiment gallantly charged the rebel cavalry who were cutting down our gunners, and drove them back in disorder. But this success was achieved at the cost of the loss of the officer commanding the squadron, Captain French, who was killed, and Lieutenant Jones, his subaltern, who was dangerously wounded.‡

The rest of the troops having formed up, now went

* Colonel Malleson is in error in making out that they had just traversed that morning forty-eight miles. This distinguished writer says (see pp. 93, 94, vol. ii. of his "History of the Indian Mutiny") that Colonel Greathed on the 9th October was at Bijeegurh, forty-eight miles distant from Agra, and that in consequence of urgent entreaties, Greathed sent forward the cavalry and artillery from Bijeegurh at midnight, and that four hours later he followed with his infantry, mounting his men on elephants, carts, and camels, and overtook his artillery and cavalry, and with them crossed the Jumna under the walls of the fort of Agra. This could not have been the case, for had such a prodigious feat been performed I must have heard of it, being on the spot. Moreover, the whole thing is impossible; for sixteen hundred men could not possibly have been conveyed forty-eight miles in five or six hours by means of elephants, carts, and camels.

† Raikes states that "on the morning of the 10th the magistrate and other officials assured Colonel Greathed that the enemy had fallen back." See Raikes' "Notes," p. 73.

‡ He recovered with the loss of an eye.

M

at them with a will. The enemy in their turn were surprised at finding themselves attacked by such a strong force of Europeans and Sikhs, and so many guns. Pearson's battery gave a check to the rebels, which was improved by a well-timed charge by Watson and Probyn, and a second charge of the Lancers with two squadrons of Hodson's horse quite overpowered their capability of further resistance; the sight of the 9th Lancers especially inspired the enemy with dread, since many of them had made a very unpleasant acquaintance with the gallantry of that distinguished regiment at Delhi.* The rebels then gave way and retreated in haste and disorder along the Gwalior road. Colonel Greathed followed them for three miles. Then Colonel Cotton came up with the 3rd Europeans, and assumed the command as senior officer. The infantry pursued the enemy for two miles farther, and the cavalry and artillery continued the pursuit as far as the Kalee Nuddee, a rivulet about ten miles from Agra.

The rebels lost all their guns, thirteen in number, their standing camp, and at least five hundred men in killed alone. By the time the pursuit was over, Greathed's cavalry and artillery had marched sixty-four miles, and the infantry fifty-four miles, in thirty-six hours; Greathed's loss in the action was sixty-seven killed and wounded. The wounded were carried into the Motee Musjid, in the Fort. Inside this marble temple rough wooden cots were hastily arranged, and the mattresses, pillows, and quilts made by the ladies were now turned into use. Mrs. Raikes and many other ladies tended the poor sufferers by night and day.

> "Oh woman! in our hours of ease
> Uncertain, coy, and hard to please;
> And variable as the shade
> By the light quivering aspen made:
> When pain and anguish wring the brow
> A ministering angel thou!"

* I was told that the mutineers were heard crying out, "Fly, brothers, there are the Lancers from Delhi!"

TROUBLED STATE OF RAJPOOTANA.

The soldiers felt deeply all this kindness, and when those who recovered became convalescent, they invited their lady nurses to an entertainment in the beautiful gardens of the Taj Mahal, and then these rough veterans thanked their compassionate benefactresses who had fed and waited on them in their sickness. The column halted at Agra three days following the battle, and I took the opportunity of purchasing a fine tulwar * from a soldier (who had taken it from one of the enemy); they then marched towards Cawnpore. Greathed was, however, superseded a few marches from Agra by Brigadier Hope Grant, Lieutenant-Colonel of the 9th Lancers, who overtook the column, and assumed the command as senior officer. Agra was now quite safe, and things all around us in October were as prosperous as could be expected, excepting perhaps the news that reached us about this time of the disturbed state of Rajpootana, with the damage done to British prestige by Colonel Lawrence's retiring to Ajmere after his unsuccessful attack upon the Jodhpore legion on the 18th September at Awah,† followed by the murder at Kotah, on the 15th October, of the political agent there, Major Burton, with his two sons, by the mutinous regiments of the Rajah of that state; and, lastly, of the defeat of four hundred men with two guns and a Mortar under Captain Tucker, on the 23rd October, by the Mundisore rebels at Jeerun near Neemuch, when Captain Tucker himself was killed, and four other officers were killed and wounded. The rebels were, however, in greatest strength at Lucknow, and thither it behoved Sir Hope Grant with his column, in conjunction with the Commander-in-Chief, to bend their steps as soon as possible to effect the second relief of that city; since Havelock and Outram found themselves in their

---

* Native sword.
† The English force consisted of 200 men of H.M. 83rd Foot, 250 of the Mhairwara Battalion, two squadrons of 1st Bombay Lancers, and seven guns and mortars.

turn besieged in the very place they had relieved. Throughout October there had been much severe fighting, and something like starvation stared the English garrison in the face, so that the advent of Sir Colin Campbell with his army was most anxiously expected. Sir Colin Campbell had arrived at Calcutta as Commander-in-Chief on the 13th August, and on the 28th October His Excellency having taken his departure from the city of palaces for the scene of action, reached Cawnpore on the 3rd November, and on the 9th he joined Sir Hope Grant, who with his column had been awaiting the Chief's arrival at Buntheera, six miles from Alum Bagh; and on the 14th November Sir Colin advanced towards the Alum Bagh at the head of about five thousand men. His force consisted chiefly of the movable column from Delhi, the formation of which has been already given; besides which, Sir Colin had with him the 93rd Highlanders, which had been diverted by Lord Elgin from the China Expedition, H.M. 53rd Foot, and the Naval Brigade, consisting of about two hundred and fifty sailors with six 68-pounders, two 24-pounders, and two rocket tubes under Captain William Peel (son of the celebrated Premier Sir Robert Peel), who in his way up had already fought one very sanguinary battle.* After giving a little rest to his troops at Alum Bagh, and receiving from Cawnpore a reinforcement of about six hundred and fifty men, consisting of detachments of H.M. 23rd and 82nd Foot, artillery, and engineers, the Commander-in-Chief, on the 14th November, advanced against

---

* This happened at Khujna on the 1st November, when a force of five hundred men, consisting of a party of sailors under Peel, with a detachment of H.M. 53rd Foot under Colonel Powell, attacked and defeated the Dinapore mutineers and other rebels to the number of about four thousand, with three guns. Captain Peel took the command on the death of Colonel Powell, who received a musket-ball in the forehead. Our loss was however heavy, amounting to ninety-five. Another detachment of the 53rd, with some Sikhs, under the command of Major English, had the month before defeated three thousand rebels at Chuttra after a hard fight, the English loss being heavy.

Lucknow, and carried the Dilkhoosha Park and the Martinière.

Two days afterwards (16th of November) His Excellency attacked the Secunder Bagh, a high-walled enclosure of strong masonry loopholed on all sides for musketry. Captain Blunt opened fire upon it with his six guns, followed by Captain Travers, who did the same with two 18-pounders. By their fire a breach was made in the wall sufficient to admit of two men abreast; the 93rd Highlanders and 4th Punjaub Rifles rushed through this small opening, closely followed by the 53rd Foot. The rebels fought to the bitter end with the energy of despair. But after the gates had been forced in, our troops entered the enclosure in such overwhelming numbers, that the mutineers with all their desperate fighting had not a ghost of a chance. No mercy was shown to the rebels. Cawnpore was the watchword of the enraged British soldier, and a terrible slaughter of the enemy took place; as, when at last our soldiers were masters of the place, more than two thousand corpses were found heaped one upon another, and it is said that only four rebels escaped from this fearful charnel-house. The Shah Nujeef was captured the same day (16th of November). Next day (17th) the mess-house and the Motee Mahul were stormed by Captain Garnet Wolseley.*

The second relief of Lucknow was now accomplished, and the interestingly historic meeting of the three Generals, Outram and Havelock with the Commander-in-Chief, now took place (17th of November). The English loss in these operations amounted to forty-three officers, and about four hundred and seventy men killed and wounded. The enemy's loss throughout the same was exceedingly severe, since about four thousand were found slain. On the 20th November, Sir Colin began to carry out his purpose of withdrawing the sick and wounded, with the women and children, from Luck-

* Now Sir Garnet Wolseley, K.C.B.

now, under cover of a bombardment of the Kaiser Bagh, and on the night of the 22nd of November the long train of noncombatants* commenced their retreat from the Oudean capital. The Commander-in-Chief and his army remained at the Dilkhoosha during the day and night of the 23rd of November. But having completed his arrangements, Sir Colin on the 24th marched to the Alum Bagh, where the same day that Christian hero, and brilliant general, the pious Havelock, breathed his last on earth. He succumbed to dysentery, brought on by excessive fatigue. "I die," said the Christian warrior, "happy and contented. I have for forty years so ruled my life that when death came I might face it without fear." He had, as a distinguished writer† justly observed, fought a good fight, and had died as he had lived, in the performance of duty. Havelock was buried in the Alum Bagh on the 26th November, on which mournful occasion his gallant son, Sir Colin Campbell, Hope Grant, Outram, Inglis and others attended the funeral. Leaving Sir James Outram behind at the Alum Bagh with three thousand five hundred men, Sir Colin started for Cawnpore on the 27th November at the head of about three thousand men, including the remnant of the 32nd Foot. The Chief reached Mungulwar next day (28th), and the same evening His Excellency with his staff galloped across the bridge into Cawnpore, where he heard of Windham's defeat by the Gwalior Contingent. Major General Charles A. Windham, C.B., the hero of the Redan, was in command of about two thousand three hundred men there, nearly two thousand of whom were Europeans. His force consisted of portions, or the whole, of the following Regiments: H.M. 64th Foot, the 82nd (a regiment diverted from the China Expedition),

---

* The sick and wounded, with the women and children, under the convoy of Sir Colin's force, amounted altogether to about two thousand. (See Malleson, vol. ii. p. 222.)

† Colonel Malleson's "History of the Indian Mutiny," vol. ii. p. 221.

and detachments of three regiments, H.M. 34th, 88th, and 2nd Rifle Brigade, which had been ordered to India from England about a fortnight after the scare produced by the receipt of the news of the mutinies at Meerut and Delhi. Windham had besides the 27th Madras N.I., some Artillery, a hundred Sikh Cavalry, together with some seamen belonging to the Naval Brigade. Having learnt that some twenty thousand rebels, consisting of the Gwalior Contingent and other mutineers under Tantia Topee, were within twenty miles of him on the Calpie road, he marched out on the 26th November with about one thousand two hundred Infantry, one hundred Sikh Cavalry, and eight guns and defeated a division of them at Pundoo Nuddee, eight miles from Cawnpore. But finding this was but their advanced column, he fell back and encamped outside the town. Next day (27th) Windham's camp was attacked by the rebels in overwhelming numbers, who began with a terrific cannonade. Assailed from three sides at the same time, and perceiving after five hours' fighting that his flanks were being turned, that the enemy were also getting into the city, and were about to attack the entrenchment near the bridge of boats, Windham resolved to fall back on that position, as his present post was no longer tenable. The so-styled retreat was, in point of fact, a regular *sauve qui peut* affair. Our men rushed back in time to save the entrenchment; but they suffered severely from the fire of their pursuers, who captured the English camp and burnt five hundred tents. The English General next day (28th November) attempted to recover the ground he had so ingloriously lost; but it only resulted in an increase of humiliation. Windham divided his force into four columns. One, under Colonel Walpole, was to defend the advanced portion of the town; a second, under Colonel Wilson, was to hold the entrenchment; whilst a third, under Brigadier Carthew, was directed to hold the Bithoor road; and the fourth, under Windham himself, was to defend that portion of the town nearest the Ganges on the left of the canal. A severe struggle now ensued. The Gwalior Contingent, having been joined by a force under the infamous Nana Sahib, now numbered twenty-one thousand men, and, flushed with victory, were eager for the fight. Walpole on his side was pretty successful, inasmuch as he repulsed a vigorous attack of the enemy. But Carthew, who struggled from morning till night against a most formidable body of the enemy, was at last compelled to fall back upon the intrenchment to prevent his being cut off, as Colonel Wilson, who had sallied out to his assistance with his column, chiefly consisting of H.M. 64th Foot, was driven back to the entrenchment with great loss. That officer, with his men, after almost reaching some of the enemy's guns, encountered a large rebel force hitherto hidden, who outnumbered the assailants by ten to one, and who rendered their further advance quite impracticable. Colonel Wilson himself was here killed, as were also Major Stirling, Captains McCrea, and Murphey, whilst many other officers were wounded, and the slaughter of the rank and file of the 64th was proportionately great. By the evening the whole force retired into the entrenchments. Windham's loss in the three days' fight amounted to three hundred and fifteen. But the loss of prestige was of still greater consequence; for the English were completely vanquished.

Moreover, the town of Cawnpore, and houses full of clothing and stores prepared for the reception of the convoy of Lucknow fugitives, fell into the enemy's hands. They also captured ten thousand rounds of Enfield cartridges, the mess plate of four Queen's regiments, Paymasters' chests, and other property. On the following morning (29th) the rebels began to bombard the entrenchments and the bridge of boats. But this judicious movement on the part of the sagacious foe

SIR COLIN CAMPBELL'S STRATEGY.

was interfered with by Sir Colin Campbell, who at this crisis appeared on the scene. This day (29th) and the following His Excellency was engaged crossing to Cawnpore with his small army and their precious charge; but even when this was accomplished, Sir Colin was still content to remain a little longer on the defensive, as the first thought of the gallant Chief was for the safety of the women and children; nor was His Excellency provoked even by the cannonade which the enemy opened on his tents on the 2nd of December to alter his plans.

But at last, in the night of the 3rd of December, these helpless ones were despatched under a strong escort to Allahabad, and three days afterwards, when they had got a good start, Sir Colin felt free to act. The enemy's force was now about twenty-four thousand strong, only one-half of whom, however, were trained soldiers; the remainder consisted of the undisciplined followers of the Ranee of Jhansi and the Nana Sahib. They occupied a strong position, with their centre in the city of Cawnpore, the principal streets of which were barricaded, their left in the old cantonments, whilst their right stretched away beyond the Grand Trunk Road and the Canal, which positions were defended by forty guns. But Sir Colin's quick eye discerned a weak point in their position, which was that one wing of their army was so isolated as to be incapable of receiving support from the other divisions, provided it were properly attacked; that, in fact, the enemy's right was in such a position that if vigorously attacked it could be driven from its position without assistance being able to come to it from any other part of the line. The Commander-in-Chief's force consisted of about five thousand Infantry, six hundred Cavalry, and thirty-five guns. His infantry were divided into four Brigades, beginning with that which was called the 3rd, consisting of the 8th, 64th, and 2nd Punjaub Infantry, under the command of Brigadier Greathed; the 4th, commanded by

Brigadier Adrian Hope, was composed of the 42nd* Highlanders, the 53rd Foot, 93rd† Highlanders, and the 4th Punjaub Rifles; the 5th was under the command of Brigadier Inglis, and was composed of the 23rd Fusiliers,† the shattered 32nd Regiment and the 82nd;† and the 6th was commanded by Brigadier Walpole, and consisted of the 2nd* and 3rd* Battalions Rifle Brigade, and a detachment of the 38th Regiment. The cavalry, consisting of the 9th Lancers, and detachments of the 1st, 2nd and 5th Punjaub Cavalry, and Hodson's horse, were under the command of Brigadier Little.

The artillery consisted of the Naval Brigade, led by Peel, the troops of Blunt and Remington, the batteries of Bourchier, Middleton, Smith, Longden, and Bridge, and was under the command of Dupuis. Brigadier Hope Grant acted as second in command to the Commander-in-Chief. On Sunday the 6th of December Sir Colin drew his sword, and went at the enemy in earnest, with the design of cutting them up in detail by first severing the rebel right wing from the main body. The battle was commenced by a brisk artillery combat, which lasted about two hours. A slackening of Windham's cannonade from the entrenchment announced that the time for attack had now arrived. The cavalry and horse artillery made a sweeping détour with the object of menacing the enemy's rear, while the whole line advanced against the rebel right wing. H.M. 53rd Foot and 4th Punjaub Rifles with admirable gallantry rushed on in the face of a very heavy fire of shot and shell, and drove the enemy from their position on the mounds. They next rushed at the bridge, where guns were planted, whilst the enemy's Infantry, having rallied, poured upon them incessant volleys of musketry, and seemed prepared to offer a stubborn resistance, when Peel and his sailors brought forward a 24-pounder, and opened a very

* These regiments were ordered out from home to India in July in consequence of the Mutiny scare.
† These were the regiments diverted from the China Expedition.

effective fire. " Nothing," says Sir Hope Grant, "could withstand the impetuous attack of the Sikhs and Europeans."* The 53rd Foot, the 4th Sikhs, and the Highlanders, passing by the guns, rushed upon the enemy, captured their guns, and drove them back helter-skelter. The defeated rebels were then pursued for fifteen miles on the Calpie road. Thus Sir Colin's stratagem of severing one wing from the main body was crowned with success; but His Excellency did not succeed so well in carrying out the rest of his design, as the enemy's centre and left managed to retreat with their guns to Bithoor.† The English loss in this important victory only amounted to ninety-nine in killed and wounded. Sir Hope Grant started off with a strong column in pursuit on the 8th December, and overtook the rebels next day at Serai Ghaut, twenty-five miles from Cawnpore, where they were about to cross by the ferry into Oude. Grant defeated them, and captured fifteen guns belonging to the Gwalior Contingent, his own loss being nil! The victor's despatch was so remarkable for its pious tone, that it deserves to be specially recorded. " I am truly grateful to God," wrote the devout Brigadier, "and happy to say, that though the fire of the grape from the enemy was most severe, and well placed, falling among the artillery like hail, I had not a single man even wounded, and only one horse of Captain Middleton's Battery killed. It was truly marvellous and providential."

Thus did Grant honour his God in his professional calling as a General. Would that all similarly placed in authority did likewise! But it is time now to return to Agra. November passed with us in quiet. The Jodhpore legion, defeated at Narnol by Colonel Gerrard‡ on the 16th of November, crossed the Jumna

---

* See Sir Hope Grant's " History of the Sepoy War."

† Bithoor is north-west of Cawnpore; their retreat so far was, therefore, in a different direction to that pursued by the defeated right wing.

‡ Colonel Gerrard lost his life in the engagement.

between Alygurh and Agra, but without coming near enough to disturb our equanimity. Next month a detachment of my regiment served with Brigadier Seaton's column at the battle of Gungeree (14th of December), on which occasion the Carabiniers, in charging the enemy's guns, lost three of their officers, Wardlaw, Hudson, and Vyse, who were killed, and Lieutenant Head, who led a handful of Lancers, was dangerously wounded. The rebels were, however, completely defeated, and lost their guns. The same detachment of my regiment was also present at the battle of Puttialee, on the 17th of December, on which occasion the rebels were pursued for seven miles, and it was computed that not less than 600 of them fell in the field or during the pursuit. They also lost thirteen guns. But it is time now to turn from chronicling the doings of my regiment to an event of the greatest importance concerning myself. This was my trial by Court-martial on the 10th of December, 1857, on the following charge :—

"With having, at Agra, on the 10th of October, 1857, when under arrest, and expressly prohibited from appearing in public, broken his arrest, and in violation of it proceeded to the parade ground of his regiment in the Fort of Agra, between the hours of 9 and 11 o'clock, at the time the regiment was assembled on the parade." My defence was based on three grounds. First, the extreme unjustifiableness of the imposition of the arrest in question, since I had committed no fault whatever to deserve it, and which was on grounds so utterly untenable, that it was not thought advisable to have me tried thereon, and that the whole business, in fact, arose from my right to appeal against the harsh treatment of me by my Commanding Officer being denied me, as I showed, by incorporating in my defence a true copy of my letter to the Commander-in-Chief, for writing which I was placed under arrest on a charge " of un-officer-like and litigious conduct." But the Court did not think it prudent that the Commander-in-Chief should see a true copy of his own letter! They therefore, for fear of giving offence to the local authorities, expunged the whole of this part of my defence bodily from the Court-martial proceedings, and so my defence was thereby shorn of part of its strength in consequence of the embarrassing circumstances of my antagonism to the station and divisional authorities, which made the Court afraid to offend them by allowing to go up to headquarters this essential part of my defence. Thus I experienced once more that a subaltern has no chance of getting strict impartial justice, when his judges have in trying him to pass an indirect sort of judgment upon their immediate superiors, who have it in their power to do so much, either to advance or to mar the interests of these temporary judges; and it only shows the necessity of having a professional lawyer, qualified by legal abilities, an independent position, and the possession of a judicious restraining power to secure the ends of justice, so as to prevent the guilty from escaping with impunity, and more especially to prevent the commission of downright injustice towards the innocent who happen to be obnoxious to the local military authorities. The second ground of my defence was that I had reason to expect that I should be allowed to go out with my regiment to the battle then raging in cantonments, inasmuch as an officer when under arrest actually went out to the battle of Sussia on the 5th of July, 1857, without being brought to a Court-martial, whereas I, on being refused permission to go out on the 10th of October, manifested my subordination by going back quietly to my quarters. The third reason adduced in my defence was that my intentions were innocent and honourable; that "I did not leave my quarters to go to a ball, picnic, card-table, billiard-room, or the mess; but I went with the warm feelings of an English soldier eager to do battle in a just cause."

I protested my unconsciousness of harm in the following words, viz.: "As an officer who is in the habit of making the performance of all known military duties a matter of conscience (in the discharge of which duties, I desire not merely to approve myself to my military superiors, but also to my Heavenly superior). As such, as a God-fearing man, I deny that I have been guilty of anything mentally criminal in this matter." This solemn protestation of my innocence was treated as long-winded cant, since the Court found me guilty, and sentenced me to be cashiered. This was followed by a recommendation to mercy "on account of the peculiar circumstances" in which I broke my arrest, viz., my desire to accompany my corps into action.* I have no patience, even at this distance of time, to speak of the hard-heartedness of several officers composing the minority of the members of the Court, who, by their declining to join in the recommendation to mercy, condemned an innocent man, as far as they could, to temporal ruin. I consider their conduct worse than the bitterest enemies I have ever had in my whole lifetime. My Commanding Officer hated me with all his heart, and, consequently, it was but natural that he should do his best to get rid of me. But these officers (whose names I am glad to be ignorant of) were supposed to be impartial judges of the merits of the case, and were sworn to administer justice without favour, partiality, or affection, and therefore I cannot find the slightest excuse for their hard-hearted conduct. It is very remarkable, so at least I think, that nearly all who were in any way concerned in bringing me to this Court-martial on the 10th of December, 1857, met with extraordinary deaths within a few months afterwards.

My Commanding Officer, it is true, did not die, but not many months afterwards, when we were at Dholpore, he was the talk of many mouths, because he did not proceed with the 3rd Europeans to the attack on Gwalior, in pursuance of the orders sent him by Sir Hugh Rose, commanding the Central Indian Force. But

* See "General Court-Martial Proceedings."

though Colonel Riddell lived to retire from the service some years afterwards, a different fate befell the others. The Adjutant of my regiment died of heat apoplexy on the line of march, and here a sort of burial question cropped up. For, by a strange coincidence, through indisposition and other causes, I became the senior available officer to command the burial party and conduct the funeral service. So here the difficulty arose, for the Colonel knew that I should refuse to read the Church of England burial service over the grave, since I had given offence before in declining to read that service over soldiers of my company I had buried. My reason for this was that I considered it a solemn mockery of God to use such words over the graves of men I believed to be unconverted, as those in the prayer speaking of the Almighty of his great mercy taking unto Himself the soul of "our dear brother," and of our therefore committing his body to the ground "in sure and certain hope of the resurrection to eternal life through our Lord Jesus Christ."

Colonel Riddell, not wishing to have anything unpleasant occurring at the funeral of his Adjutant, proposed a compromise, which I at once consented to; which was, that having marched the funeral procession to the grave, I should then request one of the junior officers to read the burial service. Then Colonel Cotton, commanding the fort and station of Agra, died suddenly a few months after my trial. The General of Division was killed in an ambuscade on the 30th of April, 1858. He was marching by night to Budaon when he was all at once attacked in the dark at Kukraolee, whilst riding at the head of the advanced guard. Penny was never seen alive again; his charger, it appears, took fright, and carried him right into the ranks of the enemy, where his body was afterwards found, shot, stripped, and gashed. The General's military adviser, the Assistant-Adjutant-General Meerut Division, was, I believe, about a fortnight afterwards murdered by some rebels near Ferozabad in the middle of the night whilst travelling by gharee with another officer. It is not pleasant to speak of these sad matters, but I feel impelled just to notice them, occurring under the particular circumstances, and at the particular time they did, which I do without any comment.

But I must return to Agra, to mention its condition at the beginning of 1858. British rule had some two or three months before been re-established, and Anglo-Indians had resumed their ordinary employments. In January, the Fort was in the course of being abandoned by every one who had a house which could be made decently habitable. But many people were compelled to prolong their residence within its walls, as so many houses had been so completely destroyed that it would take a considerable time before they could be made fit to live in.

On the 22nd of this month (January) a strong force left Agra for Cawnpore in charge of the siege train of nineteen guns, and 1,500 carts loaded with stores, and ammunition for the Commander-in-Chief's use; several ladies here took advantage of this opportunity to pack up, and go to Calcutta. January passed without my hearing anything about the result of my Court-martial, nor did I get the slightest hint about what that might be. But, though I could not but be very anxious to know whether I was to be cashiered or not, yet, thanks be to God, I was surprisingly composed, considering it involved a question of utter ruin in regard to temporal concerns. I poured out my heart to God, and he heard me. My heart was stayed, trusting in the Lord, so that I enjoyed a considerable degree of mental tranquillity. I was certainly far more at ease than my dear old mother at home, who was actually very ill with anxiety on my account. "My love to you is," wrote my mother, "and ever has been, of so ardent and tender a nature, that I feel if you were in the distress that this (being cashiered) would involve you in, I should either die or my mind would go." Though under arrest I was ordered to proceed with my regiment to take part in the hot weather campaign of 1858. But here two serious difficulties arose. The first was that if I were cashiered, which is the sole and particular punishment awardable for breaking one's arrest, that then I might be kept for months without pay, without being able to leave my regiment to return to Agra, except at the imminent risk of being murdered on the way by rebels. But this difficulty did not prevent my Commanding Officer taking me with him. The second difficulty was this, that all my tents had been looted by the budmashes on the 5th of July, and, placed as I was, I had no opportunity of purchasing such requirements for the line of march.

This embarrassment was disposed of by granting me an exemption from my arrest for one day, to enable me to purchase such tents as I might require, besides which I required a pony. On the 11th of February I left Agra with my regiment in company with the great convoy of women and children (among whom were my wife and children) that were bound for Calcutta. At last, some days after leaving Agra, a letter came from the Commander-in-Chief's camp, then at Cawnpore, relative to my Court-martial. I then heard what a severe sentence had been passed by the Court, and that the Commander-in-Chief had not confirmed it, but had instead directed my release from arrest and my return to duty without conveying the slightest censure to me for anything I had done![*] On my sword being restored to me, I returned at once to the performance of my regimental duties; but I ought immediately to have been appointed as Interpreter and Quartermaster to my regiment, as that post had been vacated by Lieutenant F. Stephenson, and I was the only qualified[†]

[*] See General Order, in my possession. See also "Court-Martial Proceedings."
[†] Duly qualified according to the regulations of the service, by having passed the military interpreter's examination.

officer of the 3rd Europeans present with the regiment.

But Lieutenant S——, an officer more than six years junior to me, and belonging to a regiment that had mutinied, was suffered to hold an appointment that was mine by right. Had Lieutenant S—— been a high-souled man, anything like Outram, he would at once have thrown up the appointment, and told Colonel Riddell that he could not think of depriving me of my rights. Lieutenant S——, however, did nothing of the sort; he was wise in his generation, and acted on the principle that possession is nine-tenths of the law. I thus lost an extra allowance of £200 a year which by right was mine.* Acting under the impression that I was entitled to the Interpretership and Quartermastership on the grounds already stated, I appealed to the Commander-in-Chief against the Interpretership of my regiment being held by an officer from another regiment to my prejudice. But I was forestalled by my Commanding Officer's making an unfavourable report of me in those privileged communications which are received as truths not to be questioned, and so instead of justice I only got a reprimand for my pains. But still, though I had no opportunity of rebutting the false report that prejudiced my case, I was determined to wait patiently, expecting that the time would come when my rectitude would be acknowledged. *Magna est veritas, et prevalebit.* I had to wait till the end of the following year for this to happen, and in the interim things got worse and worse, as the most ungenerous and cruel taunts were heaped on me, such as his openly telling me at orderly

* The truth of this can be shown by what happened in 1870, when I was appointed Interpreter to H.M. 4th Hussars, stationed at Meerut, and when on my proceeding there to take up my appointment I found that the Commanding Officer of that cavalry regiment would not acknowledge my nomination, though it was made by the Commander-in-Chief himself, because a young officer of the 4th Hussars whom he wanted to be Interpreter had just passed the required examination; and so the Commander-in-Chief had to cancel his own appointment, and appointed me Interpreter to a regiment in the Punjaub instead.

room, that I had better resign the service, as I should be better off as a clerk on fifty rupees a month; and injustice was added to injustice, till at last I was actually compelled, when stationed in 1859 at Morar (Gwalior), to perform Interpreter's work in addition to my regimental duties, without receiving an Interpreter's pay, and this at a time when qualified officers were in such great demand that there were only six who had passed the prescribed Interpreter's examination with forty-nine of H.M. Royal regiments of infantry and cavalry in the Bengal Presidency. Moreover, in the most flagrant defiance of the rules and regulations laid down on the subject, there were no less than fifteen officers appointed Interpreters to these regiments who had only passed in the rudimental examination known as the colloquial test (though it were more fitly described as the vernacular farce), whilst five more of these precious regimental Interpreters had not even passed in this simplest of examinations,* and this at a time when they might have had at any moment to interpret in cases of life and death! Whilst I could not get even one of these contemptuously treated appointments, simply because my Commanding Officer, who hated me like poison, stabbed my character behind my back without my having any opportunity given me of refuting his assertions. So that in one way I was treated more unfairly than even the persecuted Apostle Paul, for he at least had the opportunity of answering his accusers face to face (Acts xxiv.). But I could not obtain this opportunity, not even when Colonel Riddell had the assurance to tell me, on the 23rd of February, 1859, that he had reported to the Commander-in-Chief that he could not trust me for any independent command on the grounds of my incapacity as an officer. For, feeling that my very livelihood was imperilled by such a malicious report, I sent in an appeal to the Commander-in-Chief through the regular channels of communication, entreating as a

* See Bengal Army List, corrected to July, 1859.

matter of justice to me that he would order a strict inquiry into the matter. But, as usual, I could not get my appeal forwarded by either Brigadier or General.* If I had obtained an inquiry I could have completely confounded my accuser by two questions:

1st. Why, if he could not trust me, was I allowed to lead a company in every battle from 1857 to 1859?

2nd. In the hot weather campaign of 1858, when we were facing the enemy at Sheregurh Ghaut with only the river between us, and when Colonel Riddell on a certain day appeared to be under great apprehensions of a night attack, then if he could not trust me, why did he on that particular night entrust me with the responsible duty of ascertaining the designs of the enemy? and did I not perform this duty to his entire satisfaction, and to the removal of his anxiety?†

He must have answered in the affirmative, or he would have been met with the question: Why, if he was not satisfied with my report, did he not adopt such special extra precautions as though he expected a night attack? I might also have asked, Why, if I was unworthy of trust, was I employed to hold a village with my company at the action at Sheregurh Ghaut on the 15th of May, 1858? I should have also asked some very awkward questions to answer, as to how my authority had been upheld amongst my junior officers and the men of the regiment. The fact is, that I was badgered and worried to that degree, that there were some moments when I have felt a strong inclination to do something desperate. But excepting such transient moments, when passion unknown to any human eye shook my frame, I maintained an attitude of surprising calmness; so that my mother, who was most anxious for me to keep quiet, expressed her great satisfaction

---

* See public letter of Brigade Major and Assistant-Adjutant-General, in my possession.

† This I performed with much difficulty, groping about on hands and knees in the rugged ravines of the river.

with me. "It is a manifest injustice," she wrote, "making you do Interpreter's work and not giving you the pay, but your wise and temperate conduct is a match for any that are unfriendly to you." I attribute this to the fact that I was trusting in the Lord, and expected that matters would be so ordered by One above that it would all come right in time ; and so it did, for towards the end of 1859, Lord Clyde, Commander-in-Chief, came to Morar (Gwalior), and thus I got the very opportunity I wanted, for I was determined to have a few quiet words with the Chief. So, donning my full dress, I went to the General's house, where Lord Clyde was staying as an honoured guest. I at once asked and obtained an interview. Without giving the whole of the long conversation that ensued (though it was so very interesting to me that I committed it to writing verbatim immediately on my return home), I may yet mention the salient portions thereof. In the first place I told His Excellency about my very hard case in having been kept out of an Interpretership so long, and my having been made to do the work of Interpreter without receiving the pay. I then went on to speak of my grievance of the unredressed personal violence done me, and said, that feeling myself aggrieved, I had appealed to His Excellency. I laid stress on this part of my speech, maintaining that the articles of war allow an officer in such a case to appeal.

This his Lordship did not deny. It was then Lord Clyde's turn to speak. His Excellency told me that I might have an inquiry. Whereupon I expressed my delight, and here the interview might have ended, only the Chief, after making an observation about some inconvenience to the service this would occasion, addressed me in the following words: "What you want now is an appointment. Send in an application through your Commanding Officer." I then, after a little further conversation, took my leave, and immediately sent in my application for an Interpretership through Colonel Darvall, who had recently been appointed to the command of the 3rd Europeans, and next month my name appeared in General Orders as Interpreter to H.M. 6th Foot.* Moreover, some months afterwards, when on his departure for England he gave a grand levee at Calcutta, I had the honour of being specially noticed by his Lordship, who entered into a kind conversation with me. I think all this shows that Lord Clyde felt that I was an injured man.†

But it is now full time to return from this long digression to give an account of the movable column I belonged to, and of the hot weather campaign of 1858. Having taken leave of my wife and children at Mynpoorie, I marched afterwards with my regiment to Etawah, where we stayed a considerable time. Our mess supplies were good and abundant, notwithstanding the disturbed state of the country. We had a good mess manager who arranged things for us economically and well. In regard to drinkable commodities, wine, beer, or brandy were not to be had for love or money. The choice lay between tea, water and country rum, and ginger beer. I spent a good deal of my leisure time in the ruined church, which was my favourite place of lounge. I think it was whilst we were there that we heard of the conquest of Lucknow by Sir Colin Campbell. This important event must now be told. But first it will be desirable to notice a few preliminary events; which may be summed up briefly as follows:—On the 3rd January, 1858, Futtygurh was reoccupied by the Commander-in-Chief after the rebels had been completely defeated, and

* See General Orders by Commander-in-Chief, 30th January, 1860.

† I feel sure that this was long afterwards the impression that prevailed at the Adjutant-General's Office, for towards the end of 1872, when I applied for two years' furlough, I had for the first time to send in with my application, for the information of the Home Government, a record of all my Courts-martial. I was then allowed, as a very special case, to send it in interspersed with various pungent remarks of my own, and stating a few grave facts completely vindicating my conduct as an officer, and showing how abominably I had been ill-used; and this document, I suppose, may now be seen at the India Office, unless it had been torn up on my retirement from the service in 1875.

pursued for several miles with terrible slaughter the previous day. His Excellency then having ordered a siege train to be sent from Agra for use against the Lucknow rebels, returned to Cawnpore on the 4th February, and on the 28th February Sir Colin crossed the Ganges for the conquest of the Oudean capital, at the head of a splendid army, which comprised nearly half of the whole force sent out from England* for the suppression of the Mutiny. During this month the enemy had been making a succession of desperate attacks on the position of Sir James Outram, whom Sir Colin, as already mentioned, had left behind at Alum Bagh. Outram had with him H.M. 5th, 84th, 90th, and 98th Regiments, the 1st Madras Fusileers, the Ferozpore Regiment, 27th Madras N.I., and the Madras Sappers. Twenty thousand rebels attacked the Alum Bagh on the 21st February, and were driven back with the loss of three hundred and forty men killed and wounded; and they were again defeated when they to the number of thirty thousand made a desperate attack on Outram. But it is time now to speak of an important diversion which had been made in our favour by Jung Bahadur, the Prime Minister and virtual ruler of the independent Kingdom of Nepaul, who had already sent a force to our aid, which had fought for us in the Azimgurh district and had defeated the rebels in three engagements in September and October. Afterwards, in conformity with an agreement entered into with Earl Canning, Jung Bahadur himself, in the last month of that most momentous year, descended into the plains, and expelled the rebels from Goruckpore, on the 6th January, 1858. Then, having for several weeks been engaged in suppressing bands of insurgents in the Goruckpore district, he and Brigadier MacGregor with the Nepaulese army entered Oude on the east to cut off the rebels in that direction,

* Throughout 1857 and up to April, 1858, there were sent over to India forty-two thousand royal troops and five thousand Europeans belonging to the service of the Honourable East India Company.

and to join in the final capture of Lucknow. Notice must here be taken of the Jaunpore Field Force, which was marching from the east *viâ* Fyzabad to join His Excellency before Lucknow. This strong division, under the command of Brigadier-General Franks, C.B., had been employed in expelling bands of rebels from the Azimgurh, Allahabad, and Jaunpore districts, and had defeated the insurgents in several engagements. His force comprised H.M. 10th, 20th, and 97th Regiments, six regiments of Goorkhas, and twenty guns, representing a total of two thousand three hundred Europeans, and three thousand two hundred Goorkhas. Franks, a most energetic officer, having crossed the frontier of Oude, defeated the rebel leader Bunda Hoosein on the 19th February at Chandah, and Nazim Hoosein the same day at Humeerpore, in both which engagements the enemy lost eight hundred men in killed and wounded and six guns; and on the 23rd February Franks completely defeated the main body at Sooltanpore, consisting of twenty-five thousand men (of whom, however, only six thousand were disciplined troops) and twenty-five guns. In this battle the rebels lost eighteen hundred men in killed and wounded, with twenty guns and their camp, which were captured by the victors, who then pushed forward unmolested towards Lucknow, where they joined the Commander-in-Chief on the 5th March. Before, however, coming to the narration of the capture of that city mention must be made of the gallant achievement of Sir Hope Grant, who, with a movable column consisting of three thousand two hundred and forty-six men, captured by storm the strongly fortified town of Meeangunje (between Lucknow and Futtygurh) on the 20th February. In the assault, which was admirably and gallantly performed, not less than five hundred rebels were killed, whilst Grant's loss was only two men killed and nineteen wounded.

And now I shall give an account of the closing event in this chapter, the taking of Lucknow. But a few words must first be given to the state of affairs there. Grant tells us that in the interval between Sir Colin Campbell's return to Cawnpore and his final advance on 2nd March, 1858, "the rebels had fortified their stronghold to the utmost extent of which they were capable;" and that in addition to the erection of earthworks and stockades, every house had been loop-holed, and placed in a state of defence.* That highly distinguished officer computes the strength of the insurgents at thirty thousand Sepoys, fifty thousand volunteers, and a hundred pieces of ordnance. Whilst Colonel Malleson estimates the number of men belonging to trained regiments, new levies and irregulars, in Lucknow at ninety-six thousand men, which with artillery and the followers of the Talookdars he computes at not less than a hundred and twenty thousand men.† Whilst Mr. Charles Raikes, who was Civil Commissioner with Sir Colin Campbell, estimates the number of armed men in Lucknow at about two hundred thousand. The rebels in Lucknow ‡ were animated by the presence of Huzrut Muhul, the Begum of Oude, a woman of indomitable energy but of impure morals, who had been the soul of the insurrection. This lady, who professed to be the regent for her son, a minor, the scion of Wajid Aly, the deposed King of Oude (then a state prisoner at Calcutta), was very naturally at the head of the opposition against the English, since they had unjustly deprived her husband of his throne.

The next leader of importance was the Moulvie, a noted opponent of British rule. On the 1st March Sir Colin Campbell arrived in the vicinity of Lucknow. Several days were occupied with preliminary operations. On being joined by Brigadier Franks' division, the total force at the disposal of the Commander-in-Chief on the 5th March, for the capture of the rebel city, amounted

* See Sir Hope Grant's "History of the Sepoy War."
† Malleson's "History of the Indian Mutiny," vol. ii. p. 360.
‡ Raikes' "Notes of Revolt of N.W. Provinces," p. 98.

to twenty-six thousand men and two hundred guns, which six days afterwards was still further strengthened by the arrival of the Nepaulese army under Maharajah Jung Bahadur. On the 2nd March Sir Colin advanced with a portion of his army against the Dilkhoosha palace, which was occupied by our troops the following day. On the 6th of March Sir James Outram with a strong force* and thirty guns crossed the river Goomtee, over two floating bridges made of empty beer casks lashed to cross pieces of wood, covered with a firm roadway of planking, at a point of the river where it was about forty yards wide, and pitched his camp on the left bank near the Fyzabad road so as to cut off access to the city from the north. This operation was accomplished with the loss of only a dozen men killed and wounded. Next day (7th) Outram was attacked by the enemy in great force. He, however, repelled them, and fairly drove them back; and on the 9th March, after some further fighting, Outram advanced to the Badshah Bagh, which he occupied, and whence he commenced an enfilading fire on the Kaiser Bagh. The Martinière was the same day (9th) taken by storm by the troops under the command of Sir E. Lugard, the enemy making but a feeble resistance. The Begum Kothee (Queen's palace) next fell into our hands on the 11th March, being stormed by the 93rd Highlanders and 4th Punjaub Rifles. The Sepoys fought well; but the Highlanders and Sikhs, emulating each other in bravery, expelled the enemy, who left six hundred corpses behind them. This fight was described by Sir Colin as "the sternest struggle which occurred during the siege." Amongst those who fell on our side (and our loss was comparatively small) was Captain Hodson, the captor

---

* Comprising H.M. 23rd Fusileers, 79th Highlanders, two battalions Rifle Brigade, the 1st Bengal Fusileers, 3rd Punjaub Infantry, H.M. 2nd Dragoon Guards, 9th Lancers, detachments of 1st, 2nd, and 5th Punjaub Cavalry, D'Aguilar's troop Horse Artillery, Remington's troop R.A., M'Kinnon's troop, Middleton and Gibbons' light field batteries.

of the King of Delhi. The Imambara of Ghazee-oo-deen Hyder was taken by storm on the 14th March. Directly this was done Brassier's Sikhs, pressing forward in pursuit of the fleeing enemy, entered the Kaiser Bagh unopposed, which thus unexpectedly fell into our hands with seventy guns. The booty found here was immense, consisting of diamonds and emerald necklaces, pearls, and jewels of every description,* and shawls, which were quickly seized by the soldiers. Whilst this was going on, Sir James Outram had been co-operating on his side of the river by cannonading the enemy's position, and he had, moreover, occupied the left bank of the river as far as the iron suspension bridge.

Next day (15th) twenty thousand rebels escaped from Lucknow to Fyzabad. On the 16th Outram crossed the river, and marched through the city amidst some hard fighting at one point, and then he rested for the night at Azof-oo-Dowlah's Imambara. The Commander-in-Chief was now virtually master of Lucknow, and he was so in every sense on the 21st March, as on that day the Oudean capital was completely cleared of rebels after a sharp contest with the Moulvie, who was dislodged from his stronghold in the city by the 93rd Highlanders and 4th Punjaub Rifles, under Sir E. Lugard, whose cavalry pursued and cut down the flying rebels for six miles. The British loss from the 2nd March up to this date amounted to one hundred and twenty-seven officers and men killed, and five hundred and ninety-five wounded. All resistance at Lucknow was now at an end, and the Oude army was broken up into several columns, which were dispatched in different directions where they were needed. But Sir Colin Campbell was deprived of the full fruit of his great achievement by the escape of by far the greatest part of the mutineers, a very inconsiderable part only of them having been killed in all these operations leading to the capture of the rebellious city. It may be open to some

* See Sir Hope Grant's "History of the Sepoy Revolt."

doubt as to whether a city of such magnitude as that of Lucknow could be properly invested with the forces at the Commander-in-Chief's disposal. But still I cannot help thinking that the easy escape of the mutineers was in a very considerable degree attributable to the excessive caution of the cautious Scot, in wishing to spare the lives of his men. For it appears that Sir Colin Campbell would not sanction Outram's plan for cutting off their retreat, as Colonel Malleson informs us that when, at a critical period of the advance, Outram proposed to co-operate with the Commander-in-Chief, in a manner that would have rendered the victory of the latter absolutely decisive, the proposal was refused in language unworthy of Sir Colin Campbell, he (Outram) being forbidden to cross the iron bridge "if he thought he should lose a man."[*] And Dr. Russell says,[†] "Had Sir Colin Campbell not bound Outram's hands so tightly the advance would have taken place, and a tremendous slaughter of the enemy must have followed." I have never seen Sir James Outram, and have never been in any way benefited by him, but I never throughout my Indian service knew personally or by reputation any one whose character I so lovingly admired. He is well known as the Bayard of India. This grand title was spontaneously accorded to that noble man by the general acclamation of the Indian public, who have bestowed that proud appellative on no second individual. It is time now to notice the grand doings of Sir H. Rose. But the narration of the brilliant successes achieved by that able commander must be told in the next chapter.

[*] See 2nd volume Colonel Malleson's "History of the Indian Mutiny."
[†] See "My Diary in India," by W. H. Russell.

CHAPTER VII.

Commander-in-Chief's Operations in Rohilcund—Defeats Rebels and Captures Bareilly—Brilliant Campaign of Sir H. Rose—Defeats Tantia Topee near Jhansi—Captures the City—Takes the Fort by Storm—Victories of Koonch and Gulowlie—Capture of Calpie—Doings of our Column in co-operation with Sir H. Rose—Engagement at Shereghur Ghaut—Narrow Escape of being Shot in Bed—Defeat of the Maharajah of Gwalior by Tantia Topee—Flight of Scindiah to Agra—We march to Dholpore—Remain there though ordered to Gwalior—Sir H. Rose captures Gwalior—Napier's Victory over Tantia Topee—Successful Operations of the Columns of Showers, Stuart, and Rowcroft—Disaster of Colonel Milman—Victories of Lord Mark Kerr, Sir E. Lugard, and Brigadier Douglas—Second Disaster of Arrah—Victories of Lugard, Havelock, Roberts, and Whitlock—Blunder of Walpole—Victories of Walpole, Hope Grant, Seaton, and Jones—We return to Agra—Illness—Placed under Arrest—Released by the Brigadier—Transferred to the Service of the Crown—Queen's Proclamation—Cold Weather Campaign of 1858-59—Defeats of Tantia Topee—Serve under Brigadier Showers—Battle of Dowsa—Complete Suppression of the Revolt—Operations of Lord Clyde—Victory of Sir Hope Grant—The Nana and other Leaders driven into Nepaul—Remarks—Ordered to Gwalior—Curse of Drinking and Debt Exemplified—Ordered to Futtygurh—Description of an Indian March—Leave my Regiment to take up an Appointment at Benares—Ordered to Barrackpore—Stationed there—Bitten by a Widow—Awfully Sudden Death of an Acquaintance from Drinking—Capricious Conduct of Commanding Officer—Ordered back to my Regiment at Futtygurh—Serious Embarrassment—Interview with Sir Hugh Rose—His Kind Consideration of my Hard Case—Appointed Garrison Interpreter, Fort William—Pleasant Life at Calcutta.

IN giving an account of the hot weather campaign of 1858, I shall describe rather more at large the brilliant achievements of Sir H. Rose, commanding the Central Indian Field Force, with which the column I belonged to was supposed to be co-operating. But before doing this, it will be well briefly to notice the movements of the Commander-in-Chief, who, with the force from Futtygurh, joined to that of Walpole, arrived at

Shahjehanpore on the 30th of April, 1858, when he found the place evacuated by the army commanded by the notorious Moulvie, who departed towards Oude, accompanied, as it was believed, by the Nana Sahib. So, on the 2nd of May, Sir Colin resumed his march on Bareilly. Next day he was joined by General Penny's column.* As Sir Colin was advancing towards Bareilly, on the 5th of May, a most furious assault was made by a band of a hundred and thirty-three Ghazees upon the 42nd Highlanders. Uttering loud cries of " For God and Religion," these fanatics, sword in hand, rushed furiously and with impetuous speed upon the 42nd. Sir Colin, who was with them, called out "Steady men, steady; close up the ranks, and bayonet them as they come on." A mortal struggle with these fanatical mad dogs then ensued, which was short and sanguinary. In a few minutes every one of the Ghazees were killed on the spot, whilst some eighteen or twenty of our men were wounded. This fierce skirmish occurred in the vicinity of Bareilly. Being joined on the 6th by the troops under the command of Brigadier Jones, who had fought his way from Moradabad, the two forces next day advanced and took undisputed possession of the city, since Khan Bahadur Khan, who appears to have had no stomach for fighting, fled to Pileebheet. It was, however, an unsatisfactory business, inasmuch as the main body of rebels with their leaders managed to escape. The Fyzabad Moulvie, a man of ability, taking advantage of Sir Colin's departure from Shahjehanpore, suddenly attacked it with about eight thousand men and twelve guns. The British garrison under Colonel Hale, consisting of a wing of H.M. 82nd Foot, De Kantzow's Irregular Horse with four guns, were driven into the gaol, where they sustained an incessant bombardment from the 3rd to the morning of the 11th May. On which day Colonel Hale was relieved by Brigadier

* Who was killed in an ambuscade, as has already been narrated.

Jones, who defeated a part of the rebel army at Shahjehanpore. But on the 15th May, Jones was attacked by the whole united force of the enemy under the Moulvie, Prince Ferozeshah and the Begum of Oude. The struggle lasted all day, and so large was the force of the rebels, that the Brigadier could do no more than act on the defensive. Three days afterwards Jones was joined by the Commander-in-Chief, who fought an indecisive battle the same day with the Moulvie. Through excessive caution Sir Colin resolved to postpone a decisive battle till he should have more cavalry; so being joined by Brigadier Coke on the 22nd of May, the Commander-in-Chief, on the 24th of May marched out with his whole force to attack the Moulvie; but the latter was found to have prudently taken his departure. Thus closed the summer campaign in Rohilcund; and in less than a fortnight the Fyzabad Moulvie was shot dead, in attempting to force an entrance into Powain. It is now time to chronicle the doings of the Central Indian Field Force which General Sir H. Rose took command of on the 12th of January, 1858, at Sehore in Bhopal.* That General then marched towards the strong fort of Ratgurh, which he took towards the end of the month. Then, having effected the relief of Saugor, on the 3rd of February, Rose's next movement was the forcing of the strong pass of Mudenpore, which he accomplished after a short but vigorous resistance on the 3rd March, inflicting on this occasion a severe loss on the Bundela rebels, and a week later he took possession of the territory belonging to the rebel Rajah of Shahgurh. Afterwards, on the 21st of March, Rose arrived at Jhansi, a city of about four miles in circuit, which was surrounded by a wall of solid masonry, closely loopholed for musketry, and had inside a fort strongly fortified by nature and art. The place was defended

* The Begum of this principality was remarkable for her fidelity to the British Government.

by the talented Ranee of Jhansi, with ten thousand Bundelas, and fifteen hundred Sepoys. Sir H. Rose, undaunted by all this, laid siege to the place. Tantia Topee, a relative of the Nana Sahib, with a large rebel force, which included that part of the Gwalior Contingent that had escaped from the Commander-in-Chief at Cawnpore, approached Jhansi to effect the relief of the besieged Ranee. Whereupon Sir H. Rose, whose united qualities of skill, dash, and energy constituted him a consummate commander, leaving one-half of his army to continue the siege, advanced against the relieving force with the other half of his men, and completely defeated them outside the walls of the town, pursuing them to the river Betwa. This was an important victory; since the rebels left fifteen hundred corpses behind them, and all their guns were captured. This Battle of the Betwa was capped by the capture of Jhansi by storm on the 3rd of April. In the fierce contest that ensued quarter was neither asked nor given. The slaughter was terrible; for during the storming of the fort and pursuit of the garrison, more than three thousand of the rebels were killed. The Ranee, however, managed to escape during the night with some of her troops. Sir Hugh, after some delay, departed for Calpie, and on the way he defeated Tantia Topee and the Ranee of Jhansi at Koonch, on the 11th of May. The heat on this occasion was terrible. Rose himself was three times disabled by the sun; but on each occasion he rallied and resumed his saddle wet with the buckets of water that had been dashed over him; whilst thirteen of his gallant soldiers were killed by sunstroke. He afterwards directed his march towards Calpie, which he resolved not only to take, but that all outlets for the escape of the enemy should, as far as possible, be closed. To this end he arranged that Colonel Riddell's column, consisting of my regiment,* Alexander's Horse, and two guns, should move from

* The 3rd Europeans.

the North on Calpie, and that Colonel Maxwell, with a column from Cawnpore, should advance from the east, whilst General Whitlock was requested to keep a lookout at the south. About a week afterwards Rose approached Calpie, and on the 22nd May he completely routed the enemy, nearly fifteen thousand strong, with great loss, at the battle of Gulowlie, where they made a determined attack on his camp. Next day the victor captured Calpie almost without any resistance, as the enemy fled, panic-stricken, after merely firing a few shots. Before pursuing the narration of Sir H. Rose's brilliant performances it is proper that I should at this point notice the doings of our column. In pursuance of the plan for stopping the escape of the rebels, we marched towards Sheregurh Ghaut, where we defeated the enemy on the 16th of May, and drove them out of the village right across the Jumna. Our loss was trifling, and we had only one officer killed. He belonged to the cavalry, and lingered some days with the bullet in his body before he died.

The enemy then took up a position on the other side of the river. The victor's despatch was a paltry affair; he mentioned nearly every officer under his command. But he in a marked manner left me totally unmentioned, though I with a company of my regiment held the village from which the enemy had been expelled, whilst the rest continued the pursuit. We remained thus facing each other for a whole week, which I thought very humiliating, considering that we ought to have crossed the river in their teeth and chastised them well. But we remained encamped close to the banks of the river, and so near the enemy as to be within rifle-shot, so that occasionally there was a good deal of firing going on; and once I remember Colonel Riddell was very apprehensive of a night attack. On one occasion I had a very narrow escape of being shot in my bed. It was at early dawn, just as I awoke, when a ball from some far-carrying rifle went whizzing close over my body, embedding itself in the earth a few yards from my bed. I felt disgusted at this undignified inaction, to be braved in this manner by a body of rebels who were scarcely twice as many as we were. But our Commanding Officer would not cross the river against them. Chambers* in his history is quite wrong in stating that Colonel Riddell sent the 2nd (3rd) Bengal Europeans across on the 25th, and that they captured much of the camp equipage of the rebels. The heat was frightful. I, who have walked miles in the midday sun in May, now felt the heat terribly. I do not know how to describe what I suffered; it was certainly something short of sunstroke. It seemed as if my whole nervous system was paralyzed, so that during the heat of the day I felt unfit for any mental exertion; and what was grievous to me was that I could not pray, for when I attempted to do so aloud, as was my custom, it resulted in a continued stammering. I believe that a repetition of what I then endured from exposure to the sun in the ravines of the Jumna would drive me mad.† During the heat of the day I used to lie under the table of our mess tent, inside of which the thermometer stood at 120°. And we had no cooling drinks, nothing but country rum and ginger-beer, unless we preferred water or tea. We marched northwards very soon after the capture of Calpie by Sir H. Rose, whose work, so well performed, was not yet finished. Supposing the campaign to have been over, that General, on the 1st June, 1858, had issued the following eloquent and characteristic farewell address to his troops, which he directed to be read at the head of every corps and detachment of the force:—"Soldiers! you have marched more than a thousand miles, and taken more than a hundred guns; you have forced your way through mountain passes and

---

* Chambers's "History of the Sepoy Revolt," p. 507.

† Even at this distance of time I am occasionally so wretchedly nervous that I am obliged to decline taking any leading public part in matters I am deeply interested in and conversant with.

intricate jungles and over rivers; you captured the strongest forts and beat the enemy, no matter what the odds, whenever you met him; you have restored extensive districts to the Government; and peace and order now reign where before for twelve months were tyranny and rebellion; you have done all this, and you have never had a check. I thank you with all sincerity for your bravery, your devotion, and your discipline. When you first marched, I told you that you as British soldiers had more than enough of courage for the work which was before you, but that courage without discipline was of no avail, and I exhorted you to let discipline be your watchword: you have attended to my orders. In hardships, in temptations, and in dangers you have obeyed your General, and have never left your ranks. You have fought against the strong, and you have protected the rights of the weak and defenceless—of foes as well as friends. I have seen you in the ardour of the combat preserve and place children out of harm's way. This is the discipline of Christian soldiers; and this it is has brought you triumphant from the shores of Western India to the waters of the Jumna, and establishes without doubt that you will find no place to equal the glory of your arms."

But the gallant Sir Hugh's conception of the arduous labours of his army being ended for a time was soon dispelled, by learning afterwards that on that very day (1st June) Tantia Topee, the Ranee of Jhansi, the Nawab of Banda, and Rao Sahib, nephew of the Nana, with four thousand cavalry, seven thousand infantry, and twelve guns, fought a battle at Gwalior with our faithful ally, the Maharajah. Scindiah had two or three thousand cavalry, six thousand infantry, and eight guns. But the Maharajah was completely defeated, owing to the treachery of his infantry, who had been previously tampered with by Tantia Topee. The Maharajah's body-guard proved faithful, and fought manfully, till half of them were laid low, when the rest fled. Scindiah also sought refuge in flight, and happily he escaped to Agra two days afterwards. The rebels, on the flight of the Maharajah, took formal possession of Gwalior. This was a great blow; for Gwalior, strong with its rock-built fortress, was a place of great importance. The fittest man to undertake its reconquest was unquestionably the distinguished Commander of the Central Indian Field Force.

At this time, however, Sir Hugh Rose was in ill-health, suffering from the effects of repeated attacks of sunstroke, and he was about to take leave on medical certificate. But in the true spirit of heroism Sir Hugh thrust aside all thoughts of self for the promotion of the public welfare, and set to work in right earnest. He organized two brigades. The infantry consisted of H.M. 86th Foot, a wing of the 71st Highlanders, a wing of the 3rd Bombay Europeans, the 24th and 25th Regiments Bombay N.I., and the 5th Hyderabad Infantry; the cavalry comprised wings of the 4th and 14th Dragoons, the 3rd Hyderabad Cavalry, and a detachment of the 3rd Bombay Native Cavalry, a Company of Royal Engineers, some Bombay and Madras Sappers and Miners, two light Field Batteries, a troop of Bombay Artillery, and a siege train consisting of five cannons, ten mortars, and one howitzer. The first of these brigades was commanded by Brigadier Stuart; the second, under Brigadier R. Napier.[*] Arrangements were also made for the co-operation of a third brigade from Sipree, under Brigadier Smith. Colonel Maxwell was requested to march with his force from Cawnpore to Calpie, and Colonel Riddell was instructed to march on Gwalior with his column; but instead of doing so we remained in shameful inactivity at Dholpore, about thirty-five miles from Gwalior, as Colonel Riddell declared afterwards that he had not received the order in question. It was at all events a very queer business. Sir Hugh Rose arrived at Gwalior on the 16th of June. He instantly

[*] Now Lord Napier of Magdala.

attacked the rebels and gained a complete victory. The main body of rebels, after being driven right through the cantonments, were pursued over the plain. Brought to bay, the enemy at one spot maintained a desperate hand-to-hand struggle, until their fortified trench was nearly brimful with dead and wounded bodies. Rose was now in possession of Morar (cantonments). Next day (17th June), Brigadier Smith with his brigade, which comprised a wing of the 8th Hussars, a wing of the Bombay Lancers, H.M. 95th Foot, the 10th Bombay N.I., and a troop of Bombay Horse Artillery, and Major Orr's Sepoys of the Hyderabad Contingent, engaged the rebels a few miles from Gwalior and drove them before him. In this day's fighting the Amazonian Ranee of Jhansi fell to rise no more. In trying to escape she was cut down by a hussar who was ignorant of her sex. The following day (18th) the Brigadier drove the enemy from some hills held by Tantia Topee. Next day Sir Hugh Rose captured the heights commanding the city; whereupon the enemy, struck with panic, fled in all directions, pursued by our cavalry, who cut down large numbers of the fugitives. Rose now became master of Gwalior.

There was but little more fighting. On the following day (20th) the rock-built fortress was taken by a handful of men under Lieutenant Rose of the 25th Bombay N.I., who perished in the attempt. Scindiah was now reinstated on his throne. The same day Brigadier Napier left Gwalior in pursuit of Tantia Topee, with Captain Lightfoot's troop of Horse Artillery, a troop of the 14th Dragoons, a wing of the Hyderabad Contingent Cavalry, and three troops of Meade's Horse, altogether about six hundred men and six guns. With this force he attacked and completely routed six thousand rebels at Jowra Alipore on the 21st, and captured all their guns, twenty-five in number.

Tantia Topee for several months more kept Central India in agitation, and Sir H. Rose towards the end of June resigned his command on account of ill-health. Before concluding my narrative of the hot weather campaign of 1858, it will be in place just very briefly to notice some further operations, which may thus be summed up in the following methodical order. Brigadier Showers, on the 11th of March, 1858, defeated a body of about four thousand rebels at Bah in the Agra district. In Central India, Brigadier Stuart captured the fort of Chendaree on the 17th March. And Brigadier Rowcroft completely defeated Nazim Mehndee Hoosein with other rebel chiefs at the head of fourteen thousand men, including two thousand five hundred Sepoys at Amorha in the Goruckpore district, killing and wounding near five hundred of the enemy, and capturing eight guns. Rowcroft also defeated the rebels again on the 17th of April, and once more on the 25th.

A disaster was, however, sustained on the 21st of March in the defeat inflicted by Koonwur Singh at Atrowlia on a British force of nearly three hundred men and two guns, under the command of Colonel Milman of H.M. 37th Foot, who with the loss of his camp equipage was driven back to Azimgurh, where he was besieged by four thousand rebels. Another reverse befell a small force comprising two companies of H.M. 54th Foot, a hundred Sikhs, with a few Madras Cavalry and guns, who towards the close of March were defeated by a band of rebels with six guns at Suraon in the Allahabad district. To retrieve Milman's disaster, Lord Mark Kerr, Colonel commanding 13th Light Infantry, left Allahabad on the 27th of March with a wing of his regiment for Benares, which he reached on the last day of the month, and being joined there by a troop of the Bays, and four guns, he left Benares on the 2nd of April with this force, amounting to nearly five hundred officers and men, and four days afterwards he defeated four thousand rebels, comprising a large proportion of Sepoys of the Dinapore Brigade, in the vicinity of Azimgurh. Azimgurh, however, needed the assistance of a larger force than that at the disposal of Kerr; so Sir E. Lugard, with a strong column, consisting of three regiments of Infantry, three of Sikh Horse, a military train, and three batteries of Horse Artillery, started from Lucknow towards the end of March, and after defeating the enemy, he effectually relieved Azimgurh on the 15th of April. Next day Lugard despatched Brigadier Douglas in pursuit of the enemy, with H.M. 37th and 84th Regiments, some cavalry and artillery. This officer on the 20th of April at Mannahar completely defeated the rebels under Koonwur Singh, who fled to his hereditary domain of Jugdeespore. The second disaster of Arrah now occurred. For on the 23rd of April Captain Le Grand, with one hundred and fifty men of H.M. 35th Foot, one hundred and fifty Rattray's Sikhs, and fifty sailors of the Naval Brigade with two 12-pounder howitzers, sallied out from Arrah, and attacked Koonwur Singh's force, consisting of about two thousand men, without guns, in a jungle two miles from Jugdeespore. The English were completely defeated, and abandoning the howitzers they fled to Arrah, followed by the enemy, who shot and cut down many of them. The detachment of H.M. 35th suffered very severely, since no less than a hundred and two officers and men, including Captain Le Grand himself and two other officers, were killed or died from apoplexy in their flight to Arrah. Nineteen of the sailors, and nine Sikhs with their officers, were also killed. This was indeed a miserable affair. This disaster was retrieved by Sir E Lugard on the 9th of May, when he drove Koonwur Singh's[*] brother before him, and occupied Jugdeespore, and on the 27th of May Lugard defeated Ummur Singh and recaptured the two howitzers lost by Le Grand. He also defeated Ummur Singh with great slaughter on the 10th of June, and towards the end of June, Sir E.

[*] Koonwur Singh died three days after his victory from the effects of the amputation of his wrist.

Lugard resigned his command, entrusting to Brigadier Douglas the arduous duty of the pursuit of the Jugdeespore rebels from place to place. That officer gradually organized arrangements for their suppression. His right-hand man was Major Sir Henry Havelock, who with a small body of mounted riflemen and cavalry killed no less than five hundred of Ummur Singh's followers in three actions, viz., on the 19th, 20th, and 21st of October, 1858, and thereby he completely cowed the rebels. We are informed that "the average daily march of Havelock's cavalry was scarcely less than forty miles."* We must now refer to Rajpootana. Major-General H. G. Roberts, of the Bombay army, commanding the Rajpootana Field Force, marched from Nusseerabad on the 10th of March, and captured Kotah on the 30th of the month with trifling loss. The victory was gained by a clever flank movement, which turned the enemy's position, and rendered their defences useless. In Bundelcund British prestige was maintained by the capture of Banda on the 19th of April, 1858; this was accomplished by General Whitlock with a column of Madras troops, who on that day defeated the Nawab of Banda at the head of seven thousand men, killing five hundred of the enemy and taking several guns. Affairs in Oude next require attention, and here we have to chronicle a very mortifying repulse that befell our arms in that province, which happened in the following manner. General Walpole, with a strong column of about six thousand men, marched from Lucknow on the 10th of April, and four days afterwards (14th) he attacked the Fort of Rooya, fifty miles distant from Lucknow, which was defended by about four hundred rebels. This small fort, with a high mud wall loop-holed for musketry, was attacked by Walpole without using his artillery or making any proper reconnoissance.

The attacking party, consisting of two companies of

* Malleson's "History of the Indian Mutiny," vol. ii. p. 492.

H.M. 42nd Highlanders, and a hundred and twenty men of the 4th Punjaub Rifles, as might have been expected, were completely defeated, amidst yells of triumph from their concealed foes. It was in this most lamentable and wretched business that Brigadier Adrian Hope, a most gallant officer, met his death. The loss of the 42nd in killed and wounded was fifty-seven officers and men, and that of the 4th Punjaub Rifles was forty-six. The enemy quietly evacuated the fort during the night and Walpole resumed his march towards Bareilly. He was more successful on the 22nd of April, when he defeated a large body of rebels at Sirsa. His cavalry and artillery on this occasion attacked the enemy so vigorously, that they captured their guns and camp, and drove them across the Ramgunga river. A few days afterwards, he effected a junction with the Commander-in-Chief. Sir Hope Grant on the 12th of June marched by night from Lucknow, with a column consisting of the 2nd and 3rd battalions Rifle Brigade, the 5th Punjaub Rifles, the 7th Hussars, two squadrons 2nd Dragoon Guards, Hodson's Horse, a squadron of 1st Sikh Cavalry, a troop of Horse Artillery, two field batteries, and a detachment of Engineers and Sappers; and next day (13th) he attacked the enemy at Nuwabgung, when a fierce combat ensued. The rebels attempted to surround him, and destroy his men by repeated volleys of musketry. The General frustrated this manœuvre with his accustomed address, by sending a troop of artillery to the front, and a battery with two squadrons to defend the left, whilst a larger party confronted the enemy on the right. A band of Ghazees made a most determined resistance, and were killed to a man. After three hours' fighting Grant gained a complete victory. Six guns were captured, and about six hundred of the enemy were killed, whilst the wounded were much more numerous. The British loss in killed and wounded amounted to sixty-seven, but in addition thirty-three men died from sunstroke. The affairs in Rohilcund and the Futtygurh district may be dismissed with the following notice. Brigadier Seaton, with a column comprising six hundred men of H.M. 82nd Foot, four hundred Sikhs, a hundred and fifty cavalry, and two hundred mounted police with five guns, marched from Futtygurh on the 6th of April, and next day he defeated the Mynpoorie Rajah at Kankur, who was at the head of a large but ill-organized force. The rebels lost their camp and two hundred and fifty men killed and wounded. In Rohilcund, Brigadier-General J. Jones of H.M. 60th Rifles, commanding the Roorkee column, which consisted of H.M. 60th Rifles, the 1st Sikh Infantry, Coke's Rifles, the 17th Punjaub Infantry, the Mooltanee Horse, with fourteen guns, defeated the Rohilcund rebels at Nagul, on the 17th of April, and four days afterwards (21st) Jones completely defeated twelve thousand rebels with fifteen guns near Nugheena, and captured their guns; and on the 26th Colonel Coke, who was the General's right-hand man, took several rebel chiefs.

But it is time to notice the affairs of our column. After the capture of Gwalior, we returned to our station at Agra. Here, as the result of the exposure to the sun on service, I now fell into a state of ill-health, which showed itself by constant attacks of fever and ague, and just at this time I was placed under arrest by my Commanding Officer, Colonel Riddell, for a trifle light as air. It was on the assumption that I had insulted the Assistant-Surgeon of my regiment, who was attending me in his professional capacity. The facts of the case are as follows:—I asked him one day to recommend my obtaining leave on medical certificate, which he might conscientiously have done, for I was really in a bad state of health, and required a change; but instead of attending in a reasonable manner to my request, he made a rough and unfeeling reply, which so provoked me that I indignantly dismissed him from attendance on me, and called in Dr. Crozier, the Surgeon of the regiment, to attend on me instead. For this I was placed under arrest. Happily for me, the officer commanding the station happened to be an upright man. Brigadier Showers,* a most gallant officer, who had greatly distinguished himself at Delhi, fairly examined the matter, and as he was totally averse to oppress a subaltern, merely because he happened to be obnoxious to his Commanding Officer, he very properly directed my release from arrest, merely giving it as his opinion that I should express my regret to Assistant-Surgeon B—— for what I had said, which I was quite willing to do. We heard this year at Agra of the passing of the India Bill, transferring the Government of the Honourable East India Company to the Crown, whereby I at once became transformed into a Queen's officer. And on the 1st of November, 1858, the Queen's Proclamation, addressed to the princes, chiefs, and people, was published at Allahabad, by Viscount Canning, Her Majesty's first Viceroy, in person, with all due pomp and state. It announced the assumption by Her Majesty of the Government of India conducted hitherto by Her trustees, the Honourable East India Company; that the Government was a Christian one, but that no one would be either molested or benefited by his creed, and an unconditional pardon was offered to all in arms against the Government, with the exception of those who had directly taken part in the murder of British subjects, and excepting those who had willingly given an asylum to murderers, knowing them to be such, whose lives alone could be guaranteed. These terms of grace were to be extended to those concerned who should comply with the required conditions before the 1st of January, 1859. I shall now give an account of the cold weather campaign of 1858-59.

* Some years afterwards, when General Showers was commanding the Presidency Division he recommended me to the Commander-in-Chief as an officer of studious habits and a good interpreter.

Tantia Topee's defeats require first to be noticed. He was taken in hand by General Roberts, who on the 8th August routed a body of his troops near Sunganeer, and six days afterwards Roberts overtook and defeated Tantia Topee at Kattara, on which occasion great numbers of the enemy were destroyed by our cavalry and horse artillery, who continued the pursuit for ten miles. And on the 15th September General Michel gained a victory at Beora over Tantia Topee, who lost three hundred men and a considerable number of guns. That General defeated him at Sindwah on the 19th October, and again at Multhone on the 25th October, 1858. Tantia Topee had become like a hunted beast of prey, wandering about from place to place with a following of several thousand rebels. It was necessary for the pacification of Central India that this noted leader should be put down. He was a desperate man, since he was too deeply implicated in the Cawnpore massacre to hope for mercy. The Queen's proclaimed pardon was not for men who like Tantia Topee had taken active part in the treacherous murder of English men, women and children. To annihilate this arch rebel with his followers, Brigadier Showers left Agra in the cold season of 1858-59 with a column which included a detachment of the regiment to which I belonged. We marched day and night over the roadless plains of Rajpootana for several days; all which time I was literally half starved. Once I, with my party on elephants, lost our way, and were for a time in a most perplexing predicament. I felt completely worn out with this constant marching night and day, and was right glad when the bugle sounded a halt for a couple of hours' sleep on the hard ground, bitterly cold as it was. The strain was so great that at last I was on the point of completely giving way; I felt it was no use trying to keep on the elephant, as, despite the danger of falling and breaking my neck, I felt I could not keep awake. I accordingly got off and mounted my pony; but this was no better, for do what I would I could not keep awake. So I got off and thought I would walk, but drowsiness so overpowered me, that I could not keep from dozing, so letting the column pass on, I fell on the ground, and slept a sound sleep for I do not know how long. On awakening I mounted my pony, and made all haste to join the column, which I did just before dawn of day on the 14th of January, and then I learnt that we were close to the camp of Tantia Topee, who was quite unconscious of our nearness. We all fell in, and at early dawn we made a sudden dash upon the enemy, and in a few minutes our men killed about fifty or sixty of them: we could not do more because they fled so fast. I do not think they fired more than one volley before they took to their heels. The pursuit was carried on by the cavalry, who cut up some hundreds of them. It was a singular circumstance that one man was taken prisoner, and I well remember, after the action was over, that they gave this rebel a run for his life; and run he did, and several shots were fired before he was brought down. But the rest, numbering several thousands, fled such a distance that it was not considered necessary to continue the pursuit; so our part being over I was glad to go back to Agra. I returned with Captain Nixen, an officer on political employ, with whom I dined in the celebrated mud fort of Bhurtpore. The cold weather campaign of 1858-59, witnessed the complete suppression of the great Sepoy revolt, which at this period was quite stamped out.

Sir Colin Campbell, elevated to the peerage as Lord Clyde, after attending the reading of the Queen's Proclamation at Allahabad, crossed the Ganges there on the 2nd of November, 1858, and advanced into Oude with a select force. The rebels in that province, however, had no heart to meet His Excellency, who could find no worthy foe to contend with; since all the Oudean rebels thought of was to get out of his way. Once only did he succeed in coming up with the enemy, and defeating them. In fact the campaign in Oude was rather a hard marching than a fighting one. Sir Hope Grant, on the 27th November, 1858, with four thousand men, forced a passage over the Gogra river, stormed the enemy's position, and compelled them to retire. About a month after this victory (*i.e.* on the 4th January, 1859) Sir Hope again attacked the enemy near the Nepaul frontier, on which occasion the faint-hearted mutineers would not stand a moment, but ran away, abandoning their fifteen guns, which fell into Grant's possession. This was almost the closing act of the Sepoy war. Grant tells us in his work* that the wretchedness of the hunted mutineers was extreme. The remainder were driven far away over the hills into Nepaul, where they had leisure to bewail the day when they turned against the hand that had fed and pampered them for so many years. The high-spirited Begum of Oude, for whom one cannot help feeling a degree of compassion, found refuge in Nepaul. Tantia Topee was caught asleep in the jungle on the 7th April, 1859, being betrayed by his most trusted friend. He was then tried and executed. Other insurgent leaders of revolt were one after the other tracked to their lairs and punished according to their deserts. It is stated that the Nana Sahib died in the Nepaul jungle. But there is no conclusive proof of this, and I, for my part, so far discredit the report that I should not be much surprised to hear some day of the veritable Nana being unkennelled.

I do not think that there will ever be such an upheaving again, unless we drive all classes to desperation by a reckless taxation. But ever since the Mutiny I have always thought that there will some day be a last outburst of Mahomedan fanaticism. For that creed has a history of its own, and a bright future according to their way of thinking; and just as we are taught to believe in a glorious future for the Christian Church

* See Grant's "History of the Sepoy War."

at the second coming of our Lord and Saviour Jesus Christ, so the Mussulmen believe in a glorious future for their religion on the appearance of their Iman, who is to make Mahomedanism the religion of the whole earth. Therefore should any Mahomed-like impostor make his appearance professing to be this long-expected Iman, then the news would unquestionably spread like wildfire over every Mussulman town and village in India, and would produce a general rising of Ghazees, which must not be understood as a general rising of the Mussulmen, since the Ghazees are to the general body of Mahomedans what martyrs are to Protestants; and as comparatively few of the latter would be content to burn for their religion were the times of Mary I. to come over again, so the number of Ghazees represent a very small portion of the Mussulman community But the desperate courage of men excited to the highest degree by religious fanaticism, and stimulated by the soothing bhang, is by no means to be despised. Soon after our return to Agra we were ordered to Gwalior. Here there were two Government Chaplains, the one a Presbyterian for the Highlanders, the other an Episcopalian for the rest of the community. Both were earnest good men. I noticed a marked change in Lieutenant B—— of my regiment this year (1859.) He was evidently very deeply impressed by the chaplain's excellent sermons. He seemed to be almost decided. But, alas, in a little time I noticed an alteration, and I am almost certain that I know what caused him to take a fatal determination in religious matters. It was this, that he was over head and ears in debt. This made him desperate, he felt that things were against him, and that his was a hopeless case. Even at this distance of time it grieves me to think of poor B——. He was a most promising officer, and a very agreeable fellow to have anything to do with. How many officers like him have been ruined by debt, have left their homes honourable young men, and have been kicked out of the service for dishonesty. Why will young fellows buy expensive horses, buggies, guns, &c., &c., that they know well, if they chose to reflect for a moment, they cannot pay for? Then the temptations to get into debt used to be great, and occasionally in some instances expenses ill befitting his rank were forced upon him; as, for example, I remember on one occasion when my regiment gave a ball to the station of Bareilly, I was forced to pay forty rupees, or four pounds, as my share, which was much more than I as Ensign could afford to pay; besides which I was in reality paying for the benefit of the Captains, and Regimental staff, and such eligible parties as the unmarried young ladies* would deign to dance with. A poor Ensign like myself could not expect such favours. I knew an officer of my regiment, a Lieutenant drawing about £280 a year, who was reputed to be about three thousand pounds in debt. But making every allowance for exaggeration, it is most probable that he owed not less than fifteen hundred pounds. Poor B—— did what many others have done in like circumstances, and was dismissed the service, and the last I heard of him was, that he was leading the life of a wretched beggar in India. I have also seen much of the evil of drinking; for I have known officers who have died most awful deaths in a state of drunkenness. As for the soldiers, my own belief is that almost all the crimes they commit are done under the influence of liquor. Strong drink is the curse of the British army. When I was living this year at Gwalior in our mess-house, I was once placed in a rather awkward position, as late one evening a Captain of my regiment had an attack of delirium tremens when I was the next senior officer there. I, however, kept a quiet tongue in my head, and let things take their course, as there were some officers willing to take him in hand. I think this was the most prudent thing

* Who in those days were scarce commodities in the North-West Provinces.

to be done under the circumstances; for had I reported the state of my senior officer, very probably a base motive would have been imputed to me. At the end of the year we were ordered to Futtygurh. This was the last march I made with my regiment. An Indian march has its discomforts certainly, but it is not altogether devoid of interest. It has its excitements in time of war, and when in the usual course of relief in the olden time, a four months' march was nothing like so monotonous as a voyage round the Cape, for at all events there was shooting on the way, seeing a great number of towns and villages, and occasionally a British cantonment, &c., &c. Then there was the free and easy conversation, the early smoke, and cup of coffee. Talking about smoking reminds me of one of my bon-mots on the line of march. I was then only an Ensign, and therefore it was excusable. The fact is, that to spare my own cigars I used always to accept one whenever it was offered to me. At last this attracted so much observation, that my brother officers in a pleasant way wanted to know how it was that I never refused the gift of a cigar. "Why," I replied unblushingly, "I am just following the maxim of the Duke of Wellington to live on the enemy." "Surely," they laughingly replied, "you don't call us your enemies." "Yes," I replied in the same strain, "you are; for you are more enemies to me than I am to myself." I flatter myself that on this occasion I had the better of the argument in every point of view.

Another time I was held in great esteem for some interesting information I happened to pick up whilst going along, and by recounting to my amused hearers a ludicrously stormy scene I had witnessed between Brigadier Wheeler* and our Colonel. The conversation amongst us was generally good-humoured, though light and somewhat frothy—anything serious and of a melancholy nature was put aside. I shall never forget

* Afterwards Major-General Wheeler, massacred at Cawnpore.

when poor Scott, who had only just been married, and was marching with his wife in company with the regiment, one day went out shooting, and killed a neelgau, in doing which he accidentally shot himself dead, that though Scott was much loved in the regiment, yet after the first day all conversation about him seemed, by general consent, to be tabooed, because the thought of his untimely death made them feel melancholy. He seemed almost to have a presentiment that something was going to happen to him, as he two or three times returned to take leave of his wife (who was a missionary's daughter), which so impressed her, that she begged her husband not to go out. But, poor fellow, he went, and having mortally wounded the neelgau, he impetuously rushed forward to secure his prize, when his gun went off, and the contents entered his breast, from the effects of which he expired before he could be brought into camp. His last words were, " Oh, what will become of my poor wife ?" Serious conversation, as I have said, was not liked, but once a question I put to our gay Colonel sobered him for the time.

I said in an earnest manner to him one day on the line of march, " Well, Colonel, have you never been seriously impressed ?" The earnest question startled him into returning the quiet reply that he had, and then he went on to relate to me how it happened. It was easier marching with Native troops than with European for one reason, because in the case of European soldiers the officers have to look so much after their comforts, whilst Native soldiers are, or used to be, willing to be of use to their officers. Things, whether with a European or a Native regiment, worked so much pleasanter when officers pulled well together; then they resembled a large family, each feeling for the honour of the other, and *esprit de corps* bound them together like a band of brothers. Then, when we arrived at the end of our march, what appetites we had for our breakfast, which was soon ready for us in the great mess tent! But I must now bring my reminiscences of an Indian march to a close. I remained but a short time at Futtygurh, when I proceeded to take up my appointment as Interpreter to H.M. 6th Foot, stationed at Benares. How glad I was to leave my regiment! I hired a dawk gharee to take me to Cawnpore, and thence I went by rail to Allahabad, for the line was then open that distance, and from Allahabad I went by gharee to Benares. I was here but a very short time when I had to leave with the 6th, which was ordered to Barrackpore. We travelled all the way to Raneegunge in wretched jolting country carts. I was very glad to be once more stationed at Barrackpore. I at once commenced studying for high proficiency in Persian. But I eventually gave up in disgust my prosecution of the study of the native languages, because when I wrote to the Military Secretary to the Governor-General, inquiring whether I might hope to get any civil employment by passing any further high examinations in the languages, I was informed in reply that the examinations I had already passed in were quite sufficient for anything, leaving me to draw the inference that as I had already received the money-prize of a thousand rupees for two languages, it would be of no practical use for me to pass for high proficiency in Persian; so, metaphorically, I at once threw my books to the dogs. At Barrackpore I was joined by my family. Here I took a large house, sub-letting part of it to a widow, who eventually left without paying her share of the rent. It was very provoking, because I reckoned on her paying her quota. But, as I took the house, I had to pay the landlord the whole amount. Dishonestly as Mrs. —— behaved, I never for a moment thought of suing her for the money, for I hate going to law if I can help it. An awfully sudden death of an officer I knew occurred this year at Barrackpore. I noticed his servant one day rushing along in great haste, as if something serious had happened, so I asked him what was the matter; upon which he informed me that his master was taken alarmingly ill, and that he was going for the doctor So I went at once, till the surgeon should come. I found poor —— perfectly unconscious. He had, as I was informed, been in the habit of taking a bottle of brandy a day for a year past, which no doubt accounted for the state I found him in. In about ten minutes or a quarter of an hour the doctor came, and having examined the prostrate body, he uttered the dreadful words, "He is dead." He died, no doubt, the victim of intemperance; but he was buried as though he were a good Christian. Though it is hard to perceive why a man who deliberately drinks himself to death is more deserving of a Christian burial than the man who, in his senses, from inability to face impending ruin, blows out his brains.

I now desired to get something better than an Interpretership, so I wrote on the 1st of June, 1860, to Captain Rose, Officiating Military Secretary to Sir H. Rose, K.C.B., Commander-in-Chief, requesting him to solicit His Excellency to bestow on me an appointment as Adjutant, or second in command of a Native regiment.

I was informed in reply, that His Excellency wished to know my qualifications as an officer, and required on this account a Commanding Officer's certificate. Sir H. Rose, moreover, was pleased to grant me an interview, at which I particularly requested I might have an examination to test my qualifications as an officer. His Excellency very kindly expressed his willingness to accede to my request in this matter. But being informed some time afterwards (2nd of July) by Colonel H. J. Warre, C.B., Military Secretary, that the production of a Commanding Officer's certificate was absolutely necessary, I wrote to Colonel Warre, acknowledging my inability to procure such a document, on account of the very peculiar and extraordinary circumstances of my case in relation to the records of my regiment (the 3rd Europeans), and requesting that, under such peculiar circumstances, His Excellency would graciously be pleased to dispense with the production of a Commanding Officer's certificate in my particular case. This I requested the Military Secretary to submit, when perfectly convenient, for the Commander-in-Chief's consideration. The very next day (3rd of July) Colonel Warre sent me a letter informing me that His Excellency had ordered a Board to assemble at Barrackpore to report upon my proficiency as a military officer as regards the interior economy of a regiment, courts-martial, and field exercise, and evolutions of infantry in the field.* In due time the Board of examiners met. The examination lasted four days, and I felt confident that I got through the first three days with credit and success. But on the third day, being told beforehand of the programme for the following day, I very unwisely gave expression to my gladness at finding I was well up in it.. But when I came next day to be examined I found, to my astonishment and dismay, that advantage had been taken of my candour, so that the programme was entirely changed, and I was examined in something else that I was not at all well up in. The result was that I failed to pass my examination. But this was so unfair and spiteful (so it appeared to me), that had Sir H. Rose been acquainted with it, I think he would have given me another chance. But for this, I might, humanly speaking, have now been a Commanding Officer of a Native regiment, instead of a retired officer from a service I have dearly loved from my boyhood.

This disappointment was followed by my being ordered back to my regiment. This was owing to the capricious conduct of the officer commanding H.M. 6th Foot, who informed the Commander-in-Chief that he did not want an interpreter to his regiment. This placed me in a very serious embarrassment, as I had

* See letters in my possession.

joined the regiment at Benares at my own expense, and having been there a very short time I had gone with the 6th to Barrackpore, where I had taken and furnished a house, and now, after having held this poorly paid appointment* only about half a year, I was, at the mere caprice of a Commanding Officer, ordered back to my regiment at my own expense! I was indeed in a most doleful predicament; for my finances were quite exhausted, and I had not the means to go back. In such a desperate case the only thing I could think of was to obtain an interview with the Commander-in-Chief. This I accordingly did, when Sir H. Rose received me very graciously, and listened to the representation I made of my hard case, and, what was still better, considerate acts followed kind words; since the kind-hearted Sir Hugh appointed me Garrison Interpreter at Fort William, Calcutta. This appointment I held from 1860 to 1865. Here I spent a very pleasant time. I got on well with the General (Showers), who recommended me favourably to the Commander-in-Chief,† and with the Fort Adjutant, from whom I received my orders. This was Captain Parlby, a capital fellow, enormously tall, and very popular, being called as good as he was big. I always found him very obliging, and I am very sorry that he is dead. Instead of coming home for his health, he went to the hills, where he died some years ago. I also got on very well with the other officers. I had, as Interpreter, two or three passages with officers conducting the prosecution at Native Courts-martial, who wanted to have some part of the evidence taken down in a manner more consonant with their wishes than what was deemed by me a faithful translation. And though it mattered nothing to me whether the prisoner was convicted or not, yet it did very much matter to me, as one sworn to translate faithfully, that the evidence

* A hundred rupees or £10 a month, out of which a moonshee had to be kept, was the Interpreter's allowance, in addition to the pay of his rank.
† See true copy of letter in my possession.

should be correctly recorded. I therefore, when it came to a push, declared that I would not sign the proceedings, if they persisted in putting down as my translation that which was not mine but theirs. This had the desired effect, as no sentence could have taken effect without my signature. On one occasion a prosecutor so far forgot himself as to endeavour to intimidate me by threatening to report me as a bad Interpreter; but this also failed. Surrounded by my family, and having some esteemed friends, I enjoyed a thorough rest. My dearest friend there was an old missionary, the Rev. A. Leslie. He was a bluff, honest, plain-spoken man, who called a spade a spade. For this fine Scotchman I conceived a warm friendship, which was reciprocated. I regularly attended his chapel, and taught in his Sunday-school, and at his house I spent many a pleasant evening in social conversation. One of his anecdotes, from my fondness for history, was decidedly interesting to me; it was when he chatted about a very old pensioner, an acquaintance of his, who died at Monghyr* about the year 1830, at the age of 103. This veteran as a youth had taken up arms under James II.'s grandson, Prince Charles, in the rebellion of 1745-46. After which he fought in the American War of Independence; and, lastly, this wonderful man served a long time in India.

I have in a former chapter described Calcutta, therefore it would be superfluous to give a repetition of the public places there which I now frequented. It will suffice to say that I was perfectly content, finding Calcutta to be a sort of earthly paradise. I never felt dull that I can remember. Occasionally I partook of the hospitalities of Government House, where I saw assembled all the great in Church and State. I felt a particular interest in attending interesting trials at the Supreme Court, where through my friend Mr. R.

* Monghyr was where my aged friend, Mr. Leslie, had been stationed as a missionary.

Belchambers holding a high position there, I always managed to get a good seat. I remember two cases in particular I was interested in, which at the time attracted great attention in India. One was the celebrated Neel Durpun case, where a missionary was fined and imprisoned. The other was the trial of a military officer for perjury, arising out of the abduction of a pretty and very young girl, the daughter of Captain C——. But here it will be well to end this long chapter.

CHAPTER VIII.

Amalgamation Scheme arrives in Calcutta—Its unsuitability to me—My Regiment (3rd Europeans) becomes H.M. 107th Foot—Visit Chota Nagpore—Spread of Christianity among the Coles—Their extraordinary Belief in the Power of Witches—Arrival of Cannibals in Calcutta—Become Lieutenant and Brevet-Major under Government Scheme of 1864—Description of the Dreadful Cyclone at Calcutta—Illness—Resign my Appointment—Appointed to Convalescent Depôt, Darjeeling—Journey there—The Hillmen—The Snowy Range—Animal Life—Pleasant Society—Severe Affliction—Promoted to Captain—Obtain Leave to England—Place my Infant at a Ladies' School—Strange Affair there—Embark for England—Description of Affairs on Board the *Blenheim*—Nearly Wrecked in a Hurricane—Pleasant Stay at St. Helena—Hospitable Reception there—Arrival in England—Admitted to the Staff Corps as Major—Two Months' Continental Tour—Return to India—Last Passage round the Cape—General Description of these Long Voyages—Arrival at Calcutta—Suicide there of a Fellow-Passenger—Apply for the Vacant Appointment of the Persian Translatorship to Government—Disappointment for want of Interest—Ordered to Gwalior—Description thereof—Appointed Interpreter to 92nd Highlanders at Jullundur—Visit to Lahore—Strange Case of Suicide of an Officer—Promoted to Lieutenant-Colonel—Resign the Interpretership—Visits to Simla and Mussoorie—Take my Furlough to England—Stay at Delhi—Description of the Palace, &c.—A Week at Bombay—Remarks on Missionary Work in India—Thoughts about Indian Servants—Overland Journey to Genoa, and through Europe—Retirement from Service.

In 1861 the Amalgamation Scheme and the institution of the Staff Corps came out. But though it offered great advantages to those who had been for a certain number of years in Staff employ, yet it was totally unsuited to me; as under its provisions I should have had to wait some years before I could get my Captaincy, though I was then an officer of sixteen years' service; I therefore preferred to remain as I was. Next year, 1862, my regiment, the 3rd Europeans, became H.M. 107th Foot, and had I chosen to be transferred to that regiment, I might have expected to have got my promotion at once. But I still prudently preferred to remain a local officer. This year I took six months' leave; when I and my family then went by train to Raneegunge, and then by gharee dawk to an obscure place on the Grand Trunk road; where we got out and went by palkee dawk to Hussareebagh, and after staying some time there, we proceeded thence to Chota Nagpore, a district inhabited by the Coles, who are said to be the aborigines of India. The Commissioner of this district, Lieutenant-Colonel E. T. Dalton, Bengal Staff Corps, formerly belonged to my regiment (3rd Europeans). I liked much what I saw of the Coles. They appeared to be a simple people, with, as far as I can remember, none of the stupid caste prejudices of the Hindoos, and, what was still better, they had by thousands embraced Christianity. The honoured instruments in bringing about this most important and happy change in them was a band of German Missionaries. One of the most remarkable characteristics about this simple race was their extraordinary belief in the power of witches; and I was informed on good authority that this belief resulted in the commission of many murders, as they take the law into their own hands, and kill the man whom they believe by witchcraft to have killed some member of their family. They have also a singular way of killing wild beasts like the tiger, by setting a bent bow with an arrow ready to go off, in such a manner, in a particular spot where they know the animal will pass, that when some days afterwards they go there, they frequently find the tiger lying dead, transfixed by their arrow. Chota Nagpore, from its considerable altitude above the sea-level, enjoys a pleasant climate, being much cooler than the places of Bengal or Northern India. Next year (1863) I attended the installation of the Earl of Elgin at Government House, Calcutta. There is nothing more worth recording of anything I did or saw this year, except it be the arrival of a set of reputed Cannibals from the Andaman islands, which I think happened about this time. These sight-seeing savages walked about the fort as bold as brass. It was of no use our trying to converse with them, as no one knew their language, or it would have been somewhat interesting to know what these uncouth barbarians thought of the city of palaces. But as their language was totally different to that spoken in India, it was not the slightest use attempting to find out whether they were capable of appreciating the magnificence of the Metropolis of India. In the following year (1864) the Government scheme for remedying the supercession of local officers by the Staff Corps made its appearance, and caused great dissatisfaction. We asked for bread and they gave us a stone. Under its operation, on the 10th of December I became a Brevet-Major, though I was only a Lieutenant in the cadre of my regiment, whilst Stephenson of the same regiment, whose commission as Ensign bore the same date as that of mine, was a Substantive Major on the Staff Corps. Not only was the Government remedy a mere mockery, but it was worse; for, as Lieutenant and Brevet-Major, I had afterwards, at another station, to perform double duty, one week as a Subaltern, and another week as a Field Officer! But I must return from this digression, to notice a curious meteorological event which happened on the 24th March, 1864, on which evening there was a wonderful hail-storm. I never before saw such large hailstones as those I gathered, and used as ice to cool my beer at dinner that day, and the rest, which I preserved in a blanket, I used up the following day. These hailstones were really enormous; since they were considerably larger than grapeshot, and some were nearly as large as small oranges. Next month I was on a Court-martial as Interpreter for the trial of a European soldier, one of the coolest fishes that ever I saw. His cheek was quite remarkable. As, for instance, when asked whether he pleaded guilty or not, he coolly said to the Court, " I leave you to find that out." And on another occasion he actually snapped his fingers in defiance at the Court, saying, " I don't care that for you." The most noteworthy event of 1864 was the dreadful cyclone which, on the morning of the 5th October, burst upon Calcutta, and lasted till evening, doing great injury on the river. I thought by barring my door with a strong iron bar, and placing a large box against it, that I should be all right; but a sudden blast of the awful storm blew the door open as if the iron bar and heavy box were a straw. So we took to our heels, not knowing what in the world was going to happen; and as the masonry of the wall seemed to be giving way to a rather alarming extent, we felt it advisable to seek refuge in a more central room. Moreover, the verandah had to some extent given way, and the other corner of Royal Barracks had suffered severely. The Fort itself looked very much like a place taken by storm, the enemy being the stormy wind, which had blown down a great many trees, which were lying about in all directions inside the fortifications. Next day (6th October) I walked a long way on the river side, and most dismal were the sights of wrecks that met my eyes; and the worst appeared to be on the other side of the river, where the ships had run foul of one another, and were in the most extraordinary state of disorder conceivable. It was indeed an awfully novel sight. I saw one large steamer driven right ashore opposite the Metcalf Hall; and I saw part of a ship that had gone right down. I do not know whether the exceeding heat we experienced in June, in consequence of the rains not setting in till the very end of that month, had anything to do with this marvellous commotion in the elements: this is for meteorologists to decide. The previous month I was taken very ill, and some months afterwards, in consequence of ill-health, I resigned my appointment of Garrison Interpreter, and was appointed to do duty at the Convalescent Depôt, Darjeeling. So on the 24th of February, 1865, I and my wife and children crossed the river* to Howra, the railway terminus. Thence we went by the morning train to Burdwan.

Here I left the train, hired a gharee for a drive, and showed my children over the Rajah's fine zoological gardens. We returned the same evening to the station, and left at midnight for Sahibgunge, which we reached at 7 A.M. on the following morning. Here my wife was greatly grieved by receiving a telegram informing her of the death of her only brother. After experiencing a good deal of trouble in getting my baggage, which had previously been sent by the goods train, we left Sahibgunge, and having steamed about twenty-six miles, we anchored. After which, having got a wretched two-wheeled cart with worthless springs called a champooney, drawn by oxen, we jolted on to a place of rest called Caragola, which we left about 8 P.M. on the 26th of February, by palkee dawk, and after a miserable stormy night we reached Purneah early next morning, the 27th. Here we were provokingly detained several days, for on going to the Purneah and Darjeeling Transit Company's manager, I learnt that he had not received the post-office order I had sent him for 160 rupees to lay our dawks, so we had to wait here till the 1st of March, when our dawks being laid we set off, and in a few days we reached Punkabarree, at the foot of the hills. An accident befell my poor dear wife on the way, which led to serious consequences in her particular condition, as, whilst the bearers were carrying her along, the palkee pole suddenly snapped, when down came the palkee with such force to the ground as to inflict a severe shock to her in the delicate state she was in. At last we reached Darjeeling, on the

* There being no bridge over the Ganges at Calcutta, the passengers had to cross to Howra either by the steam ferry or by native boat.

6th March. Our quarters were at Jullapuhar, the Convalescent Depôt, where we were not at all comfortable, as our furniture had not arrived. The dilatoriness of the hill porters, men of immense strength in lifting burdens, is something incredible. The supply being very far below the demand, I was informed that a lot of these stalwart fellows would at one and the same time engage to take up to Darjeeling a great many boxes, barrels of beer, &c., belonging it might be to several parties, and there being comparatively few porters to convey these things to their destination, they would first carry a certain number of boxes a certain distance, and then go backwards and forwards for ever so long, till the whole were carried so far, and so they would go on all the way to Darjeeling, a distance of about twenty miles from Punkabarree. I believe their reputed dilatoriness was anything but exaggerated, for what with other delays on the road, I have been three or four months in getting heavy packages from Calcutta. I was enchanted with the beautiful view of the snowy range that met my eye. Gazing at Kunchunjingee (only fifty miles distant as the bird flies), one cannot help feeling that it is the grandest sight in the world. It is a great place for a butterfly collector. For thirty rupees I bought a splendid collection of the most magnificent butterflies and beetles. But with so much in nature to please the eye, there was one drawback, and that consisted in the rats, which from their fierceness constituted a great nuisance, since I heard at Darjeeling instances where these bold animals had flown up and bitten at least two people, one an English lady, and the other an English tradesman. I was pleased in April to read in the *Home News* my own case brought forward in an editorial, extracted from the London *Standard*. And next month I heard that the House of Commons, by sixty-nine to thirty-six, had voted an address to the Queen for the redress of our grievances. On the 5th of June I was one of the pall-bearers at the funeral of Lieutenant-General Loyd, who commanded at Dinapore during the Mutiny. This month I saw my name in orders promoted to Captain in the cadre of my regiment. I had some very pleasant Christian society here. I was on particularly friendly terms with Lieutenant-Colonel Shelton, an officer who had long been sorely tried by a worthless wife, from whom, I believe, he afterwards procured a divorce. I was also very friendly with Mrs. Coombs, a pious lady, whom I knew when I belonged to the 42nd Regiment N.I., and with Mr. Niebel, the Baptist Missionary. We had very pleasant Bible meetings at the house of the Chaplain, whose church I attended, as I much liked his preaching. There was one sermon on wasted opportunities that went straight to my heart, for I felt I was the man. I can say from experience that it is a most bitter thing to feel how much brighter one's career would have been but for one fatal step. The feeling is much the same many years afterwards, when the heart cries in remorse—"Oh that I had acted differently on that turning point of my life." This year, 1865, was one of great gloom to me, for in April I lost my dearest wife in childbirth, and in June I lost my darling boy, my only son, a handsome and sweet child of nearly two years old. The Chaplain would not bury him because he had not been baptized, but, for all that, there can be no doubt that the dear one's spirit, on quitting the body, fled to the region of the blest. I now got a medical certificate to England, so, on the 14th of November, I left Darjeeling with my children.

But my youngest child, who was only an infant of eight months, I left behind in charge of a Miss Wight, who kept a ladies' school there. That lady, about a year after my departure, became (as I was informed) a bankrupt, and about a month after Miss Wight had received from me a year's payment in advance, my poor Louie was turned adrift on the mercy of strangers, till

I could be written to to make fresh arrangements for her, which of course I lost no time in doing. But I must return from this digression to say that I and the rest of my children, three girls, reached Calcutta on the 22nd of November, and put up at a very comfortable boarding-house, where my daughter Annie was taken alarmingly ill, but happily she recovered in time for me to embark on the 9th of December on board the *Blenheim*, which left next day full of passengers for London *viá* Madras, which latter place we reached on the 18th. We of course went ashore there amidst a good deal of excitement whilst forcing our way in a Massoola boat through the raging surf. I found Madras a very benighted place in comparison with Calcutta, where I had spent so many years of my life. We left Madras on the 23rd of December. It will be well now to say a word or two about the parties on board. The Captain of course comes first. Of him I have only to say this, that I found him a most disobliging and very disagreeable man. One consequence of his disagreeableness was the difficulty I experienced in getting salt water for my ablutions. I found him dreadfully stingy whenever I sent to him to be helped to anything nice; and he used to watch the wine I drank in a most offensive manner. I never experienced anything at all like it in any of my five voyages round the Cape; and on one occasion at least my children could not get enough meat to eat. It was really too bad, considering the large sum I had paid for our passage, and the *Blenheim* was a regular A1 passenger ship. I have not much to say regarding the passengers. There is nothing like a long sea voyage for discovering the selfishness of human nature. There was the usual amount of squabbling; but this I shall pass over as not of sufficient interest to relate. But there was one display of female vanity amusing enough to be mentioned. It was the attempt made by Mrs. E——n, the wife of a Major of the Bengal staff corps to make the passengers believe she was twenty years younger than she really was. The conversation happened to turn upon the ages of people, when Mrs. E——n, who I believe was fifty, graciously volunteered information as to her own age. She did not care about people knowing her age. The fact was (so she said) she was thirty. This declaration was made in an offhand manner, as though she were laying down the law on a matter of fact that admitted of no dispute. No one of course openly manifested any incredulity; but this I venture to affirm, that every one present must have been laughing in his or her sleeve to hear a lady of ordinary sense, who looked quite fifty, unblushingly declare, and in such a manner, that she was only thirty. How can sensible ladies tell such incredible falsehoods about themselves? I can only attribute such ridiculous folly to an excess of feminine vanity resembling that of Queen Elizabeth, who was so vain in her old age as to be gratified by receiving compliments on her good looks. The event of the voyage, however, was the terrific hurricane we encountered off the Mauritius on the night of the 12th and morning of the 13th January, 1866. Just before its commencement I saw a sailor fall from one mast to another, and then from that to the deck. Poor man! he was taken up alive, but died two days afterwards. Soon after the above-mentioned accident the fearful storm broke upon us. Great and widespread was the alarm when the stern cabin, occupied by Lady Leeds and family, was burst in by the fury of the angry waves, and the mizzen-mast went by the board. I was praying most of the night, feeling that the *Blenheim* was in great danger of being wrecked. Our clever carpenter, however, managed to stave off the greatest source of danger by fixing a substitute for a door, which stopped the water from coming in through the breach in the stern cabin. About 3 P.M. on the 13th, thinking the danger of going to the bottom was over, I went to sleep under a comparative sense of security. The fury of the hurricane was, at least up to that time, truly dreadful, and we were no doubt in great danger. But, by the mercy of the Lord, it ended at last, and we were safe. Next day we were becalmed. This was indeed a most strange contrast. But is it not so sometimes with the Christian, that after passing through a terrible ordeal, wherein he was all but engulfed in absolute ruin, the storm has passed away, the sky clears, and is followed by a calm? I have experienced this myself, and have no doubt but that others have done so too. The next event of interest was our arrival at St Helena on the 24th February, after being seventy-seven days from Calcutta. I went ashore to see my friend Mr. Janisch,* with whom having dined I returned on board in the evening. I experienced great hospitality from Mr. and Mrs. Janisch, who next day welcomed most kindly not only myself but all my children to their house, where we stayed one night and two days; on one of which I went with Mr. Janisch up the hill and saw Napoleon's tomb; on which occasion my friend informed me that we had gone up as high as two thousand feet. After a pleasant visit we returned on board ship on the evening of the 26th, and the *Blenheim* left St. Helena the same day. I have nothing further to chronicle of the homeward voyage except that about a month afterwards I was taken very ill with liver complaint, and that on the 4th of April we turned about to go to the Azores, having run short of provisions. But as on the following day we came up with a ship from which we got the provisions that were required, we returned to our former homeward bound course.

On the 13th of April we took a pilot on board, and next day I, with a number of the passengers, got into a boat that came alongside (paying £1 12s. as my share), and landed at Folkstone. It does not fall in with the scope of this to say anything of my prolonged stay in England beyond this: that I was this year, 1866, admitted to the Staff Corps as Major, and that I went

* Now Governor of the island.

for a two months' continental tour, first to Rotterdam, thence to Cologne, then by steamer ~~down~~ the Rhine to Mayence and St. Moritz in the Engadine, where I stayed some weeks, and then turned my steps homeward *viâ* Homburg, where I stayed a week or two, and travelled home *viâ* Strasburg and Brussels. Having taken my passage by the *Shannon*, one of Green's ships, I went on board on the 10th August, 1869, and arrived after an uneventful passage at Calcutta about the middle of November.* This being my last and fifth voyage round the Cape of Good Hope, I will take this opportunity of summing up what I have to say on the subject of these long sea voyages, which have occupied about twenty months of my Indian service up to this time. The very strong distaste I have conceived for them is not so much on account of the miserable ordeal of sea-sickness one has to pass through, as their dreadful monotony, unrelieved by any incident of a more pleasing description than the occasional talking by signals with a passing ship, as sometimes happens; or of falling in with a ship in mid-ocean, and sufficiently close as to be able to converse with those on board by word of mouth. This, with an occasional glimpse of land, watching the flight of the fearless albatrosses coming so near the ship as to be easily shot into the water by cruel sportsmen, or looking at the flying fishes as they wend their flight out of the water and through the air, probably to avoid some enemy of the finny tribe, together with promenading the deck, eating and drinking and smoking, constitute the maximum joys of boardship life. There are, it is true, other incidents which help to keep people alive, such as the quarrels of passengers of various tempers and dispositions, who are *nolens volens* forced to eat and drink and live together for three or four months within the narrow limits of their floating wooden cage; and I am bound in truth to say that the fair sex were not far behind in

* After having been about a year without pay.

these rows. Those get on best who make the most fuss, or who have some one to make a fuss for them. Nothing brings out into full play one's natural selfishness like life on board ship. One source of the greatest wretchedness, whilst it lasts, is of course sea-sickness. But even after this is over, there are other serious discomforts from the oppressive heat in the proximity of the equatorial line, on which occasion I have sometimes been compelled to have my port put down, which made it so very close and hot as to be nearly suffocating, and was certainly more unbearable than the heat in India. I have therefore a strong repugnance to the wearisomeness and monotony of a long sea voyage. This being my case, with nothing to complain of in respect to my food and cabin, what must such a life be to the poor midshipman, with his hard salt junk to eat and other hardships to bear? A blacksmith's lot is far preferable, in my opinion, to his. In short, the great event of the voyage, which everybody with a grain of sense in his head looks forward to, is its end; and next to this is the vessel's touching at some intermediate port, such as the Cape or St. Helena. At Calcutta I put up at Mrs. Waters's boarding-house, where I spent a month very pleasantly. Here I made the acquaintance of a very pleasant American gentleman, of the name of Atterbury (a descendant of the celebrated Jacobite Bishop of that name), who was making the tour of the world. A few days after my arrival in India I went to call on a fellow-passenger of the *Shannon*, a weak-minded young Ensign, and when I got to his room I found to my horror that he had only just blown his brains out with his pistol. It seems that he had by some folly or other lost every rupee he had in the world, and that an engagement to be married had been broken off, which things together appear to have reduced him to such a state of despair as to have emboldened him to commit suicide. About this time, learning that the appointment of the Persian translatorship to Government was vacant, I immediately applied for it, on the strength of the examinations I had passed in the Native languages, and I was in all fairness entitled to it, which would have suited me exactly, as translating was my particular forte. But here I met with a cruel disappointment, as an objection was raised against my application on the grounds that I had not passed for two examinations in "honours." This was a technical objection, and showed me plainly that I only missed the mark because I had no one to say a single word in my favour; since the prize in two languages which I had passed in, was quite as difficult as the examination in honours. This I know, because I have studied for honours in Hindee, when I read through the "Subha Bilas," one of the test books for that examination, and partly read the celebrated "Ramayn," which is the other. It was soon followed by a second disappointment, because it resulted in a serious injury to me. This was my application that the time I had been on medical certificate might count as service, on the grounds of my ill-health being brought on by exposure to the sun on service, in 1857-58. But this was not acceded to by the Indian Government, on the grounds of the number of years that had intervened between 1858 and 1865, the year of my taking furlough. This adverse decision proved of serious consequence to me afterwards; for had I obtained medical certificate in 1858, when I wanted Assistant-Surgeon B—— to recommend me for leave on sick certificate, then I should eventually have retired on a Lieutenant-Colonel's pension, instead of that of a Major.

Being ordered to do duty at Morar (Gwalior), I crossed the river and went by train to Agra; whence I travelled about sixty-five miles by gharee dawk to my destination. A description of the capital of the Maharajah Scindiah's dominions may here fittingly be given. The Mahratta town of Gwalior is not very interesting to look at, being irregularly built and dirty. It is famed principally for its hill fortress, which is situated high up on a solid rock, a mile and a half long, by about a quarter of a mile broad, which rises in some places to a height of three hundred and forty feet, is in many parts perpendicular, and is quite isolated from the other hills in its vicinity. This fortress, once deemed impregnable, has ever since the Mutiny been held by British troops, and is a place which might be held by ten thousand resolute soldiers against a hostile force of hundreds of thousands. The city of Gwalior is situated along the eastern base of the rock; and the British Cantonment of Morar, where I was stationed, was on the opposite side of the town, and completely separated therefrom. I was here but a short time, and was not sorry to leave Morar, on account of the great scarcity of houses. In 1870 I was appointed Interpreter to H.M. 92nd Highlanders, cantoned at Jullundur in the Punjaub. Here I was stationed three years. I went this year by rail on leave for a short period to Lahore, the capital of the Punjaub, a city of about a hundred thousand inhabitants, situated about a mile from the river Ravee. I put up at a very comfortable hotel, kept by a Mrs. Goose, where I met an old Calcutta friend, and in a few days I saw all that was worth seeing. It contains many large buildings, and is principally celebrated for the Shalimar Gardens. But the Museum, to my mind, is the place most worth seeing. My stay at Jullundur was a very uneventful one. The only event out of the common was my being a President and Interpreter on a Court of inquest on a young officer of the 92nd Highlanders who had committed suicide. The apparent cause of his committing the rash act was of a most trivial description, being nothing more than a slight pecuniary embarrassment. But before he expired he made a remarkable statement, showing the terrible power which is exercised on earth by the great enemy of souls.

On the 10th December, 1870, I became Lieutenant-

Colonel, and resigned my Interpretership, and was appointed to do duty at Jullundur. I found Jullundur very dull, but a happy thought struck me which employed a good deal of my time, which was writing a small History of England. I was President of the Station Prize Committee, and as such I paid many scores of men prize-money for Delhi, Lucknow, and Calpie, which they ought to have had years ago. In 1871 I went to Simla. As I have in a former chapter already described this most fashionable sanatorium, there will be no occasion to say more than that I found Simla charming, and thoroughly enjoyed the change. I put up at a very comfortable boarding-house, where all the meals were served à la mode table d'hôte. I also partook of the hospitalities of the Viceroy, Earl Mayo, who a few months afterwards was assassinated on a visit to the Convict Settlement of Port Blair. There was this year an exhibition of paintings held at Simla, which I attended. Next year I took six months' leave to Mussoorie, where, as at Simla, I put up at a comfortable boarding-house. I was delighted with the picturesque hill scenery and cool climate of this lovely health resort, and derived much enjoyment from picnicking excursions to various places. I also attended an interesting trial which created a great sensation that year, in which an attempt was made to destroy the reputation of a young lady, a Colonel's daughter. On one occasion I made an excursion to the top of the Camel's Back. I do not know what others have felt, but I remember well that when I stood on the highest point of the Camel's Back I felt a particularly queer sensation, which I should not care to experience again. One of my picnics was to the Batta Waterfalls. The cascade here was really charming, and repaid one for the trouble of going down a break-neck sort of road to get to it. This year a Government order appeared, offering a pound a day to all unemployed Lieutenant-Colonels desirous of residing in England, till they should be entitled to Colonel's off reckonings. The offer was in due course made to me, and I accepted it conditionally, that I should first enjoy the two years' furlough I was entitled to. This was undoubtedly the best thing for me to do, for I felt nettled at having it thrown in my teeth that I was drawing a large amount of pay for doing very little work; and sometimes, in the newspapers, we unemployed officers were spoken of as military loafers. Having obtained two years' furlough, I left Jullundur on the 6th February, and went by train to Delhi, where I remained sight-seeing for several days. I first put up at an hotel, but the fare was so disgusting that I was very glad to change my quarters, and go to the Dak Bungalow, which I found decidedly better, and the day after my arrival at this walled city I drove to the Fort, where I saw the marble palace of the King of Delhi. How charmed I was as I stood gazing with admiration at the grandeur of a past age, when the great Moghul sat on his magnificent peacock throne in a palace of incomparable splendour! The matchless grandeur of this palatial building may to some extent be imagined, if the reader will but picture to his mind's eye a superb hall of white marble, with pillars and arches of exquisite symmetry, elaborately inlaid with jewelled devices of birds, flowers and fruits arranged with perfect taste, which is entered by a series of beautiful gateways sculptured with flowers and inscriptions from the Koran. At the same time I saw all that was worth seeing in the Fort. My visit to the Jumma Musjid must next be mentioned, as this building is certainly a masterpiece of the workmanship of Islam. Passing over the various curiosities which the Mussulman priest showed to me, I give instead the following description of a building that is to the Mahommedans of Delhi what St. Paul's is to the citizens of London. The Jumma Musjid, which is situated in the centre of the city, was built more than two hundred years ago by the Emperor Shahjehan.

This immense Mahommedan mosque is built of a dark red stone, with a marble court containing a fountain for purposes of ablution. It has three domes of white marble, and two minarets of white and rose-tinted marble, rising respectively to a height of 120 feet. On the 12th I started in an open carriage, and drove about ten miles to see the Kootub, a colossal column of triumph, erected by the Mussulman conqueror Kutuboodeen, to commemorate his conquest of the Hindoo capital.* It is a pillar of immense height, and one must go to see it, otherwise he cannot boast of having properly performed the sight-seeing business. Near the Kootub is a fine archway, built in the fourteenth century. I also went over the ruins of ancient Delhi, which is a few miles from the Kootub, and which was the capital of a Hindoo kingdom long before its conquest by the Mussulmen. I saw several Hindoo temples in ruins; one of which I took particular notice of, because it was reputed to be two thousand years old, and I noticed some graven images which it contained were in a wonderful state of preservation, considering their great antiquity. To antiquarians there is much in old Delhi that is well worth seeing. After viewing all that was worth seeing in the ruins of this ancient city, I went to the well to witness the wonderful feats of the divers, who jump from an immense height into the water to get bukhsheesh. It was a fearful-looking performance. After all this sight-seeing I got home about 6 P.M. Next day I visited some localities of interest associated with the siege of Delhi; such as the place where the gallant General Nicholson fell mortally wounded, the tomb of that noble fellow, and the monument erected to the memory of those officers and men who fell during the memorable siege. After seeing all this I drove back through the city. The streets of Delhi are mostly narrow; the chief exception is that of a handsome street full of fine shops, called the

* Delhi was occupied by Kutuboodeen in 1206.

"Chandnee Choke," which is about three-quarters of a mile long and fifty yards wide, and is crowded all hours of the day by well-dressed Mussulmen and Hindoos. Delhi has seven gates on the land side, viz., the Lahore, Ajmere, Turcoman, Delhi, Moree, Cashmere, and Agra gates. The population is computed at a hundred and sixty thousand, half Hindoos and half Mussulmen. After seeing all the sights I went to see the Baptist Mission here. My remarks on Missionary work will be found further on, and therefore I shall pass on in my narrative. I, like others, bought a lot of curiosities. Here a word of caution is necessary, which is that purchasers cannot be too cautious. For though I have not bought much jewellery, yet on two occasions I was regularly cheated. Once when I gave fifteen or sixteen rupees for what I believed to be a gold locket, but which, though resembling gold, was made of some base metal, and was not worth sixpence. The other was when I bought a gentleman's gold ring, which turned out to be made of sealing wax with a covering of gold. On the 15th I arrived by train at Allahabad, and put up at the Great Eastern Hotel, where I stayed a few days. There is not anything of much interest to be seen here. Of course I went and saw the stone Fort, situated on the confluence of the two rivers Ganges and Jumna, which is a place of great strength. On the 19th I left Allahabad by train for Jubbulpore, which I reached the same day, and put up at Kelner's Hotel, and on the morning of the 21st I left by the train for Bombay, which I reached about seven on the 22nd February, when I put up at Watson's Hotel. Here I stayed a week. I liked Bombay very much. It is certainly a very formidable rival to Calcutta, so much so that I do not know which to award the palm to. One would almost think, from its greater proximity to London, its native population,* which somewhat

* The population of Bombay amounts to nearly six hundred thousand.

exceeds that of Calcutta, its great importance as the general port of embarcation, and from its representing the senior Presidency,* that it ought to take the place of Calcutta as the metropolis of British India. The chief drawback appears to be this, that Bengal is, and according to precedent ever must be, the superior Presidency, unless the three Presidencies became amalgamated into one, with one Governor-General and one Commander-in-Chief. There is one advantage which Calcutta as a port of embarcation enjoys that Bombay does not possess, or at least did not at the time I am speaking of, which is, that I noticed all the way from Jubbulpore to Bombay (which is more than six hundred miles), there appeared to be no signs of an hotel, which any one might be taken to in case of sickness or over-fatigue; since I neither saw nor heard of anything beyond a few station refreshment rooms; whereas, were a traveller to be journeying towards Calcutta the same distance, he would find three or four hotels where he might break his journey. Bombay does not require a lengthy description. Suffice it to say, that it is a place where the Parsees represent a very considerable part of the population. The island on which the city is situated extends to about eight miles, with an average breadth of some three miles or thereabouts. The streets in Bombay are wide, and the buildings are handsome. The most remarkable buildings besides the Fort, are Government House, Byculla Club, and numerous churches, &c. Having first gone to the pier, I hired a boat to see the steamer on which I had taken my passage. Afterwards I went to the public gardens, where the band was playing. The scene was animating, great numbers of Parsees dressed in a variety of colours, but all looking clean and nice. I have often wondered at such a highly intelligent set of people as the Parsees being fire-worshippers. The chief object of interest at this time at Bombay was

* Being acquired in the reign of Charles II.

the Exhibition, which of course I visited, and was much pleased with what I saw; such as most gorgeously worked cloth and velvet, and several large pieces of brocaded carpets worked entirely in precious stones and seed pearls, which were regarded as so valuable that they were guarded by soldiers with fixed bayonets. On the 1st of March I embarked on board one of the Rubatino line of steamers, and arrived at Aden on the 9th. Here we stayed a week to repair some damage that had happened to the machinery, in consequence of the screw of the engine having gone down on entering the harbour. The heat at Aden was truly frightful. We left Aden with its oppressive heat (after seeing everything that was worth looking at) on the evening of the 17th, and arrived at Suez on the 24th, and left next day; but about an hour after starting, the steamer grounded on a sandbank, rolled on one side, and so completely stopped all traffic in the Suez Canal for some time. This created considerable alarm; several of the passengers rushed out of their cabins to know what had happened; everything rolled off the table, and a grand smash took place. It was not till the morning of the 28th that we were able to start again, and we reached Port Saïd next day, and arrived at our destination, Genoa, on the 6th April. I stayed three days here sight-seeing, and then went to Turin, staying there part of a day, and then pushed on through the Mont Cenis Tunnel to Paris, where I stayed four days, and arrived in England on the 15th April, 1873, and in April, 1875, I retired, after a service of thirty years, on a Major's pension, with the additional annuity provided for by the retirement scheme, that had recently come into operation.

In drawing my narrative of Indian Reminiscences to a close, I feel I cannot do so without saying something about a matter of such great importance as the work of evangelizing the people amongst whom so great a part of my life has been spent, especially as I have taken so much interest in the subject, and have myself had much religious conversation with both Mussulmen and Hindoos for many years. I have invariably taken an interest in the schools and other efforts put forth to Christianize the people by the missionaries, with whom I have ever maintained a warm friendship. These workers in the Lord's vineyard need no recommendation from my pen, since their work is so well known now-a-days, that there is no necessity for me to give any description thereof, which at the best would be but an imperfect one. I may remark, however, that I sympathize most with those efforts that are made towards making the native churches independent; increasing greatly the number of independent native ministers; educating the people in the vernacular rather than an English education, as the latter, which is given in the Government schools, tends, so it appears to me, to make them ungratefully self-conceited; educating as Christians the native women by zenana visiting, and the formation of orphanages. I shall commence by endeavouring to give a clear and intelligible account of those influences which have struck me after about twenty years' religious conversation with the Hindoos, to present the greatest obstacles to the spread of the gospel in India. The first evil influence on my catalogue is Hindoo pride, and of all the difficulties which I am going to describe, that self-complacent pride so characteristic of the Hindoo, which leads him to regard himself as of pure birth and divine origin (and partaking of the divine nature of a Brahmin), in conjunction with that self-righteous pride, the trusting in something to do to merit God's favour, presents one of the greatest barriers to the reception of the humbling doctrine of the Cross brought to them by the foreigner whose very touch he regards as pollution. To tell the Hindoo, puffed up by the self-righteous belief taught him in his Shastres that he is able to perform certain very virtuous and heaven-meriting works, such as venerating and feeding Brahmins and cows, invocation of their favourite deities, Ganges bathing, pilgrimages, idol worship, &c.—to tell him that none of these are meritorious, but are on the contrary high treason in the sight of God, whose will it is that man should entirely owe his salvation to Christ's atoning merits, is to arouse in the Hindoo's heart the most indignant and scornful feeling; as in the case of my Pundit, for example, who taught me Hindee for some years, whom I found to be a most bitter enemy to the doctrine of the Atonement; for when I told him of the blood of Christ Jesus cleansing from all sin, he at once sunk the fawning nature of the dependent, and quite forgot himself in the intense hatred and rancour which he manifested to a doctrine so repugnant to his Brahminical pride, which he consequently hated with all the hatred of the self-righteous fukeer (devotee), who said that rather than owe his salvation to another, he would prefer to be damned: there was no time-service with my Pundit on this occasion, for he did not care to offend me, which he rather did by somewhat worsting me in the argument by the indignant vehemence of his talk. Then there are the Hindoo devotees, whom I saw a good deal of when stationed with my regiment at Benares, who, besides acquiring a high position as saints, expect to obtain absorption into the Supreme Being as a reward of their religious austerities; such as the observance of religious vows, like that of silence, abstinence of rest taken in a recumbent position, and infliction of bodily pain in certain prescribed modes, pilgrimages performed by crawling all the way, &c. Now only conceive with what scornful anger these wild-looking Hindoo saints would regard the announcement of their fancied righteousnesses being no better than filthy rags in God's sight, and that to be saved they must descend from this pinnacle of their fancied merits, and take their stand with the common herd of guilty, hell-deserving sinners, and thankfully receive salvation as God's free, unmerited gift to sinners! Could they find words to express their rage, it would doubtless be in the same strain as that of the self-righteous fukeer already quoted. What a miracle of grace it is for such monsters of pride to be converted, and become humble Christians! When such trophies are won to redeeming grace, let us see to it that we give God all the praise.

2nd. Another great hindrance arises from the Hindoo's conscience being so blunted by the practice of the grossest sensuality, and by the debasing and polluting influences of his idolatrous creed, and being besides so ill-informed that it requires to be reformed from its chaotic state by being taught what sin really is, as the words in the Hindee language for sin and holiness fail to convey their proper meaning to the polluted mind of the Hindoo. But dark and unenlightened as his conscience undoubtedly is, yet after an experience of many years' religious conversation with the natives, I am fully convinced that it is the most profitable plan to make an earnest appeal in that quarter, looking to God for blessing, and with a heart empty of self and full of Christ. I do not say but that it may sometimes be advisable to show up the absurd geographical errors of their Purans or Shastres—such as the existence of seas of milk and butter, and a mountain (Mount Sumeroo) hundred of miles high; the description of the earth as a plain surface, the Shastre account of sunrise and sunset being caused by a sort of game of "bo-peep" between that luminary and a certain mountain; and to point out the very contradictory and irreconcilable accounts of the Supreme Being recorded in their Shastres, and that gods so vile and depraved as they are described in those books can have no claim on our respect or worship, and cannot be the god and judge of the whole earth. Their belief in transmigration affords matter for a good laugh, exercising, as it does, its influence in daily life. For instance, I have heard of an

Indian king who, on the death of his queen, prohibited the poor fishermen in his dominions from following their occupation for a certain time, from the fear that his deceased wife, who he believed had become a fish, would be caught and eaten. Again, the uselessness of all religious austerities, and in fact of all religious duties beyond the invocation of one of their favourite gods, may be urged; for who would give a pound for what he could get for a penny? I have, therefore, sometimes said, "Why do anything beyond merely calling out 'Ram! Ram!' sitting at ease in your houses, since that is all you need to do for your salvation according to your Shastre?" But beating them soundly with their own books causes warmth, and is often a mere selfish, vainglorious proceeding; and reviling their gods irritates them; and though you may come off with flying colours in the argument, yet it is the old story:

> "He that's convinced against his will
> Is of the same opinion still."

For instance, when I conceived I had quite overcome a Hindoo, after much talk on the merits of Hindooism, the same man has afterwards taken leave for the express purpose of running back to his idol, the sin and folly of worshipping which I had so clearly shown him.

3rd. Another hindrance is in reference to the deep degradation of the female sex, the entire absence of anything in them to work upon—nothing, for instance, like the example of a pious father, the loving memory of a pure-minded sister, or the remembrance of a mother's teaching and prayers, which in more favoured lands have been productive of such blessed results. For talk to a respectable and educated Hindoo about his mother (the speaker being necessarily a lady, on account of the strangely jealous temper of the Hindoo, who cannot bear a man taking an interest in his female relations), and what reminiscences will that fond name conjure up? Well, certainly nothing of a purifying or ennobling nature for the missionary to ground an appeal upon to the better feelings of his heart. There will be the remembrance of feelings wounded by the foulest and most telling abuse, through the vehicle of a mother's and sister's name; for it is a strange peculiarity of the Hindoo to pour out the vials of his wrath through the female relations of the object of his anger. Then there will be the remembrance of his mother's position in his father's household, viz., one of a group of his father's wives, a zenana prisoner, or, in other words, a domestic slave, illiterate of course, and without much more intellect than a cow, and hardly so much valued as that animal, according to the following popular saying of theirs, viz., "If your house is on fire, save yourself first, your cow next, and then your wife." Again, should his mother have been left a young widow, there are most probably degrading reminiscences, owing to the inveterate Hindoo prejudice against the remarriage of widows, who, previous to the abolishment of suttee by Lord William Bentinck in 1829, used to immolate themselves on their husbands' pyres. Such, no doubt, are some of the things that present themselves to his mental vision when he thinks of his mother; and no thoughts of a more elevating nature will suggest themselves on thinking of a beautiful, bright-eyed sister; for, to begin with, the Hindoosthanie word "sala" (brother-in-law), denoting her husband's relationship to him, is, incomprehensible as it may seem, a very common term of bitter abuse, to understand which, one must understand the very low estimate that is taken of woman's moral character in the East. Confinement under lock and key, and not education or religion, being the great Hindoo safeguard for the female honour of between twenty and thirty millions of females, together with the fear of summary vengeance for deviation from the path of female rectitude. It will help to throw light on the subject if we consider what are the Hindoo ideas on womanly loveliness; they all relate to the body, and

R

not to the mind, for to be accomplished (except in a few isolated cases) would be scouted in one of the softer sex, who best fills her proper place as the mere convenience and drudge of her husband and master. The lovely female is invariably described as follows, viz., one with hair like the clouds, deer's eyes, parrot's nose, dove's throat, teeth like a necklace of pearls, tiger's waist, a peek-bird's voice, and the gait of an elephant, with whom every one falls in love at sight. It is much to be wished that a deputation of strong-minded women from the "women's rights" party could be induced to proceed to India for the purpose of teaching the husbands more correct views of what positions their wives ought to fill. And should their representation of the humane side of the question prove ineffectual, a forcible appeal might still be made to their self-interest, for they can never expect to ascend much in the social scale so long as they hold their wives and daughters in such deplorable bondage and ignorance, whose degradation is their own, and that of their children.

Again, in addition to the vacuum of working material in a social point of view, they are besides such sophists and such adepts at evading an argument that there is no grasping hold of them, for they elude your grasp just when you think they must yield, by suddenly attacking you with some sophism about the irresponsibility of the Almighty, covered by objections regarding the origin of sin and Satan, &c. Such cavillings I have had to answer when insisting on the holiness of God, and that consequently the gods of the Shastres, who are depicted as monsters of impurity, cannot be God.

Another way they have of extricating themselves from a dilemma is this: such as when they have told me that this is the Kuljoog (the iron age), and that we are all wandering about, under the power of "Maya," a most subtle delusive influence, and know literally nothing; and when, to expose this fallacy, I have asked, "Surely there can be no doubt that you are this moment talking with me, and that that [tapping my table] is a table?" the reply has been, "I think so, but don't know, being under the power of Maya." Thus they endeavour at the same time to evade your argument and to disown all responsibility, which is, besides, almost obliterated by their fatalistic notions expressed by their proverb, "What Brahma has written in my forehead can never be obliterated," and the usual stoical remark of "What was to be, that has happened," on the occurrence of any dire calamity. I have found it very difficult to make any deep and abiding impression on the Hindoo mind; for during the twenty years I have had religious talk with them I have not had the pleasure of being the honoured instrument of effecting a single conversion. I have seen some, to all appearance, deeply impressed by the truth as I have set it before them, but nothing more. I had great hopes of the conversion of my Hindoo bearer, who went through a regular course of instruction with me in Bible truths, in which he succeeded in acquiring much head-knowledge; but there, I am afraid, the matter ended, at least as far as I know.

4th. Caste, every one knows, is a great hindrance, as the loss of it is regarded by Hindoos as the greatest earthly calamity and disgrace. It has four primary divisions—Priest, Soldier, Writer, and the Soodra, or low caste; besides which there are a variety of subdivisions. But there is no such thing as promotion, every Hindoo always remaining, and his descendants after him, in the caste into which he is born. The Hindoo, I need hardly say, has to submit to the loss of this much-prized distinction when he makes a public profession of the Christian Faith in baptism, and he must be prepared to lose his wife and children, who often abandon him, and refuse to hold any social intercourse with him. And for such a sacrifice, which may also be attended with the loss of his vocation, he will meet with little or no sympathy from the mass of mere professing Christians, and often the reverse, as I have had frequently to defend their character against the scorn heaped upon them as a body. Renouncing caste is the strongest proof of sincerity. I was informed by a missionary in 1873 that in the large native city of Delhi, where he was stationed, he believed there were a thousand secret Christians, who had given up Hindooism for Christianity without making an open profession.

6th. The Mussulmen, who, I should think, form nearly a fourth of the population, have their objections, which are different in their nature from those of their Hindoo countrymen. Their principal objection is against the divinity of Christ, whom they speak respectfully of as a good man, but inferior to Mahomet. I say this subject to correction, as I have been told that Christ is spoken of as the "Word of God" in the Koran, which is a book I have not read. They hate us politically for having wrested from them the country which they obtained by conquest from the Hindoo, and they are imbued with a feeling of strong hatred of our religion. On the other hand, it must be admitted that there are some exceptions, for I have sometimes met with quiet attention from them. For instance, my landlord at Bareilly, Sadut Ally, listened with the most profound attention when I freely and earnestly set before him the blessed doctrine of Redemption without uttering a single objection, which is the more remarkable, because a Mussulman cannot bear to hear the name of Jesus mentioned as the Son of God. He confessed to me that he felt his heart inclining to the doctrine propounded by me, and wished that I might always be near to instruct him. I made him a present of a Bible in his own language, and can only hope that it, with my conversation, may have been blessed to him.

I always insist on Christ being God, and as the Mahometans acknowledge the Old and New Testaments to be a Divine Revelation, I generally quote the inspired words of the apostle in refutation of the claims of Mahomed—" But though we or an angel from heaven preach any other doctrine to you than that which we have preached to you, let him be accursed." If the Mussulman happens to be a man of education, a warm contest then ensues, he declaring that the Old and New Testaments in my possession are not the genuine Old and New Testaments, which, he says, were destroyed ages ago by order of a wicked king. I then warmly contend that this could not be, on account of the early multiplication of copies of the Scriptures all over the known world. However, after all, I think the best plan in dealing either with the Hindoo or Mussulman is to make an earnest appeal to his conscience. I often used to hire a congregation of the poor, the maimed, the halt, and the blind, who, attracted by a small sum of money which each would receive before leaving, would gladly come into my compound to listen to a discourse which I would preach to them from a text in my Hindoosthanie or Hindee Bible, and sometimes a leper would appear standing afar off. By this means I was able to make known to a good many poor people the good tidings of salvation through faith in a crucified Saviour. I hope that some text of Scripture may have sunk deep into the hearts of some of these degraded creatures, and that these efforts may not have been as water spilt on the ground. The theme of my sermon was almost always the atonement of Christ, which I explained to them as simply and plainly as I could, and eternity will show with what results. The very day I left Jullunder for Bombay, on the occasion of my final departure from India, I gave as earnest an address as I could command to my assembled servants. Probably it was my own fault that I did not see some conversions amongst them; at all events, God's word, wherever it is faithfully explained, is and must be productive of some result; it must be either a savour of life unto life or a savour of death unto death.

And now, in conclusion, let me say that I think we ought to give our warmest sympathies to the Lord's servants working in a tropical climate like India, with such mighty obstacles and sometimes great discouragements to contend with; for they much need our prayers that their zeal fail not; for long years of daily contact with idolatry has a deadening influence as the first fresh impressions of abhorrence by degrees lose their strength. Hence, as it appears to me, there is danger of deteriorating in Christian character; for we can hardly help suffering spiritual injury from becoming so familiarized with any sin that has ceased to be as hateful as it once was, for the less sin is hated the more must one's spirituality suffer.

We should therefore uphold these workers in the Lord's vineyard with our prayers, that they may increase rather than go back in zeal for the truth, and be strong in faith, and possess a yearning compassion for the perishing heathen, leading them to delight more in testifying for Christ than in testifying against the false gods of the heathen.

I shall conclude with making the following remarks in regard to Native Servants:—As a general rule a good master will generally get a good set of servants, whom on the whole he will find honest—surprisingly so, considering the disadvantage of their creed. There are, no doubt, masters who shamefully ill-treat their servants; and, on the other hand, there are others who treat them well. But even a kind and considerate master will sometimes, under great provocation, be driven to exercise a little discipline, such as a slap for some grave fault, when, in all probability, the bearer, or whoever the offender may be, will virtually acknowledge his offence by deprecatingly saying to his master, "Ap mā bāp hain" (you are my father and mother). I do not defend the boxing of a native's ears—I merely state the facts of the case. Great supervision is required on

the part of parents to counteract the evil influence brought to bear on little English children by the Ayahs, who have charge of them most part of the day, and who take every opportunity to initiate them into the way of lying. The greatest care is necessary to guard English girls of tender age against the seductive influences of the men-servants, who in every way may be seen to take every opportunity of ingratiating themselves with the "Missy babas." The patience of the Ayahs is something wonderful. You can see them for hours together sitting with the little ones, amusing them, and never seeming to get tired; and you may see an Ayah perhaps for hours sitting with a baby in her lap, trying to lull it to sleep. Many years ago I had an Ayah of the name of Puddoo, a very simple body, who I fancy scarcely knew more than one nursery song. At all events, I heard it so often—scores if not hundreds of times—that I can't get the stupid thing out of my head. The inane lullaby was as follows:—
"Kul ka muchlee Kiyā Kiya Soono to bāba Soono tō;" the interpretation of which is, "What have you done with yesterday's fish? Listen, child, listen!" This she would repeat over and over again by the hour together *ad nauseam*. She used to shrink back at the sight of me, either in real or affected modesty; but when she had been drinking—which sometimes happened—then she became bolder in her demeanour. I need say nothing about their lying propensities, this being so well known. But sometimes one could not help laughing to observe into what ludicrous dilemmas it landed them. For sometimes, in telling his master something that was not true, a servant would forget some previous lie he had told, which at once stamped the falsehood of what he was now saying. But they are so accustomed to utter untruths that a conviction from their own mouths would not greatly abash them. If he were a Hindoo, he might pull his ear as a tacit acknowledgment of his fault. The natives are very

polite in their language, though very often they contradict you, which is sometimes very provoking. They are glib in such phrases as "Ap kee Mihrbānee se," or "Ikbāl se," &c., and such genteel modes of expression as "Sahib ārām furmāte hain" (the Sahib is ordering rest for himself); instead of saying simply, "Sahib sota hai" (the Sahib is asleep), which is a vulgarism. Also, when a "bura Sahib" dies, it is unpardonably impolite to state the plain fact. The polished form of expressing the melancholy fact is by the words " Rehlut furmaye hain" (he has ordered the march of departure to the other world).

My narrative is now ended. I must now bid adieu to the land of beautiful birds, wild beasts, snakes, and amphibious creatures—a land swarming with animal life, from the enormous elephant to the skunk-rat that runs about near your bed at night with its hideous squeak and nasty smell; the domestic lizard, that drops from your walls to the floor with a gentle thud; the paroquets and crows that come into your verandah, down to the unwelcome, buzzing mosquito, ever on the look-out for his sleepy prey; and yet, after all, to the land where I have spent many happy days!

CHAPTER IX.

Narrative continued of E. S. the Atheist—Our Final Meeting in Calcutta—E. S. takes his Discharge—His Bright Prospects Ruined by his own Folly—He Re-Enlists—His Wretched Death—Remarks—Concluding Argumentative Remarks.

It is time now to continue the narrative of the Atheist, E. S., who, having served as a private throughout the Crimean War, returned to India in 1857, and took part in the suppression of the Sepoy Revolt. I did not at this time meet with him, for he served with his regiment in Oude, whilst I served with mine, as already particularized, in the North-West Provinces from '57 to '59. One would have thought that this opportunity of seeing so much service would have proved the means of his regaining a commission. But it was not the case, and I have been informed on good authority that he bore the character of a "discontented and ill-conditioned soldier."

Shortly after the complete suppression of the Mutiny I was appointed Garrison Interpreter, Fort William, Calcutta, and here at last, at the end of 1864, I met my old Barrackpore neighbour. It was on the occasion of his going home, previous to taking his discharge. Although he had behaved so ill to me, when he was an officer, yet I could not see him in such sadly altered circumstances without trying to do something for him. Military etiquette prohibited my showing him Indian hospitality, as I should of course have endangered my own commission had I asked him to sit down and dine with me. However, I helped him with money, which he told me he was in need of, and I did my best to convince him of the unreasonableness of Atheism, and got him to read the best book on the subject I could procure in Calcutta. All my efforts were, however, of no avail, as this poor fellow (whose whole career was one of folly) entirely refused to believe in the existence of an All-wise God; and one of the last things he said to me on the subject was to deny the existence of any Supreme Being, and to account for things as they are by some absurd speculative theory of his own. Yet one would think that any one with a grain of common sense must perceive that such a beautifully constructed world as ours, displaying such wonderful wisdom, order, and grandeur, must be the work of some great designer; since to think otherwise one may as well believe that a watch is not the work of a watchmaker, or that some cleverly constructed mechanical contrivance made itself. And to see the incomparably superior workmanship of the Almighty Creator of the Universe, let any one with a good microscope compare the work of God as seen in the dust of a butterfly's wing with the finest workmanship that can be produced by man, and notice the difference!!! This meeting at Calcutta was a final one; I never saw the unhappy Atheist again. S. went to England, and was discharged in May, 1865, whilst I went home on furlough the same year. I heard nothing further about him till 1869, when, being again stationed at Gwalior, I met with an officer of the regiment he originally belonged to, from whom I learnt the following surprising particulars, which I will now relate. It seems that after taking his discharge a bright future opened to him. Some friends interested in his welfare agreed to give him a large sum of money on condition that he would go and settle in the colonies. Now this really was a splendid opening, affording a fine opportunity for retrieving his past follies, and one would think it was the very thing for a man who had roughed it as a private through the Crimean and Mutiny campaigns, and must, consequently, be inured to hardship, being besides in the prime of life, and possession of great physical strength. Well, what did E. S. do? He accepted the money on these stringent conditions, booked his passage to the colonies, and actually went on board when the ship was near sailing, as if he really meant to go in her. But it was all pretence, for when the ship was on the point of departure, he slipped down the side into a boat and went ashore. But he had been watched, and he was pounced upon at once, and made to refund the money he had taken on false pretences. Now, how can such consummate folly be accounted for? Poor fellow, this was the last opportunity afforded him of retrieving his lost position, as far as I am acquainted with his history. Indeed, after this it is not probable that any friends would persist in trying to help one who would not be helped; and thus it happened that he re-engaged as a soldier in May, 1865. Assuredly he was under the influence of a withering blight, the result of Atheism. And can we doubt but that the curse of God, even in this world, does rest upon those who totally deny the existence of any Supreme Being whatever! In corroboration of this view, I give the following extract to show how Infidelity, though not quite so bad as Atheism, brings with it blighted worldly prospects:—" I have," says the writer, "recently visited the prison at Sing Sing. As I went from cell to cell I met an old man. . . . . He said that when young he was one of a company of youths who formed an Infidel club, and who met once a week for talking Infidelity, gambling, and drinking, and I was shocked as he told me of the end to which his companions came. 'One,' said he, 'died by his own hand, another by violence, some in State prisons, some in delirium tremens, and, as far as I know, I am the only one of them surviving; and here I am in the garb, and daily at the work, of a felon.' "[*]

I have not much left to say, having merely to add

[*] Dr. Prime's "Power of Prayer," p. 291.

that the subject of this sketch appears to have died a violent death. For shortly after my arrival at Jullunder, in 1870, I read of the death of E. S., at Plymouth, in an English paper. It appeared from this account that he was found lying in a solitary road in a dying state, unable to speak; that there was every appearance of a severe struggle for life with some one, who had made good his escape; and that this wretched man expired soon after in the hospital, without being able to state how he came by his death. Poor fellow, with his natural advantages, how different his career might have been! Here, truly, was a melancholy ending to an unhappy life! But there is a life beyond the grave. But here, compassion to him we knew as a young officer, full of life and strength, bids us drop the curtain on this mournful scene. Let us hope that, like the thief on the cross, he may have repented at the last. More than this charity will not admit of our saying, in consideration of some whom we hope may derive some benefit from the solemn warning conveyed by the life of an Atheist. I have never been able to learn anything concerning his last days; but I have heard this, that he never evinced any disposition to retrieve his youthful follies, which certainly does not encourage the hope that he repented of his evil ways.

In conclusion. One can hardly, we should think, read the history of the life of E. S. without being convinced that the surest way to blight one's prospect for both worlds is to become an Atheist. Beware of any attempt made to undermine your belief in the truth of the Bible; do not listen to people making jocose remarks on its contents. Esteem the Bible as a treasure, and walk by its precepts, in order to secure happiness lasting as eternity. Remember how short time is at the longest, and how long eternity is! How soon you may be summoned from time to eternity, perhaps so suddenly as not to leave you the opportunity of crying to God for mercy. Make up your mind at once, for delay is dangerous;

defer it not; to-morrow may be too late, so now, while it is called to-day, flee to the loving arms of Christ, who stands ready to receive the sinner coming to Him.

> " The cross! it takes our guilt away,
> It holds the fainting spirit up;
> It cheers with hope the gloomy day,
> And sweetens every bitter cup.
>
> " It makes the coward spirit brave,
> And nerves the feeble arm for fight;
> It takes the terror from the grave,
> And gilds the bed of death with light."

Come now, what shall be your answer? Is it for the pleasures of sin, which are but for a season? Well, but remember, that after death there is a judgment to come, and hell is truth seen too late! Does not your heart creep at the very thought? Think again, will you deliberately barter your hopes of eternal happiness for a few sinful delights, which last but for a season? As you have seen in the case of a companion cut off in the hey-day of youth, and in the enjoyment of those pleasures your heart is set upon? Or will you embrace the fanciful notions of poor E. S., and deny the existence of a Supreme Being? If so, you may expect a blight to rest upon you; so that you will not prosper even in this world. And think of the expected heaven of the infidel; (viz.,) annihilation; can you think of it and bear the idea of such a thing? How much better to decide for Christ; you will not desire annihilation then, you will not fear the dreadful judgment-day then; for there is no condemnation to them who are in Jesus. No, if you will but make a surrender of your heart to Christ, you will expect, and receive in due time, that incorruptible inheritance spoken of in the 1st chapter of the 1st Epistle of Peter, which is reserved in heaven for you, and will be upheld by the mighty power of God through faith unto salvation. Should this fall into a soldier's hands, I have a word of advice suited to his position.

With such a prize before you, dare to be singular in differing from your drunken, blaspheming, dissolute companions, and look up to God your Father for help and strength in every difficulty, and He will bless you, and He will most likely bless you to others, if your life corresponds with your profession. Go on, therefore, in the strength of the Lord, who cares for His people and will cause all things to work together for their good. You must not expect things always to go smoothly with you; or be disappointed if some turn out differently to what you hoped and expected; nor must you be dismayed by the difficulties of the way; though doubtless you do find it a hard struggle in the barrack-room, exposed as you are to so much temptation; for remember that the Christian life is a warfare, which we must all wage in order to obtain the crown. But though you have to fight, you need not fear, when you know that you are on the winning side. Look forward then to that happy coming time, when you will receive the crown of victory, and in the meantime keep out of the way of temptation; for your safety consists in putting your trust in the Lord, which you would show you were not doing were you unnecessarily to put yourself in the way of temptation. Seek God's help and guidance, however severe may be the fight within and without, and you will come out of the ordeal a conqueror through your sympathizing Saviour, who will not allow any enemy to pluck you out of His hand. Lastly, do not be discouraged if you have seen some, who, after making great professions, have turned back to their former wicked ways; for, remember, that their backsliding in no way alters the truth of God's promises, so precious to the believer. Think how foolish it would be to set no value on the current coin of the realm, because you have been deceived by the reception of a few counterfeit shillings! We must not be kept from pursuing the plain path of Christian duty because we fear we may fall. I repeat it, therefore, go on in the strength of the Lord; walk humbly with your God, and then when your earthly pilgrimage is over your eternal holiday will commence. Think of that bright future as much as you possibly can, and take for your motto in life the inspired words contained in Proverbs iii. 5, 6: "Trust in the Lord with all thine heart; and lean not unto thine own understanding. In all thy ways acknowledge him, and he shall direct thy paths. I humbly hope that what I have said may induce some who have hitherto neglected their Bibles, to obey Christ's command to search the Scriptures, which proclaims pardon and peace through the blood of the Lamb, which cleanseth from all sin.

> " There is life for a look at the Crucified One,
> There is life at this moment for thee;
> Then look, sinner, look unto Him and be saved,
> Unto Him who was nailed to the tree.
>   Look! look! look and live!
>   There is life for a look at the Crucified One,
>   There is life at this moment for thee.
>
> " Oh, why was He there as the Bearer of sin,
> If on Jesus thy guilt was not laid?
> Oh, why from His side flowed the sin-cleansing blood,
> If His dying thy debt has not paid?
>
> " It is not thy tears of repentance or prayers,
> But the blood that atones for the soul;
> On Him then who shed it, thou mayest at once
> Thy weight of iniquities roll.
>
> " Then doubt not thy welcome, since God has declared,
> There remaineth no more to be done;
> That once in the end of the world He appeared,
> And completed the work He begun.
>
> " Then take with rejoicing from Jesus at once,
> The life everlasting He gives;
> And know with assurance thou never canst die,
> Since Jesus, thy righteousness, lives."

I shall conclude my book with the following remarks:—

1st. Contrast the alleged discrepancies of Scripture with the abundant discordant statements and inaccuracies to be found in the works of the most celebrated writers which our enlightened country has produced, and the contradictory utterances on important questions made by the most renowned of our statesmen at different periods of their political careers.

2nd. Reflect, that a spiritual eye is required to understand the paradoxes of Scripture, which, though they appear to involve contradiction, are all really true in the sense in which they are meant, such as the following: 1 Cor. iii. 18; 2 Cor. vi. 10; and 2 Cor. xii. 10.

3rd. It must be borne in mind that there are some difficulties arising from taking certain passages literally which were never meant to be taken in that sense; but figuratively, conveying a spiritual meaning, such as those in John vi. 52 to 60; or which by comparison, the highest duty of loving God above ought else is taught, as in Luke xiv. 26; and it is obvious that those verses speaking about God's repenting are not to be taken in a literal sense; since the Almighty is immutable. He never changes, James i. 17. The same remark applies to those passages where God condescends to use language suitable to our finite comprehensions, such as those contained in Isaiah lix. 1; Jeremiah xxi. 5; Luke i. 51; and 1 Peter iii. 12.

4th. There are some apparent contradictory statements in regard to doctrine; but on careful examination it will be seen, that they all contain accurate views of the same truth from different stand-points.

5th. Do not for an instant admit the command for the utter destruction of the Amalekites to be at variance with the divine attribute of mercy; for remember it is the prerogative of the Almighty to take away the life he bestows in any way he pleases, and being unrestricted as to means, he may with equal propriety employ the swords of the Israelites to execute his righteous wrath upon the wicked Amalekites, as to call for fire and brimstone from heaven to destroy the people of Sodom and Gomorrah, or to put an end to human existence in any way he pleases. Moreover, it was necessary for the spiritual welfare of God's own people that the Israelites should show no mercy to the heathen, since the return made by them was, that by enticing them to serve their gods, they became thorns in the sides of the Jewish nation.

6th. Do not be disconcerted by certain appeals to false sentiment, contained in such insidious queries as: What will become of the heathen world? and do you believe in the eternal punishment of the wicked? It is sufficient to know this, that the weight of Scripture, even the emphatic and reiterated words of our Saviour, support the doctrine of the everlasting punishment of the finally impenitent, and that the Judge of the whole world will certainly deal rightly and justly by his creatures. Moreover, I would submit this thought for serious consideration, that, as sinners ourselves, we are not in a position to gauge the magnitude of sin, and the infinite guilt of transgression against God's holy law, and that the Almighty alone is competent to decide this all-important question. Once more with regard to those heathen who have never heard of Christ; it may be observed, in the first place, that the inspired apostle Paul tells us:—

" For when the Gentiles which have not the law, do by nature the things contained in the law, these, having not the law, are a law unto themselves: which show the work of the law written in their hearts, their conscience also bearing witness, and their thoughts the meanwhile accusing or else excusing one another," Rom. ii. 14, 15.

It is my belief, that the conscience of the heathen does not acquit them of sin. For having lived long and conversed much with them, I fearlessly assert, that without punishing them for the rejection of a gospel they have never heard, there is so much guilt contracted in their daily lives, according to the standard of their own consciences, as to demand heavy punishment; for instance, a Hindoo has ingenuously confessed to me the most gross impurities which are practised in the families of his idolatrous countrymen. Then let any one acquainted with the subject think of the atrocities committed by the heathen during the Indian Mutiny!! Moreover, what is the entire sacrificial system of heathenism, but a confession that it feels guilty before the bar of conscience?

7th. Do not choke yourself with mysteries that are well in their place, but don't concern you. Leave it to angry disputants to discuss the doctrines of election and freewill; and waste not your time in arguing with those who desire to mystify you with captious questions about such things as the existence of sin and Satan in God's universe. Be content to leave all such matters till the light of eternity clears up all mysteries (which are now, as it were, secrets of state), and then everything will be fully cleared up with universal satisfaction, and cavillers will be speechless. For the present we may safely leave these things with One who is too wise to err, and too good to be unkind.

Caution is necessary to be observed against taking for granted the correctness of infidel quotations of Scripture, or of anything they may state in depreciation of the Bible upon the presumption of their superior learning; and I remember several years ago, when spending the hot season at Mussoorie, having a religious conversation with a sceptical gentleman, who boldly asserted that a considerable portion of the New Testament was spurious, and gave the name of a well-known writer as his authority. I consequently procured the book referred to, which I read only to find that his assertion was as mendacious as it was audacious.

Moreover, it is necessary to be on one's guard against disjointed quotations from the Bible; since mischievous notions might be founded on some fragmentary portions severed from the concluding portion which supplies the key to the meaning; for instance, if an idle, ignorant man read no further than the words, "Labour not for the meat that perisheth" (John vi. 27), he might, if so inclined, construe the passage to mean that he need not work for his daily bread; and a man of choleric disposition, reading just these words, "Surely the wrath of man shall praise thee" (Psalm lxxvi. 10), might possibly say that he saw no harm in giving way to anger.

8th. There are several objections to the credibility of miracles, overlooking the fact that the miracles of the New Testament are attested to by witnesses of unimpeachable integrity; whilst the objectors readily accept as truth statements regarding earthly matters on much less evidence; whilst the integrity and sincerity of the evangelists are shown by the surprising ingenuousness with which they recorded events so much to their discredit: and not only were they themselves ready to give up their lives for the truth of the gospel, but hundreds of thousands, at different times, have endured torture and death, rather than deny those truths. Some miracles are especially selected as objects of ridicule or objection; such, for instance, as Joshua's miracle of the prolongation of day, recorded in Joshua x. 12, 13; which I feel no difficulty in accepting in a literal sense. Nor do I find any difficulty in believing with regard to the 8th verse of the xxxviiith chapter of Isaiah, that the shadow of the degrees of the sundial of Ahaz was supernaturally brought back ten degrees, and that the sun, as it were, returned ten degrees, by the earth being stopped in its revolution, and made to revolve backwards ten degrees. I care not one atom what scientific men may say of the physical derangement this would cause if this globe were made to revolve backwards; for the Bible tells me that the Almighty "turneth wise men backward, and maketh their knowledge foolish," Isaiah xliv. 25. It is only cursed unbelief that makes a difficulty. The laws of nature, as they are called, are under the absolute control and disposal of the Great Creator, just as clay is in the hands of the potter.

I once heard an infidel officer, at the mess-table, attempt to demolish all reverence for the Bible, by turning into ridicule, what he looked upon as the absurd story of Jonah's being swallowed by a whale, as containing a physical impossibility, on account of the smallness of the whale's throat. There is really no force in the scoffings of that infidel, whose military career, I may remark *en passant*, terminated in infamy. The Scripture says, Jonah i. 17, that the Lord prepared a great fish to swallow Jonah, and that fish our Saviour called a whale, Matthew xii. 40. The Almighty, as I conceive, therefore, either miraculously removed the natural disqualification existing in that particular whale, or else created a whale for the very purpose, in whose stomach the prophet remained three days.

9th. It will be well to allude to a Biblical reference difficulty. At Benares, I was once puzzled for the time by an unbeliever referring me to the 9th verse of the 27th chapter of Matthew, and requesting me to verify the reference therein contained, which I could not do. But there is a satisfactory solution of this difficulty, which I gathered from Ryle:—

1. That the prophecy quoted by Matthew was really delivered by Jeremiah, though not written, and only handed down and recorded by Zechariah: or,

2. That the name of Jeremiah, as some think, was applied by the Jews to the books of the prophets, including, of course, Zechariah, in the 11th chapter of which the reference is to be found: or,

3. That as some say that Matthew originally wrote the words "The prophet," without quoting the name of any one in particular, and that the word "Jeremy" was inserted by an ignorant copyist. In favour of this view the Syriac version, one of the oldest extant, simply says "The prophet," and omits Jeremy's name. The Persian version also omits it.

10th. With regard to the various fulfilled prophecies of the Bible. I cannot forbear asking the sceptic to compare the 53rd chapter of Isaiah, containing the prediction of Christ's sufferings and expiatory death, with its exact fulfilment more than seven hundred years afterwards, as recorded in the New Testament; remembering this, that the authenticity of these future prophecies is fully established by the fact, that the prophecies we have in our Bible are in perfect harmony with the same which the Jews have in their Bible; and it is impossible that there should be any collusion between Jews and Christians.

11th. The truth of the Bible may be shown by reasoning that a child may understand: as, for instance, the Bible must be the word of God; because if not, who could have written it? Bad men would not have written a book inculcating holiness and so totally condemning all their evil ways. And good men surely would not be such wicked deceivers as to say, "Thus saith the Lord," if the Lord had not spoken by them. Consider the wonderful adaptability of the Gospel to the temporal and spiritual necessities of the human race; the predicted hostile reception it has encountered throughout the world, and yet it has spread and flourished, notwithstanding the terrible persecutions it has suffered from Pagans and Papists; the veracity of its description of the frightfully corrupt state of the heart of man. We have not to go far to see the truth of this. Whence arises all the misery and wretchedness that exist around us? Sin is the cause of it all, when traced to its source. What greater evidence can we have of the intimate connection between sin and misery, than the appalling suffering that not very long since overspread Eastern Europe, where every conceivable wickedness was wrought on defenceless men, women, and children, showing unmistakably the bent of human nature when free from restraint. Consider also the transforming effect upon all people who obey the Gospel. The recipient of the truth as it is in Jesus experiences a real, and a wonderful change, which is equivalent to a new birth, a passing from a state of death to life—to becoming a new creature, a mighty self-conqueror. Paul the persecutor, under its transforming influence, contends mightily for the faith he had before so zealously laboured to destroy (Rom. viii. 37; 2 Cor. v. 17; Gal. v. 24). The passionate man is influenced to curb his angry passions, the poor drunkard becomes temperate, the profligate chaste, the churlish man opens his purse-strings to relieve the poor, and the proud man becomes humble. Faith in the Gospel enables the believer to bear adversity with patience and resignation, and affords solace in the hour of death. May I ask, Do any of you, under trying circumstances of no ordinary kind, know what it is to meet with some one who has had precisely the same perplexities, and who assures you from his own experience that you may get out of your difficulty by following his directions? If so, you may well remember the confidence you felt in his advice. Well, after all, this was not confidence in your own experience, but in that of another. Accept, then, the general testimony of believers, who will tell you that the teachings of the Bible are in harmony with, and are verified in, their experience.

12th. Proof of the truth of the divine origin of the Bible, derived from personal experience, is completed when the poor sinner is translated from blindness to sight, from darkness to light, from death to life, so that he can rejoicingly affirm with the blind man whom Christ healed, "Whereas I was blind, now I see." He is able now to rejoice in Christ Jesus as his Saviour, and enjoy the sweet feeling of having passed from a state of awful danger to one of security and peace with a reconciled God; he has soul experience of the truth of God's word, which teaches man's depravity, his need of atonement, and the sufficiency of the perfect expiation of sin effected by our blessed Redeemer on Calvary's cross, "who tasted death for every man," and who bore the wrath of God against the transgressions of the whole world in His own person, when He bore our sins in His own body on the tree, and so put an end to sin by the sacrifice of Himself. He is assured and confident that it is the inspired word of God; for he has found it to be the power of God to his salvation from the time he believed in it (1 Rom. 16). And this confidence is nowise affected because it contains some things he cannot understand; for it is in the very nature of a divine revelation that this should be the case.

The Christian understands the practical value of the Bible, which is a light to his feet and a lamp unto his path. As an illustration I shall conclude this chapter with the following testimony of the German Emperor, who, in the hall of a seminary for the education of Protestant divines, recently delivered a long address to the assembled clergymen and students, in which the grand old veteran made use of the following words, which deserve to be written in letters of gold:—

"The one thing necessary was to believe in God, and His only Son Christ Jesus. There was no mode of ordering one's life in a pious and conscientious way unless upon the eternal foundations laid in the Bible."*

May the Lord add his blessing to these remarks, in so far as they are in harmony with Scripture.

* *The Standard*, 18th June, 1879.

"Follow the trail of my lazo."